David Grann is a staff writer at the *New Yorker* and the bestselling author of *The Lost City of Z*, which was chosen as one of the best books of the year by the *New York Times*, the *Washington Post* and other publications, and has been translated into more than twenty-five languages. He is also the author of *The Devil and Sherlock Holmes*. His work has garnered several honours for outstanding journalism, including a George Polk Award.

ALSO BY DAVID GRANN

The Lost City of Z:
A Legendary British Explorer's Deadly Quest to
Uncover the Secrets of the Amazon

The Devil and Sherlock Holmes:
Tales of Murder, Madness and Obsession

KILLERS
OF THE
FLOWER
MOON

OIL, MONEY, MURDER
AND THE
BIRTH OF THE FBI

DAVID GRANN

**SIMON &
SCHUSTER**

London · New York · Sydney · Toronto · New Delhi

First published in Great Britain by Simon & Schuster UK Ltd, 2017
This paperback edition published by Simon & Schuster UK Ltd, 2018

16

Simon & Schuster UK Ltd
1st Floor
222 Gray's Inn Road
London WC1X 8HB

www.simonandschuster.co.uk
www.simonandschuster.com.au
www.simonandschuster.co.in

Simon & Schuster Australia, Sydney
Simon & Schuster India, New Delhi

A CIP catalogue record for this book
is available from the British Library

Paperback ISBN: 978-0-85720-903-0
eBook ISBN: 978-0-85720-904-7

Book design by Maria Carella
Endpaper map designed by Jeffrey L. Ward

Printed and bound by CPI Group (UK) Ltd, Croydon, CR0 4YY

For my mom and dad

CONTENTS

CHRONICLE THREE:
THE REPORTER

KILLERS
OF THE
FLOWER
MOON

THE
MARKED WOMAN

◆◆◆◆

There had been no evil to mar that propitious night, because she had listened; there had been no voice of evil; no screech owl had quaveringly disturbed the stillness. She knew this because she had listened all night.

—John Joseph Mathews, *Sundown*

In April, millions of tiny flowers spread over the blackjack hills and vast prairies in the Osage territory of Oklahoma. There are Johnny-jump-ups and spring beauties and little bluets. The Osage writer John Joseph Mathews observed that the galaxy of petals makes it look as if the "gods had left confetti." In May, when coyotes howl beneath an unnervingly large moon, taller plants, such as spiderworts and black-eyed Susans, begin to creep over the tinier blooms, stealing their light and water. The necks of the smaller flowers break and their petals flutter away, and before long they are buried underground. This is why the Osage Indians refer to May as the time of the flower-killing moon.

On May 24, 1921, Mollie Burkhart, a resident of the Osage settlement town of Gray Horse, Oklahoma, began to fear that something had happened to one of her three sisters, Anna Brown. Thirty-four, and less than a year older than Mollie, Anna had disappeared three days earlier. She had often gone on "sprees," as her family disparagingly called them: dancing and drinking with friends until dawn. But this time one night had passed, and then another, and Anna had not shown up on Mollie's front stoop as she usually did, with her long black hair slightly frayed and her dark eyes shining like glass.

When Anna came inside, she liked to slip off her shoes, and Mollie missed the comforting sound of her moving, unhurried, through the house. Instead, there was a silence as still as the plains.

Mollie had already lost her sister Minnie nearly three years earlier. Her death had come with shocking speed, and though doctors had attributed it to a "peculiar wasting illness," Mollie harbored doubts: Minnie had been only twenty-seven and had always been in perfect health.

Like their parents, Mollie and her sisters had their names inscribed on the Osage Roll, which meant that they were among the registered members of the tribe. It also meant that they possessed a fortune. In the early 1870s, the Osage had been driven from their lands in Kansas onto a rocky, presumably worthless reservation in northeastern Oklahoma, only to discover, decades later, that this land was sitting above some of the largest oil deposits in the United States. To obtain that oil, prospectors had to pay the Osage for leases and royalties. In the early twentieth century, each person on the tribal roll began receiving a quarterly check. The amount was initially for only a few dollars, but over time, as more oil was tapped, the dividends grew into the hundreds, then the thousands. And virtually every year the payments increased, like the prairie creeks that joined to form the wide, muddy Cimarron, until the tribe members had collectively accumulated millions and millions of dollars. (In 1923 alone, the tribe took in more than $30 million, the equivalent today of more than $400 million.) The Osage were considered the wealthiest people per capita in the world. "Lo and behold!" the New York weekly *Outlook* exclaimed. "The Indian, instead of starving to death...enjoys a steady income that turns bankers green with envy."

The public had become transfixed by the tribe's prosperity, which belied the images of American Indians that could be traced back to the brutal first contact with whites—the original sin from which the country was born. Reporters tantalized their readers with stories about the "plutocratic Osage" and the "red millionaires," with their brick-and-terra-cotta mansions and chandeliers, with their diamond rings and fur coats and chauffeured cars. One writer marveled at Osage girls who attended the best boarding schools and wore sumptuous French clothing, as if "*une très jolie demoiselle* of the Paris boulevards had inadvertently strayed into this little reservation town."

At the same time, reporters seized upon any signs of the traditional Osage way of life, which seemed to stir in the public's mind visions of "wild" Indians. One article noted a "circle of expensive automobiles surrounding an open campfire, where the bronzed and brightly blanketed owners are cooking meat in the primitive style." Another documented a party of Osage arriving at a ceremony for their dances in a private airplane—a scene that "outrivals the ability of the fictionist to portray." Summing up the public's attitude toward the Osage, the *Washington Star* said, "That lament, 'Lo the poor Indian,' might appropriately be revised to, 'Ho, the rich redskin.'"

Gray Horse was one of the reservation's older settlements. These outposts—including Fairfax, a larger, neighboring town of nearly fifteen hundred people, and Pawhuska, the Osage capital, with a population of more than six thousand—seemed like fevered visions. The streets clamored with cowboys, fortune seekers, bootleggers, soothsayers, medicine men, outlaws, U.S. marshals, New York financiers, and oil magnates. Automobiles sped along paved horse trails, the smell of fuel overwhelming the scent of the prairies. Juries of crows peered down from telephone wires. There were restaurants, advertised as cafés, and opera houses and polo grounds.

Although Mollie didn't spend as lavishly as some of her neighbors did, she had built a beautiful, rambling wooden house in Gray Horse near her family's old lodge of lashed poles, woven mats, and bark. She owned several cars and had a staff of servants—the Indians' pot-lickers, as many settlers derided these migrant workers. The servants were often black or Mexican, and in the early 1920s a visitor to the reservation expressed contempt at the sight of

"even whites" performing "all the menial tasks about the house to
which no Osage will stoop."

—————

Mollie was one of the last people to see Anna before she vanished. That day, May 21, Mollie had risen close to dawn, a habit
ingrained from when her father used to pray every morning to
the sun. She was accustomed to the chorus of meadowlarks and
sandpipers and prairie chickens, now overlaid with the *pock-pocking*
of drills pounding the earth. Unlike many of her friends, who
shunned Osage clothing, Mollie wrapped an Indian blanket around
her shoulders. She also didn't style her hair in a flapper bob, but
instead let her long, black hair flow over her back, revealing her
striking face, with its high cheekbones and big brown eyes.

Her husband, Ernest Burkhart, rose with her. A twenty-eight-
year-old white man, he had the stock handsomeness of an extra in
a Western picture show: short brown hair, slate-blue eyes, square
chin. Only his nose disturbed the portrait; it looked as if it had
taken a barroom punch or two. Growing up in Texas, the son of
a poor cotton farmer, he'd been enchanted by tales of the Osage
Hills—that vestige of the American frontier where cowboys and
Indians were said to still roam. In 1912, at nineteen, he'd packed
a bag, like Huck Finn lighting out for the Territory, and gone to
live with his uncle, a domineering cattleman named William K.
Hale, in Fairfax. "He was not the kind of a man to ask you to do
something—he told you," Ernest once said of Hale, who became
his surrogate father. Though Ernest mostly ran errands for Hale, he
sometimes worked as a livery driver, which is how he met Mollie,
chauffeuring her around town.

Ernest had a tendency to drink moonshine and play Indian
stud poker with men of ill repute, but beneath his roughness there
seemed to be a tenderness and a trace of insecurity, and Mollie fell
in love with him. Born a speaker of Osage, Mollie had learned some
English in school; nevertheless, Ernest studied her native language

〉〉〉〉 *Mollie Burkhart*

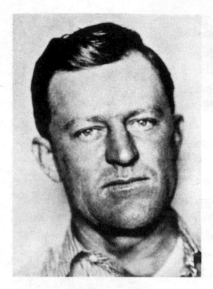

Ernest Burkhart

until he could talk with her in it. She suffered from diabetes, and he cared for her when her joints ached and her stomach burned with hunger. After he heard that another man had affections for her, he muttered that he couldn't live without her.

It wasn't easy for them to marry. Ernest's rough-neck friends ridiculed him for being a "squaw man." And though Mollie's three sisters had wed white men, she felt a responsibility to have an arranged Osage marriage, the way her parents had. Still, Mollie, whose family practiced a mixture of Osage and Catholic beliefs, couldn't understand why God would let her find love, only to then take it away from her. So, in 1917, she and Ernest exchanged rings, vowing to love each other till eternity.

By 1921, they had a daughter, Elizabeth, who was two years old, and a son, James, who was eight months old and nicknamed Cowboy. Mollie also tended to her aging mother, Lizzie, who had moved in to the house after Mollie's father passed away. Because of Mollie's diabetes, Lizzie once feared that she would die young, and beseeched her other children to take care of her. In truth, Mollie was the one who looked after all of them.

═══

May 21 was supposed to be a delightful day for Mollie. She liked to entertain guests and was hosting a small luncheon. After getting dressed, she fed the children. Cowboy often had terrible earaches, and she'd blow in his ears until he stopped crying. Mollie kept her home in meticulous order, and she issued instructions to her servants as the house stirred, everyone bustling about—except Lizzie, who'd fallen ill and stayed in bed. Mollie asked Ernest to ring Anna and see if she'd come over to help tend to Lizzie for a change. Anna, as the oldest child in the family, held a special status in their mother's eyes, and even though Mollie took care of Lizzie, Anna, in spite of her tempestuousness, was the one her mother spoiled.

When Ernest told Anna that her mama needed her, she promised to take a taxi straight there, and she arrived shortly afterward, dressed in bright red shoes, a skirt, and a matching Indian blanket; in her hand was an alligator purse. Before entering, she'd hastily combed her windblown hair and powdered her face. Mollie noticed, however, that her gait was unsteady, her words slurred. Anna was drunk.

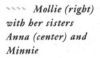 *Mollie (right) with her sisters Anna (center) and Minnie*

Mollie couldn't hide her displeasure. Some of the guests had already arrived. Among them were two of Ernest's brothers, Bryan and Horace Burkhart, who, lured by black gold, had moved to Osage County, often assisting Hale on his ranch. One of Ernest's aunts, who spewed racist notions about Indians, was also visiting, and the last thing Mollie needed was for Anna to stir up the old goat.

Anna slipped off her shoes and began to make a scene. She took a flask from her bag and opened it, releasing the pungent smell of bootleg whiskey. Insisting that she needed to drain the flask before the authorities caught her—it was a year into nationwide Prohibition—she offered the guests a swig of what she called the best white mule.

Mollie knew that Anna had been very troubled of late. She'd recently divorced her husband, a settler named Oda Brown, who owned a livery business. Since then, she'd spent more and more time in the reservation's tumultuous boomtowns, which had sprung up to house and entertain oil workers—towns like Whizbang, where, it was said, people whizzed all day and banged all night. "All the forces of dissipation and evil are here found," a U.S. government official reported. "Gambling, drinking, adultery, lying, thieving, murdering." Anna had become entranced by the places at the dark ends of the streets: the establishments that seemed proper on the exterior but contained hidden rooms filled with glittering bottles of moonshine. One of Anna's servants later told the authorities that Anna was someone who drank a lot of whiskey and had "very loose morals with white men."

At Mollie's house, Anna began to flirt with Ernest's younger brother, Bryan, whom she'd sometimes dated. He was more brooding than Ernest and had inscrutable yellow-flecked eyes and thinning hair that he wore slicked back. A lawman who knew him described him as a little roustabout. When Bryan asked one of the servants at the luncheon if she'd go to a dance with him that night, Anna said that if he fooled around with another woman, she'd kill him.

Meanwhile, Ernest's aunt was muttering, loud enough for all to hear, about how mortified she was that her nephew had married a redskin. It was easy for Mollie to subtly strike back because one of the servants attending to the aunt was white—a blunt reminder of the town's social order.

Anna continued raising Cain. She fought with the guests, fought with her mother, fought with Mollie. "She was drinking and quarreling," a servant later told authorities. "I couldn't understand her language, but they were quarreling." The servant added, "They had an awful time with Anna, and I was afraid."

That evening, Mollie planned to look after her mother, while Ernest took the guests into Fairfax, five miles to the northwest, to meet Hale and see *Bringing Up Father,* a touring musical about a poor Irish immigrant who wins a million-dollar sweepstakes and struggles to assimilate into high society. Bryan, who'd put on a cowboy hat, his catlike eyes peering out from under the brim, offered to drop Anna off at her house.

Before they left, Mollie washed Anna's clothes, gave her some food to eat, and made sure that she'd sobered up enough that Mollie could glimpse her sister as her usual self, bright and charming. They lingered together, sharing a moment of calm and reconciliation. Then Anna said good-bye, a gold filling flashing through her smile.

———

With each passing night, Mollie grew more anxious. Bryan insisted that he'd taken Anna straight home and dropped her off before heading to the show. After the third night, Mollie, in her quiet but forceful way, pressed everyone into action. She dispatched Ernest to check on Anna's house. Ernest jiggled the knob to her front door—it was locked. From the window, the rooms inside appeared dark and deserted.

Ernest stood there alone in the heat. A few days earlier, a cool rain shower had dusted the earth, but afterward the sun's rays beat down mercilessly through the blackjack trees. This time of year, heat blurred the prairies and made the tall grass creak underfoot. In the distance, through the shimmering light, one could see the skeletal frames of derricks.

Anna's head servant, who lived next door, came out, and Ernest asked her, "Do you know where Anna is?"

Before the shower, the servant said, she'd stopped by Anna's house to close any open windows. "I thought the rain would blow in," she explained. But the door was locked, and there was no sign of Anna. She was gone.

News of her absence coursed through the boomtowns, traveling from porch to porch, from store to store. Fueling the unease were reports that another Osage, Charles Whitehorn, had vanished a week before Anna had. Genial and witty, the thirty-year-old Whitehorn was married to a woman who was part white, part Cheyenne. A local newspaper noted that he was "popular among both the whites and the members of his own tribe." On May 14, he'd left his home, in the southwestern part of the reservation, for Pawhuska. He never returned.

Still, there was reason for Mollie not to panic. It was conceivable that Anna had slipped out after Bryan had dropped her off and headed to Oklahoma City or across the border to incandescent Kansas City. Perhaps she was dancing in one of those jazz clubs she liked to visit, oblivious of the chaos she'd left trailing in her wake. And even if Anna had run into trouble, she knew how to protect herself: she often carried a small pistol in her alligator purse. She'll be back home soon, Ernest reassured Mollie.

———

A week after Anna disappeared, an oil worker was on a hill a mile north of downtown Pawhuska when he noticed something poking out of the brush near the base of a derrick. The worker came closer. It was a rotting corpse; between the eyes were two bullet holes. The victim had been shot, execution-style.

It was hot and wet and loud on the hillside. Drills shook the earth as they bore through the limestone sediment; derricks swung their large clawing arms back and forth. Other people gathered around the body, which was so badly decomposed that it was impossible to identify. One of the pockets held a letter. Someone pulled it out, straightening the paper, and read it. The letter was addressed to Charles Whitehorn, and that's how they first knew it was him.

Around the same time, a man was squirrel hunting by Three Mile Creek, near Fairfax, with his teenage son and a friend. While the two men were getting a drink of water from a creek, the boy spotted a squirrel and pulled the trigger. There was a burst of heat and light, and the boy watched as the squirrel was hit and began to tumble lifelessly over the edge of a ravine. He chased after it, making his way down a steep wooded slope and into a gulch where the air was thicker and where he could hear the murmuring of the creek. He found the squirrel and picked it up. Then he screamed, "Oh Papa!" By the time his father reached him, the boy had crawled onto a rock. He gestured toward the mossy edge of the creek and said, "A dead person."

There was the bloated and decomposing body of what appeared to be an American Indian woman: she was on her back, with her hair twisted in the mud and her vacant eyes facing the sky. Worms were eating at the corpse.

The men and the boy hurried out of the ravine and raced on their horse-drawn wagon through the prairie, dust swirling around them. When they reached Fairfax's main street, they couldn't find any lawmen, so they stopped at the Big Hill Trading Company, a large general store that had an undertaking business as well. They told the proprietor, Scott Mathis, what had happened, and he alerted his undertaker, who went with several men to the creek. There they rolled the body onto a wagon seat and, with a rope, dragged it to the top of the ravine, then laid it inside a wooden box, in the shade of a blackjack tree. When the undertaker covered the bloated corpse with salt and ice, it began to shrink as if the last bit of life were leaking out. The undertaker tried to determine if the woman was Anna Brown, whom he'd known. "The body was decomposed and swollen almost to the point of bursting and very malodorous," he later recalled, adding, "It was as black as a nigger."

He and the other men couldn't make an identification. But Mathis, who managed Anna's financial affairs, contacted Mollie, and she led a grim procession toward the creek that included Ernest, Bryan, Mollie's sister Rita, and Rita's husband, Bill Smith. Many who knew Anna followed them, along with the morbidly curious. Kelsie Morrison, one of the county's most notorious bootleggers and dope peddlers, came with his Osage wife.

Mollie and Rita arrived and stepped close to the body. The stench was overwhelming. Vultures circled obscenely in the sky. It was hard for Mollie and Rita to discern if the face was Anna's—there was virtually nothing left of it—but they recognized her Indian blanket and the clothes that Mollie had washed for her. Then Rita's husband, Bill, took a stick and pried open her mouth, and they could see Anna's gold fillings. "That is sure enough Anna," Bill said.

Rita began to weep, and her husband led her away. Eventually, Mollie mouthed the word "yes"—it was Anna. Mollie was the one in the family who always maintained her composure, and she now retreated from the creek with Ernest, leaving behind the first hint of the darkness that threatened to destroy not only her family but her tribe.

A coroner's inquest, composed of jurors and led by a justice of the peace, was hastily convened at the ravine. Inquests were a remnant of a time when ordinary citizens largely assumed the burden of investigating crimes and maintaining order. For years after the American Revolution, the public opposed the creation of police departments, fearing that they would become forces of repression. Instead, citizens responded to a hue and cry by chasing after suspects. Benjamin N. Cardozo, the future Supreme Court justice, once noted that these pursuits were made "not faintly and with lagging steps, but honestly and bravely and with whatever implements and facilities are convenient and at hand."

Only in the mid-nineteenth century, after the growth of industrial cities and a rash of urban riots—after dread of the so-called dangerous classes surpassed dread of the state—did police departments emerge in the United States. By the time of Anna's death, the informal system of citizen policing had been displaced, but vestiges of it remained, especially in places that still seemed to exist on the periphery of geography and history.

The justice of the peace selected the jurors from among the white men at the ravine, including Mathis. They were charged with determining whether Anna had died by an act of God or man, and if it had been a felony, then they were tasked with trying to identify the principals and the accessories to the crime. Two doctors, the brothers James and David Shoun, who cared for Mollie's family, had been summoned to perform an autopsy. Leaning over the body, with members of the inquest huddled around them, they began to diagnose the dead.

Each corpse tells its own story. A fractured hyoid—a bone in the neck that supports the tongue—can indicate that a person has been strangled. Marks on the neck can further reveal whether the killer used his bare hands or a cord. Even a victim's torn fingernail can speak of a fateful struggle. An influential nineteenth-century manual on medical jurisprudence cited the saying "A medical man, when he sees a dead body, should notice everything."

The Shoun brothers set up a plank as a makeshift table. From a medical bag, they removed a few primitive instruments, including a saw. The heat slithered into the shade. Flies swarmed. The doctors examined the clothes Anna wore—her bloomers, her skirt—searching for unusual tears or stains. Finding nothing, they tried

The ravine where Anna Brown's body was found

to determine the time of death. This is more difficult than generally presumed, particularly after a person has been dead for several days. In the nineteenth century, scientists believed that they had solved the riddle by studying the phases a body passes through after death: the stiffening of the limbs (rigor mortis), the corpse's changing temperature (algor mortis), and the discoloring of the skin from stagnant blood (livor mortis). But pathologists soon realized that too many variables—from the humidity in the air to the type of clothing on the corpse—affect the rate of decomposition to allow a precise calculation. Still, a rough estimate of the time of death can be made, and the Shouns determined that Anna had been deceased between five and seven days.

The doctors shifted Anna's head slightly in the wooden box. Part of her scalp slipped off, revealing a perfectly round hole in the back of her skull. "She's been shot!" one of the Shouns exclaimed.

There was a stirring among the men. Looking closer, they saw that the hole's circumference was barely that of a pencil. Mathis thought that a .32-caliber bullet had caused the wound. As the men traced the path of the bullet—it had entered just below the crown, on a downward trajectory—there was no longer any doubt: Anna's death had been cold-blooded murder.

═══

Lawmen were then still largely amateurs. They rarely attended training academies or steeped themselves in the emerging scientific methods of detection, such as the analysis of fingerprints and blood patterns. Frontier lawmen, in particular, were primarily gunfighters and trackers; they were expected to deter crimes and to apprehend a known gunman alive if possible, dead if necessary. "An officer was then literally the law and nothing but his judgment and his trigger finger stood between him and extermination," the *Tulsa Daily World* said in 1928, after the death of a veteran lawman who'd worked in the Osage territory. "It was often a case of a lone man against a pack of cunning devils." Because these enforcers received pitiful salaries and were prized for being quick draws, it's not surprising that the boundary between good lawmen and bad lawmen was porous. The leader of the Dalton Gang, an infamous nineteenth-century band of outlaws, once served as the main lawman on the Osage reservation.

At the time of Anna's murder, the Osage County sheriff, who carried the bulk of responsibility for maintaining law and order in the area, was a fifty-eight-year-old, three-hundred-pound frontiersman named Harve M. Freas. A 1916 book about the history of Oklahoma described Freas as a "terror to evil doers." But there were also murmurings that he was cozy with criminal elements—that he gave free rein to gamblers and to bootleggers like Kelsie Morrison and Henry Grammer, a rodeo champion who had once served time for murder and who controlled the local distribution of moonshine. One of Grammer's workers later admitted to authorities, "I had the assurance that if I was ever arrested...I would be turned out in five minutes." A group of citizens from Osage County had previously issued a resolution—on behalf of "religion, law enforcement, home decency and morality"—stating, "That the people who believe a sworn officer of the Law should enforce the Law are hereby urged to see or write Sheriff Freas, at once, and urge upon him to do his sworn duty."

When Sheriff Freas was informed about Anna's murder, he was already preoccupied with Whitehorn's slaying, and he initially sent one of his deputies to collect evidence. Fairfax had a town marshal, the equivalent of a police chief, who joined the deputy at the ravine while the Shoun brothers were still conducting the autopsy. To identify the murder weapon, the lawmen needed to extract the bullet that was apparently lodged in Anna's skull. Using their saw, the Shouns cut through her cranium, then carefully lifted her brain and placed it on the plank. "The brains were in such a bad shape," David Shoun recalled. "You couldn't trace the bullet at all." He picked up a stick and probed the brain. The bullet, he announced, was nowhere to be found.

The lawmen went down to the creek, scouring the murder scene. By a rock on the bank were smears of blood, marking where Anna's body had lain. There was no sign of the bullet, but one of the lawmen noticed a bottle on the ground, which was partially filled with a clear liquid. It smelled like moonshine. The lawmen surmised that Anna had been sitting on the rock, drinking, when someone came up behind her and shot her at close range, causing her to topple over.

The marshal spotted two distinct sets of car tracks running between the road and the gulch. He called out, and the deputy sheriff and the inquest members rushed over. It looked as though both cars had come into the gulch from the southeast, then circled back.

No other evidence was collected. The lawmen were untrained in forensic methods and didn't make a cast impression of the tire marks, or dust the bottle for fingerprints, or check Anna's body for gunpowder residue. They didn't even photograph the crime scene, which, in any case, had already been contaminated by the many observers.

Someone, though, retrieved one of Anna's earrings from her body and brought it to Mollie's mother, who was too ill to venture to the creek. Lizzie instantly recognized it. *Anna was dead.* As with all Osage, the birth of her children had been the greatest blessing of Wah'Kon-Tah, the mysterious life force that pervades the sun and the moon and the earth and the stars; the force around which the Osage had structured their lives for centuries, hoping to bring some order out of the chaos and confusion on earth; the force that was there but not there—invisible, remote, giving, awesome, unanswering. Many Osage had given up their traditional beliefs, but Lizzie had held on to them. (A U.S. government official had once complained that women like Lizzie "keep up the old superstitions and laugh down modern ideas and customs.") Now someone, *something*, had taken Lizzie's oldest and most favored daughter before her allotted time—a sign, perhaps, that Wah'Kon-Tah had

〜〜〜 *Mollie (right)*
with her sister Anna
and their mother,
Lizzie

withdrawn his blessings and that the world was slipping into even greater chaos. Lizzie's health grew even worse, as if grief were its own disease.

———

Mollie relied on Ernest for support. A lawyer who knew them both noted that his "devotion to his Indian wife and his children is unusual...and striking." He comforted Mollie as she threw herself into organizing Anna's funeral. There were flowers to be purchased, along with a white metal coffin and a marble tombstone. Undertakers charged the Osage exorbitant rates for a funeral, trying to gouge them, and this was no exception. The undertaker demanded $1,450 for the casket, $100 for preparing and embalming the body, and $25 for the rental of a hearse. By the time he was done tallying the accessories, including gloves for the grave digger, the total cost was astronomical. As a lawyer in town said, "It was getting so that you could not bury an Osage Indian at a cost of under $6,000"—a sum that, adjusted for inflation, is the equivalent of nearly $80,000 today.

The funeral was arranged to reflect the family's Osage and Catholic traditions. Mollie, who had gone to a missionary school in Pawhuska, regularly attended Mass. She liked to sit in the pews as the Sunday morning light came through the windows and listen to the sermon of the priest. She also liked to socialize among friends, and there was plenty of that on Sundays.

The funeral service for Anna began at the church. William Hale, Ernest's uncle, was very close to Anna and Mollie's family, and he served as one of the pallbearers. The priest chanted the rhythmic thirteenth-century hymn "Dies Irae," which culminates with a supplication:

SWEET JESUS LORD MOST BLEST,
GRANT THE DEAD ETERNAL REST.

After the priest sprinkled holy water over Anna's casket, Mollie guided her family and the other mourners to a cemetery in Gray Horse, a quiet, isolated spot overlooking the endless prairie. Mollie's father and her sister Minnie were buried there in adjoining plots, and beside them was a freshly dug pit, damp and dark, awaiting Anna's casket, which had been transported to the edge of the grave site. Her tombstone bore the inscription "Meet Me in Heaven." Ordinarily at the cemetery the lid of a coffin was lifted a final time before interment, allowing loved ones to say good-bye, but the condition of Anna's body made that impossible. More troubling, her face couldn't be painted to signal her tribe and clan—a tradition at Osage funerals. If this ritual of ornamentation didn't occur, Mollie feared Anna's spirit might be lost. Still, Mollie and her family placed enough food in the casket for Anna's three-day journey to what the Osage refer to as the Happy Hunting Ground.

The older mourners, like Mollie's mother, began to recite Osage prayer-songs, hoping that Wah'Kon-Tah would hear them. The great historian and writer John Joseph Mathews (1894–1979), who was part Osage, documented many of the tribe's traditions. Describing a typical prayer, he wrote, "It filled my little boy's soul with fear and bittersweetness, and exotic yearning, and when it had ended and I lay there in my exultant fear-trance, I hoped fervently that there would be more of it, and yet I was afraid that there might be. It seemed to me later, after I had begun to reason, that this prayer-song, this chant, this soul-stirring petition, always ended before it was finished, in a sob of frustration."

At the grave site, standing with Ernest, Mollie could hear the old people's song of death, their chants interspersed with weeping. Oda Brown, Anna's ex-husband, was so distraught that he stepped away. Precisely at noon—as the sun, the greatest manifestation of the Great Mystery, reached its zenith—men took hold of the casket and began to lower it into the hole. Mollie watched the glistening white coffin sink into the ground until the long, haunting wails were replaced by the sound of earth clapping against the lid.

The killings of Anna Brown and Charles Whitehorn caused a sensation. A banner headline in the *Pawhuska Daily Capital* read, TWO SEPARATE MURDER CASES ARE UNEARTHED ALMOST AT SAME TIME. Theories proliferated about who might be responsible. Two bullets were retrieved from Whitehorn's skull, and they appeared to have come from a .32-caliber pistol—the same kind of weapon that had been suspected in Anna's murder. Was it just a coincidence that both victims had been wealthy Osage Indians, in their thirties? Or was this, perhaps, the work of a repeat killer—someone like Dr. H. H. Holmes, who had murdered at least twenty-seven people, many of them during the 1893 World's Fair, in Chicago?

Lizzie relied on Mollie to deal with the authorities. During Lizzie's lifetime, the Osage had become dramatically unmoored from their traditions. Louis F. Burns, an Osage historian, wrote that after oil was discovered, the tribe had been "set adrift in a strange world," adding, "There was nothing familiar to clutch and stay afloat in the world of white man's wealth." In the old days, an Osage clan, which included a group known as the Travelers in the Mist, would take the lead whenever the tribe was undergoing sudden changes or venturing into unfamiliar realms. Mollie, though she often felt bewildered by the upheaval around her, took the lead for her family—a modern traveler in the mist. She spoke English and was married to a white man, and she had not succumbed to the temptations that had hurt many young members of the tribe, including Anna. To some Osage, especially elders like Lizzie, oil was a cursed blessing. "Some day this oil will go and there will be no more fat checks every few months from the Great White Father," a chief of the Osage said in 1928. "There'll be no fine motorcars and new clothes. Then I know my people will be happier."

Mollie pressed the authorities to investigate Anna's murder, but most officials seemed to have little concern for what they deemed a "dead Injun." So Mollie turned to Ernest's uncle, William Hale. His business interests now dominated the county, and he had become a powerful local advocate for law and order—for the protection of what he called "God-fearing souls."

Hale, who had an owlish face, stiff black hair, and small, alert eyes set in shaded hollows, had settled on the reservation nearly two decades earlier. Like a real-life version of Faulkner's Thomas Sutpen, he seemed to have come out of nowhere—a man with no known past. Arriving in the territory with little more than the clothes on his back and a worn Old Testament, he embarked on what a person who knew him well called a "fight for life and fortune" in a "raw state of civilization."

Hale found work as a cowboy on a ranch. Before trains crisscrossed the West, cowboys drove cattle from Texas to Osage territory, where the herds grazed on the lush bluestem grass, and then on to Kansas, for shipment to slaughterhouses in Chicago and other cities. These drives fueled the American fascination with cowboys, but the work was hardly romantic. Hale toiled day and night for a pittance; he rode through storms—hail, lightning, sand—and survived stampedes, guiding the cattle into smaller and smaller circles before they could trample him. His clothes carried the stench of sweat and manure, and his bones were frequently battered, if not broken. Eventually, he hoarded and borrowed enough money to buy his own herd in Osage territory. "He is the most energetic man I ever knew," a man who invested in his business recalled. "Even when he crossed the street he walked as if he were going after something big."

Hale soon went bankrupt—an embittering failure that only stoked the furnace of his ambition. After he started over in the cattle business again, he often slept in a tent on the cold windy plains, alone in his fury. Years later, a reporter described how he'd still pace before a fire "like a leashed animal. He nervously rubbed his hands into the flames. His rather ruddy face was aglow with cold and excitement." He worked with the fever of someone who feared not only hunger but an Old Testament God who, at any moment, might punish him like Job.

He became an expert at branding, dehorning, castrating, and selling stock. As his profits rose, he bought up more territory from the Osage and neighboring settlers until he had amassed some forty-five thousand acres of the finest grazing land in the county, as well as a small fortune. And then, in that uncanny American way, he went to work on himself. He replaced his ragged trousers and cowboy hat with a dandified suit and a bow tie and a felt hat, his eyes peering out through distinguished round-rimmed glasses. He married a school-teacher and had a daughter who adored him. He recited poetry. Pawnee Bill, the legendary Wild West showman and the onetime partner of Buffalo Bill, described Hale as a "high-class gentleman."

He was named a reserve deputy sheriff in Fairfax, a position that he would continue to hold. The title was largely honorific, but it enabled him to carry a badge and to lead posses, and he some-times kept one pistol in his side pocket and another strapped to his hip. They represented, he liked to say, his authority as an officer of the law.

As his wealth and power grew, politicians courted his support, knowing that they couldn't win without his blessing. He outworked and outwitted his rivals, making plenty of enemies who wanted him dead. "Some did hate him," a friend admitted. Still, Mollie

~~~~ *William Hale competing in a roping contest when he was a cowboy (above); a transformed Hale standing with his daughter and wife (below)*

Burkhart and many others considered him Osage County's greatest benefactor. He aided the Osage before they were flush with oil money, donating to charities and schools and a hospital. Assuming the mantle of a preacher, he signed his letters "Rev. W. K. Hale." A local doctor said, "I couldn't begin to remember how many sick people have received medical attention at his expense, nor how many hungry mouths have tasted of his bounty." Later, Hale wrote a letter to an assistant chief of the tribe, saying, "I never had better friends in my life than the Osages. . . . I will always be the Osages true Friend." In this last remnant of the American frontier, Hale was revered as the "King of the Osage Hills."

===

Hale frequently came by Mollie's house to collect Ernest, and not long after Anna's burial Hale showed up to pay his respects to Mollie and her mother. He vowed to obtain justice for Anna.

With his supreme confidence and his mastery of that secret world of whites (he often wore a diamond-studded pin from the Masonic lodge), it didn't seem to matter that he had no formal role in the murder investigation. He had always expressed affection for Anna—"We were mighty good friends," he said—and during another visit Mollie could see him huddled with Ernest, apparently talking about hunting down whoever had murdered her sister.

Members of the coroner's inquest, along with the county prosecutor, continued investigating Anna's death, and shortly after Anna's burial Mollie went to give evidence at a hearing in Fairfax. The Department of the Interior's Office of Indian Affairs—which oversaw government relations with tribes and was later renamed the Bureau of Indian Affairs—had a field agent assigned to the Osage territory who knew Mollie. He said that she was "willing to do everything she can in order to . . . bring the guilty parties to justice." The authorities had provided a translator for Mollie, but she waved him off and spoke in succinct English, the way the nuns had taught her as a child.

Mollie described for the jurors the final time that Anna visited her house. She said that Anna had left around sundown. In a later proceeding, a government official asked her, "How did she go?"

"She goes in a car."

"Who was with her?"

"Bryan Burkhart."

"Did you notice which direction they went?"

"Towards Fairfax."

"Was anyone else in the car with Bryan and Anna?"

"No, just Bryan and Anna..."

"Did you see her any more alive after that?"

Mollie stayed composed. "No," she said.

"You saw her body after it was found?"

"Yes."

"How long was it about after this time you saw her leave your mother's place with Bryan Burkhart, you saw her body?"

"About five or six days."

"Where did you see the body?"

"At the pasture... just right there."

At the inquest, while Mollie seemed eager to answer every question, to make sure that nothing was missed, the justice of the peace and the jurors asked her barely anything. Perhaps they discounted her because of prejudice—because she was an Osage and a woman. The panel questioned with greater depth Bryan Burkhart, about whom many locals had begun to whisper; after all, he was the last person seen with Anna before she went missing.

Bryan lacked the good looks of his brother Ernest, Mollie's husband, and there was something cold about his appearance; he had uncomfortably steady eyes. Hale had once caught him stealing his cattle and, to teach his nephew a lesson, filed charges against him.

The county prosecutor asked Bryan about the day that he said he'd given Anna a ride to her house. "When you brought her back, where did you go?"

"Come to town."

"When was this?"

"About 5 or 4:30."

"You haven't seen her since then?"

"No, sir."

At one point, the county prosecutor paused and asked, *"Positive?"*

"Yes, sir."

At a later hearing, Ernest was also questioned. A law-enforcement official pressed him about his brother: "You understand he is the last person seen with this woman, Anna Brown?"

"I understand," Ernest replied, adding that Bryan told him "he left her at her house. That is his story."

"Do you believe it?"

"Yes, sir."

Bryan was detained by the authorities after the first hearing. To Mollie's distress, they even held Ernest, too, in case he was covering for his younger brother. But both men were soon turned loose. There was no evidence implicating Bryan other than the fact that he'd been with Anna before she disappeared. When Ernest was asked if he had any information as to how Anna met her death, he said no, adding, "I don't know of enemies she had or anyone that disliked her."

=====

A prevailing theory was that her killer came from outside the reservation. Once, the tribe's enemies had battled them on the plains; now they came in the form of train robbers and stickup men and other desperadoes. The passage of Prohibition had only compounded the territory's feeling of lawlessness by encouraging organized crime and creating, in the words of one historian, "the greatest criminal bonanza in American history." And few places in the country were as chaotic as Osage County, where the unwritten codes of the West, the traditions that bound communities, had unraveled. By one account, the amount of oil money had surpassed

Lawmen seize a moonshine still in Osage County in 1923.

the total value of all the Old West gold rushes combined, and this
fortune had drawn every breed of miscreant from across the country. A U.S. Justice Department official warned that there were more
fugitives hiding out in the Osage Hills than "perhaps any other
county in the state or any state in the Union." Among them was
the hard-boiled stickup man Irvin Thompson, who was known as
Blackie maybe because of his dark complexion (he was a quarter
Cherokee) or maybe because of his dark heart: a lawman described
him as "the meanest man I ever handled." Even more notorious
was Al Spencer, the so-called Phantom Terror, who had made the
transition from galloping horses to speeding getaway cars and had
inherited from Jesse James the title of the region's most infamous
outlaw. The *Arizona Republican* said that Spencer, with his "diseased
mind and a misguided love of adventure," appealed to the "portion
of the population of the country that fed on false idolatry." Members of his gang, including Dick Gregg and Frank "Jelly" Nash,

Al Spencer Gang members jokingly hold up others in their crew.

were themselves ranked among the most dreaded outlaws of the day.

A more unnerving theory about Anna's death was that her killer was living among them in sheep's clothing. Mollie and others began to harbor suspicions about Anna's ex-husband, Oda Brown, who called himself a businessman but spent most of his time carousing. In retrospect, his distraught manner had seemed almost too theatrically intense. An investigator wrote in his notes, "This may have been real grief or … for effect." After Anna had divorced him, she had denied him any inheritance, leaving virtually all of her fortune to Lizzie. Since the burial, Brown had hired a lawyer and had tried unsuccessfully to contest the will. The investigator concluded that Brown was "absolutely no good and capable of doing almost anything for money."

Several weeks after the funeral, a man who'd been arrested in Kansas for check forgery sent a letter to Sheriff Freas claiming that he had information concerning Anna's murder. "Honorable Sir," he wrote, "I hope to be some assistance to you." He didn't divulge what he knew, however, and upon receiving the message the sheriff set out in what the press described as a "fast automobile." Hale, who had been tipped off regarding the potential breakthrough, rushed to the jail as well. Under interrogation, the forger, a fidgety twenty-eight-year-old man, claimed that Brown had paid him $8,000 to murder Anna. He described how he'd shot her in the head, then carried her body in his arms down to the creek.

Soon after his confession, a posse of lawmen swept in and seized Brown when he was in Pawhuska on business. The *Pawhuska Daily Capital* heralded the news: ANNA BROWN SLAYER CONFESSES CRIME. It added, "Oda Brown, Husband of Woman, Also Arrested." Mollie and her family were devastated by the notion that Oda was responsible for Anna's murder, but they could take solace in the thought of his facing justice, perhaps the hangman's noose or the electric chair. But within days authorities had conceded that there was no evidence to support the forger's claims—no evidence that he had been in Osage County at the time of the murder or that Brown had ever contacted him. The authorities had no choice but to release Brown. "There's a lot of talk," the sheriff was quoted as saying. "But you have to have proof, not talk."

<hr>

Like many officials, the county prosecutor owed his election at least in part to Hale. When he first ran for office, his advisers told him that he had to get Hale's endorsement, and so he made several trips to Hale's ranch. He could never find him, and finally a cattle inspector told him, "If you want to see Bill Hale, you will have to get to his ranch early—and I mean damned early." So, at three in the morning, the attorney parked his Model T at the ranch and went to sleep in the car. Before long, he was jolted awake by a fierce-looking man pressed against his window, demanding to know why he was trespassing. It was William Hale. The attorney explained his purpose, and Hale realized that he knew the attorney's parents, who had once sheltered him during a blizzard. Hale promised to turn out the vote for him. One of the attorney's advisers remarked that Hale "would not lie to anyone, and if he said he would do something, he would do it." On Election Day, the attorney carried every single precinct in that part of the county.

Hale had remained close with the county prosecutor and conferred with him and other officials about Anna's murder. Eventually, the county prosecutor decided to look again for the bullet that had eluded investigators during Anna's autopsy. A court order was obtained to unbury Anna. Scott Mathis, the Big Hill Trading Company owner who was friends with Hale and Mollie, was asked to supervise the grim task, and he went to the cemetery with his undertaker and a grave digger. The grass on Anna's plot had barely had time to grow back. The men began to prod the unforgiving earth with their spades, then reached down and lifted up the once white casket, now dirt blackened, and forced open the lid. An awful vapor, death itself, filled the air.

The Shoun brothers, who had performed the first autopsy, appeared at the cemetery and renewed their search for the bullet. This time, the brothers put on gloves and took out a meat cleaver, cutting Anna's head into "sausage meat," as the undertaker later put it. But, once again, the brothers found nothing. The bullet appeared to have vanished.

———

By July 1921, the justice of the peace had closed his inquiries, stating that Anna Brown's death had come at "the hands of parties unknown"—the same finding as delivered in the Whitehorn inquest. The justice locked away in his office the little evidence that he'd gathered, in case more information emerged.

Meanwhile, Lizzie—who'd once possessed the same energy and stubborn determination as Mollie—had grown sicker. Each day, she seemed to drift further away, to become more insubstantial; it was as if she had the same peculiar wasting illness that had consumed Minnie.

Desperate for help, Mollie turned to the Osage medicine men, who chanted when the eastern sky was red like blood, and to the new breed of medicine men, the Shoun brothers, who carried their potions in black bags. Nothing seemed to work. Mollie kept vigil over her mother, one of the last tethers to the tribe's ancient way of life. Mollie could not cure her, but she could feed her, and she could brush her long, beautiful, silvery hair from her face—a face that was lined and expressive, that maintained its aura.

One day that July, less than two months after Anna's murder, Lizzie stopped breathing. Mollie couldn't revive her. Lizzie's spirit had been claimed by Jesus Christ, the Lord and Savior, and by Wah'Kon-Tah, the Great Mystery. Mollie was overwhelmed with grief. As an Osage mourning prayer went,

> *Have pity on me, O Great Spirit!*
> *You see I cry forever,*
> *Dry my eyes and give me comfort.*

━━━

Mollie's brother-in-law, Bill Smith, was one of the first to wonder if there was something curious about Lizzie's death, coming so soon after the murders of Anna and Whitehorn. A bruising bulldog of a man, Bill had also expressed deep frustration over the authorities' investigation, and he had begun looking into the matter himself. Like Mollie, he was struck by the peculiar vagueness of Lizzie's sickness; no doctor had ever pinpointed what was causing it. Indeed, no one had uncovered any natural cause for her death. The more Bill delved, conferring with doctors and local investigators, the more he was certain that Lizzie had died of something dreadfully unnatural: she'd been poisoned. And Bill was sure that all three deaths were connected—somehow—to the Osage's subterranean reservoir of black gold.

The money had come suddenly, swiftly, madly. Mollie had been ten years old when the oil was first discovered, had witnessed, firsthand, the ensuing frenzy. But, as the elders in the tribe had relayed to Mollie, the tangled history of how their people had gotten hold of this oil-rich land went back to the seventeenth century, when the Osage had laid claim to much of the central part of the country—a territory that stretched from what is now Missouri and Kansas to Oklahoma, and still farther west, all the way to the Rockies.

In 1803, President Thomas Jefferson purchased, from the French, the Territory of Louisiana, which contained lands dominated by the Osage. Jefferson informed his secretary of the navy that the Osage were a great nation and that "we must stand well, because in their quarter we are miserably weak." In 1804, a delegation of Osage chiefs met with Jefferson at the White House. He told the navy secretary that the Osage, whose warriors typically stood well over six feet tall, were the "finest men we have ever seen."

At the meeting, Jefferson addressed the chiefs as "my children" and said, "It is so long since our forefathers came from beyond the great water, that we have lost the memory of it, and seem to have grown out of this land, as you have done.... We are all now of one family." He went on, "On your return tell your people that I take them all by the hand; that I become their father hereafter, that they shall know our nation only as friends and benefactors."

But within four years Jefferson had compelled the Osage to relinquish their territory between the Arkansas River and the Missouri River. The Osage chief stated that his people "had no choice, they must either sign the treaty or be declared enemies of the United States." Over the next two decades, the Osage were forced to cede nearly a hundred million acres of their ancestral land, ultimately finding refuge in a 50-by-125-mile area in southeastern Kansas. And it was in this place where Mollie's mother and father had come of age.

Mollie's father, who was born around 1844, went by his Osage name, Ne-kah-e-se-y. A young Osage man then typically wore fringed buckskin leggings and moccasins and a breechcloth; a finger-woven belt held his tobacco pouch and tomahawk. His chest was often bare, and his head was shaved, except for a strip of hair that ran from the crown to his neck and that stood straight up, like the crest of a Spartan's helmet.

Along with other warriors, Ne-kah-e-se-y defended the tribe from attacks, and before heading into battle he would have painted his face black with charcoal and prayed to Wah'Kon-Tah, confirming that it was time, as the Osage put it, "to make the enemy lie reddened on the earth." As Ne-kah-e-se-y grew older, he became a prominent figure in the tribe. Deliberate and thoughtful, he had an ability to study each situation before choosing a course of action. Years later, when the tribe created its first court system, which adjudicated mostly minor crimes, he was elected one of the three judges.

Lizzie also grew up on the reservation in Kansas, where she helped to provide for her family, harvesting corn and hauling wood over distances. She wore moccasins, leggings, a cloth skirt, and a blanket around her shoulders, and she painted the part in the middle of her hair red to symbolize the path of the sun. An Indian Affairs agent would later describe her as "industrious" and a "person of good character."

Twice a year, when Lizzie and Ne-kah-e-se-y were young, their families and the rest of the tribe would pack their few earthly possessions—clothing, bedding, blankets, utensils, dried meat, weapons—lash them to horses, and set out on a sacred, two-month buffalo hunt. When a scouting party spotted a herd, Ne-kah-e-se-y and the other hunters raced on their horses across the plains, the hooves pounding the earth like drums, the manes whipping the riders' sweating, gleaming faces. A French medical student, who accompanied the tribe on a hunt in 1840, said, "The race is a merciless one.... Once the bison is reached, the animal tries to escape in another direction, he doubles to deceive his enemy; then seeing himself overtaken, he becomes enraged and turns against his aggressor."

Ne-kah-e-se-y would coolly draw his bow and arrow, which the Osage considered more effective than a bullet. When a bison was fatally wounded, the medical student recalled, "the beast vomits torrents of blood and falls to its knees before sinking to the ground." After the tail was cut off—as a trophy for the conqueror—nothing was left to waste: the meat was dried, the heart smoked, the intestines made into sausages. Oils from the bison's brain were rubbed over the hide, which was then transformed into leather for robes and lodge coverings. And still there was more to reap: horns were turned into spoons, sinews into bowstrings, tallow into fuel for torches. When an Osage chief was asked why he didn't adopt the white man's ways, he replied, "I am perfectly content with my condition. The forests and rivers supply all the calls of nature in plenty."

The Osage had been assured by the U.S. government that their Kansas territory would remain their home forever, but before long they were under siege from settlers. Among them was the family of Laura Ingalls Wilder, who later wrote *Little House on the Prairie* based on her experiences. "Why don't you like Indians, Ma?" Laura asks her mother in one scene.

"I just don't like them; and don't lick your fingers, Laura."

"This is Indian country, isn't it?" Laura said. "What did we come to their country for, if you don't like them?"

One evening, Laura's father explains to her that the government will soon make the Osage move away: "That's why we're here, Laura. White people are going to settle all this country, and we get the best land because we get here first and take our pick."

Though, in the book, the Ingallses leave the reservation under threat of being removed by soldiers, many squatters began to take the land by force. In 1870, the Osage—expelled from their lodges, their graves plundered—agreed to sell their Kansas lands to settlers for $1.25 an acre. Nevertheless, impatient settlers massacred several of the Osage, mutilating their bodies and scalping them. An Indian Affairs agent said, "The question will suggest itself, which of these people are the savages?"

========

The Osage searched for a new homeland. They debated purchasing nearly 1.5 million acres from the Cherokee in what was then Indian Territory—a region south of Kansas that had become an end point on the Trail of Tears for many tribes ousted from their lands. The unoccupied area that the Osage were eyeing was bigger than Delaware, but most whites regarded the land as "broken, rocky, sterile, and utterly unfit for cultivation," as one Indian Affairs agent put it.

Which is why Wah-Ti-An-Kah, an Osage chief, stood at a council meeting and said, "My people will be happy in this land. White man cannot put iron thing in ground here. White man will not come to this land. There are many hills here . . . white man does not like country where there are hills, and he will not come." He went on, "If my people go west where land is like floor of lodge,

white man will come to our lodges and say, 'We want your land.' ...
Soon land will end and Osages will have no home."

So the Osage bought the territory for seventy cents per acre
and, in the early 1870s, began their exodus. "The air was filled with
cries of the old people, especially the women, who lamented over
the graves of their children, which they were about to leave forever,"
a witness said. After completing their trek to the new reservation,
members of the tribe built several camps, the most significant one
being in Pawhuska, where, on a prominent hilltop, the Office of
Indian Affairs erected an imposing sandstone building for its field
office. Gray Horse, in the western part of the territory, consisted
of little more than a cluster of newly built lodges, and it was here
where Lizzie and Ne-kah-e-se-y, who married in 1874, settled.

The series of forced migrations, along with such "white man's
diseases" as smallpox, had taken a tremendous toll on the tribe. By
one estimate, its population dwindled to about three thousand—a
third of what it had been seventy years earlier. The Indian Affairs

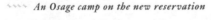

An Osage camp on the new reservation

agent reported, "This little remnant is all that remains of a heroic race that once held undisputed ownership over all this region."

Although the Osage still went on buffalo hunts, they were chasing not only food but the past. "It was like life in the old days," a white trader who accompanied them recalled. "The old men of the band were wont to gather about the campfires in a reminiscent mood and there recount the tales of prowess on the war-path and in the chase."

By 1877, there were virtually no more American buffalo to hunt—a development hastened by the authorities who encouraged settlers to eradicate the beasts, knowing that, in the words of an army officer, "every buffalo dead is an Indian gone." U.S. policy toward the tribes shifted from containment to forced assimilation, and officials increasingly tried to turn the Osage into churchgoing, English-speaking, fully clothed tillers of the soil. The government owed the tribe annuity payments for the sale of its Kansas land but refused to distribute them until able-bodied men like Ne-kah-e-se-y took up farming. And even then the government insisted on making the payments in the form of clothing and food rations. An Osage chief complained, "We are not dogs that we should be fed like dogs."

Unaccustomed to the white man's agricultural methods and deprived of buffalo, the Osage began to go hungry; their bones soon looked as if they might break through their skin. Many members of the tribe died. An Osage delegation, including the chief Wah-Ti-An-Kah, was urgently dispatched to Washington, D.C., to petition the commissioner of Indian Affairs to abolish the ration system. According to an account by John Joseph Mathews, members of the delegation wore their best blankets and leggings, while Wah-Ti-An-Kah wrapped himself in a red blanket so entirely that you could see little more than his eyes, dark wells that burned with an entire history.

The delegation went to the commissioner's office and waited

The Osage chief Wah-Ti-An-Kah

for him. When the commissioner arrived, he informed an interpreter, "Tell these gentlemen that I am sorry that I have another appointment at this time—I am sorry I had forgotten about it until just now."

As the commissioner tried to leave, Wah-Ti-An-Kah blocked his path to the door and let go of his blanket. To the shock of even his fellow Osage, he was naked, except for his breechcloth and his moccasins, and his face was painted as if he were leading a war party. "He stood there towering like some primitive god of the dark forests," Mathews wrote.

Wah-Ti-An-Kah told the interpreter, "Tell this man to sit down." When the commissioner complied, Wah-Ti-An-Kah said, "We have come [a] long way to talk about this."

The commissioner said, "Surely this man who doesn't know how to act—who comes to my office almost naked, with war paint on his face, is not civilized enough to know how to use money."

Wah-Ti-An-Kah said that he was not ashamed of his body, and after he and the delegation pressed their case, the commissioner agreed to end the ration policy. Wah-Ti-An-Kah picked up his blanket and said, "Tell this man it is all right now—he can go."

Like many others in the tribe, Mollie's parents tried to hold on to their customs. Bestowing a name was one of the most important Osage rituals; only then was someone considered a person by the tribe. Mollie, who was born on December 1, 1886, was given the Osage name Wah-kon-tah-he-um-pah. Her sisters were also known by Osage names: Anna was Wah-hrah-lum-pah; Minnie, Wah-sha-she; and Rita, Me-se-moie.

But the process of acculturation was accelerating as settlers began to move onto the reservation. They didn't look like the Osage, or even like the Cheyenne or the Pawnee. They seemed unwashed and desperate, like William Hale, who would eventually appear on his horse, in his ragged clothes—this man from nowhere. Even settlers like Hale who formed close ties to the Osage argued that the white man's road was inevitable and that the only way for the Osage to survive was to follow it. Hale was determined to transform not only himself but the wilderness from which he came—to cross-fence the open prairie and to create a network of trading posts and towns.

In the 1880s, John Florer, a Kansas frontiersman who referred to Osage territory as "God's country," established the first trading post in Gray Horse. Mollie's father, Ne-kah-e-se-y, liked to linger outside it, in the shade, and sell animal pelts, and Mollie got to know the son of a trader, who was one of the first white people she'd ever seen; his skin was as pale as the belly of a fish.

The trader's son kept a journal, and in it he noted a profound existential change experienced by Mollie and her family, though he remarked upon it only in passing, as if it were no more than a new item on a ledger. One day, he said, a trader began to refer to Ne-kah-e-se-y as Jimmy. Soon other traders began to call Mollie's father Jimmy, and before long it had supplanted his Osage name. "Likewise his daughters who often visited the store, received their

~~~~ *John Florer's trading store in Gray Horse*

names there of," the trader's son wrote. And that's how Wah-kon-tah-he-um pah became Mollie.

Mollie—who, like her mother, then wore leggings, moccasins, a skirt, a blouse, and a blanket—slept on the floor in a corner of her family's lodge and had to do many grueling chores. But there was a relative peacefulness and happiness to that time: Mollie could enjoy the ceremonial dances and the feasts and playing water tag

~~~~ *Mollie's father*
(right) in front of
Florer's trading store

in the creek and watching the men race their ponies in the emerald fields. As the trader's son wrote, "There lingers memories like a half forgotten dream, of an enchanting world dawning on a child's consciousness in its wonder and mystery."

In 1894, when Mollie was seven, her parents were informed that they had to enroll her in the St. Louis School, a Catholic boarding institution for girls that had been opened in Pawhuska, which was two days' journey by wagon to the northeast. An Indian Affairs commissioner had said, "The Indian must conform to the white man's ways, peacefully if they will, forcibly if they must."

Mollie's parents were warned that if they didn't comply, the government would withhold its annuity payments, leaving the family starving. And so, one morning in March, Mollie was taken from her family and bundled into a horse-drawn wagon. As she and a driver set out toward Pawhuska, in the center of the reservation, Mollie could see Gray Horse, the seeming limit of her universe, gradually disappear until all that was visible was the smoke rising from the tops of the lodges and fading into the sky. In front of her, the prairie stretched to the horizon like an ancient seabed. There were no settlements, no souls. It was as if she'd slipped over the edge of the world and fallen, to borrow Willa Cather's phrase, "outside man's jurisdiction."

Hour after hour, mile after mile, lurching back and forth in the wagon, Mollie crossed the wild, empty landscape, not yet carved into a country. Eventually, the light began to fail, and the driver and Mollie had to stop and set up camp. When the sun sank below the prairie floor, the sky would turn blood red and then black, the density of the darkness diluted only by the moon and the stars, from where the Osage believed that many of their clans descended. Mollie had become a traveler in the mist. She was surrounded by the forces of night, heard but not seen: the gibbering of coyotes and the howling of wolves and the screaming of owls, which were said to carry an evil spirit.

The next day, the monochrome prairies gave way to timber-covered hills, and Mollie and her driver rode up and down the slopes, past shadowy blackjacks and sunless caves—perfect places, as an Indian Affairs agent once fretted, "for ambush." (He added, "Let me tell you there are ... ignorant criminals who would do anything.") They rode until they came upon a sign of human habitation: a single-story, dilapidated, red-painted wooden structure. It was an Osage trading store, and nearby was a grubby rooming house and a blacksmith shop with an immense pile of horseshoes. The muddy trail turned into a wider, even muddier trail, with a scattering of trading stores on either side. These businesses had sagging duckboards out front to help customers avoid the treacherous mud and hitching posts for horses and weather-beaten façades that looked as if they might tumble over in the breeze, some of them with trompe l'oeil second stories to create an illusion of grandeur.

Mollie had reached Pawhuska. Although the reservation's capital then seemed a small, squalid place—a "muddy little trading post," as one visitor described it—it was likely the biggest settlement Mollie had ever seen. She was taken about a mile away, to a forbidding stone building that stood four stories high: the St. Louis Catholic missionary school, where she was left in the care of women in black-and-white habits. Mollie went through the front door—Mathews once described the entrance to another Osage boarding school as a "big, black mouth, bigger and darker than a wildcat's"—and down a labyrinth of drafty corridors; coal lanterns glowed in the darkness.

Mollie had to remove the Indian blanket from her shoulders and put on a plain dress. She wasn't allowed to speak Osage—she had to catch the white man's tongue—and was given a Bible that began with a distinct notion of the universe: "Then God said, 'Let there be light'; and there was light. God saw that the light was good; and God separated the light from the darkness."

Each hour of the day was regimented and students were lined up and marched from point to point. They were taught piano, penmanship, geography, and arithmetic, the world distilled into strange new symbols. The instruction was intended to assimilate Mollie into white society and transform her into what the authorities conceived of as the ideal woman. So while Osage boys at other institutions learned farming and carpentry, Mollie was trained in the "domestic arts": sewing, baking, laundering, and housekeeping. "It is impossible to overestimate the importance of careful training for Indian girls," a U.S. government official had stated, adding, "Of what avail is it that the man be hard-working and industrious, providing by his labor food and clothing for his household, if the wife, unskilled in cookery, unused to the needle, with no habits of order or neatness, makes what might be a cheerful, happy home only a wretched abode of filth and squalor? ... It is the women who cling most tenaciously to heathen rites and superstitions, and perpetuate them by their instructions to the children."

Many Osage students at Mollie's school tried to flee, but lawmen chased after them on horseback and bound them with ropes, hauling them back. Mollie attended class eight months each year, and when she did return to Gray Horse, she noticed that more and more girls had stopped wearing their blankets and moccasins and

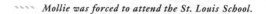

Mollie was forced to attend the St. Louis School.

that the young men had exchanged their breechcloths for trousers and their scalp locks for broad-brimmed hats. Many students began to feel embarrassed by their parents, who didn't understand English and still lived by the old ways. An Osage mother said of her son, "His ears are closed to our talk."

=====

Mollie's family was straddling not only two centuries but two civilizations. Her family's distress increased in the late 1890s as the U.S. government intensified its push for the culmination of its assimilation campaign: allotment. Under the policy, the Osage reservation would be divvied up into 160-acre parcels, into *real estate*, with each tribal member receiving one allotment, while the rest of the territory would be opened to settlers. The allotment system, which had already been imposed on many tribes, was designed to end the old communal way of life and turn American Indians into private-property owners—a situation that would, not incidentally, make it easier to procure their land.

The Osage had seen what had happened to the Cherokee Outlet, a vast prairie that was part of the Cherokees' territory and was near the western border of the Osage reservation. After the U.S. government purchased the land from the Cherokee, it had announced that at noon on September 16, 1893, a settler would be able to claim one of the forty-two thousand parcels of land—if he or she got to the spot first! For days before the starting date, tens of thousands of men, women, and children had come, from as far away as California and New York, and gathered along the boundary; the ragged, dirty, desperate mass of humanity stretched across the horizon, like an army pitted against itself.

Finally, after several "sooners" who'd tried to sneak across the line early had been shot, the starting gun sounded—A RACE FOR LAND SUCH AS WAS NEVER BEFORE WITNESSED ON EARTH, as one newspaper put it. A reporter wrote, "Men knocked each other down as they rushed onward. Women shrieked and fell, fainting, only to

~~~~ *The land run*
of 1893

be trampled and perhaps killed." The reporter continued, "Men, women and horses were laying all over the prairie. Here and there men were fighting to the death over claims which each maintained he was first to reach. Knives and guns were drawn—it was a terrible and exciting scene; no pen can do it justice.... It was a struggle where the game was empathically every man for himself and devil take the hindmost." By nightfall, the Cherokee Outlet had been carved into pieces.

Because the Osage had purchased their land, it was harder for the government to impose its policy of allotment. The tribe, led by one of its greatest chiefs, James Bigheart—who spoke seven lan-

guages, among them Sioux, French, English, and Latin, and who
had taken to wearing a suit—was able to forestall the process. But
pressure was mounting. Theodore Roosevelt had already warned
what would befall an Indian who refused his allotment: "Let him,
like these whites, who will not work, perish from the face of the
earth which he cumbers."

By the early twentieth century, Bigheart and other Osage knew
that they could no longer avoid what a government official called
the "great storm" gathering. The U.S. government planned to break
up Indian Territory and make it a part of what would be a new state
called Oklahoma. (In the Choctaw language, "Oklahoma" means

"red people.") Bigheart had succeeded in delaying the process for
several years—the Osage were the last tribe in Indian Territory
to be allotted—and this had given the Osage more leverage as
government officials were eager to avoid any final impediments to
statehood. In 1904, Bigheart sent a zealous young lawyer named
John Palmer across the country "to keep his finger on the Washington pulse." The orphaned son of a white trader and a Sioux woman,
Palmer had been adopted as a child by an Osage family and had
since married an Osage woman. A U.S. senator from Oklahoma
called Palmer "the most eloquent Indian alive."

For months, Bigheart and Palmer and other members of the
tribe negotiated with government officials over the terms of allotment. The Osage prevailed upon the government to divide the
land solely among members of the tribe, thereby increasing each
individual's allotment from 160 acres to 657 acres. This strategy
would avoid a mad dash on their territory, though whites could
then attempt to buy allotments from tribe members. The Osage
also managed to slip into the agreement what seemed, at the time,
like a curious provision: "That the oil, gas, coal, or other minerals
covered by the lands … are hereby reserved to the Osage Tribe."

The tribe knew that there were some oil deposits under the reservation. More than a decade earlier, an Osage Indian had shown
John Florer, the owner of the trading post in Gray Horse, a rainbow
sheen floating on the surface of a creek in the eastern part of the
reservation. The Osage Indian dabbed his blanket at the spot and
squeezed the liquid into a container. Florer thought that the liquid
smelled like the axle grease sold in his store, and he rushed back
and showed the sample to others, who confirmed his suspicions: it
was oil. With the tribe's approval, Florer and a wealthy banking
partner obtained a lease to begin drilling on the reservation. Few
imagined that the tribe was sitting on a fortune, but by the time of
the allotment negotiations several small wells had begun operating,
and the Osage shrewdly managed to hold on to this last realm of
their land—a realm that they could not even see. After the terms

of the Allotment Act were agreed upon, in 1906, Palmer boasted to Congress, "I wrote that Osage agreement out in longhand."

Like others on the Osage tribal roll, Mollie and her family members each received a headright—essentially, a share in the tribe's mineral trust. When, the following year, Oklahoma entered the Union as the forty-sixth state, members of the tribe were able to sell their surface land in what was now Osage County. But to keep the mineral trust under tribal control, no one could buy or sell headrights. These could only be inherited. Mollie and her family had become part of the first underground reservation.

=====

The tribe soon began leasing areas to more and more white prospectors for exploration. Mollie saw workers—tool dressers, rope chokers, mule peelers, gang pushers—toiling furiously. After lowering a torpedo filled with nitroglycerin into the belly of the earth, the muddied workers would detonate it, occasionally turning up a fragment of an ancient American Indian spear or an arrowhead. They'd stare at it in bewilderment. These men built wooden structures that ascended into the sky, like temples, and they chanted their own private language: "Bounce, you cats, bounce. Load up on them hooks, you snappers. That's high. Ring her off, collar-pecker. Up on the mops. Out, growler-board." Many wildcatters dug dry wells, or "dusters," and scurried away in despair. An Osage remarked that such white men "ack like tomorrow they ain't gonna be no more worl'."

In the early twentieth century, George Getty, an attorney from Minneapolis, began his family's quest for oil in the eastern part of Osage territory, on a parcel of land, Lot 50, that he'd leased for $500. When his son, Jean Paul Getty, was a boy, he visited the area with him. "It was pioneer days," Jean Paul, who founded the Getty Oil Company, later recalled. "No motorcars, very few telephones, not many electric lights. Even though it was the beginning of the twentieth century, you still very much felt the influence of the

Workers strike oil in Osage territory.

nineteenth century." He went on, "It seemed a great adventure. My parents never saw the charm of it all that I did. We used to go often to Lot 50, about nine miles into the Osage, in a horse-drawn wagon. It took a couple of hours and we had to cross a river to get there."

Before encountering the Indians, Jean Paul had asked his father, "Are they dangerous? Will we have to fight them off?"

His father laughed. "No," he said. "They're rather quiet and peaceful."

One damp spring day in 1917, Frank Phillips—a wildcatter who'd previously sold a tonic to prevent baldness—was out with his workers on Lot 185, less than half a mile from Lot 50. They were on a platform drilling when the derrick began to tremble, as if a locomotive were rushing by. From the hole in the ground came a rumbling, gurgling sound, and the workers began to run, their screams smothered by what had become a roar. A driller grabbed Phillips and pulled him off the platform just as the earth burst open and a black column of oil spewed into the air.

Each new find seemed more breathtaking than the last. In 1920, E. W. Marland, who was once so poor that he couldn't afford train fare, discovered Burbank, one of the highest-producing oil fields in the United States: a new well generated 680 barrels in its first twenty-four hours.

Many of the Osage would rush to see a gusher when it erupted, scrambling for the best view, making sure not to cause a spark, their eyes following the oil as it shot fifty, sixty, sometimes a hundred feet in the air. With its great black wings of spray, arcing above the rigging, it rose before them like an angel of death. The spray coated the fields and the flowers and smeared the faces of the workers and the spectators. Still, people hugged and tossed their hats in celebration. Bigheart, who had died not long after the imposition of allotment, was hailed as the "Osage Moses." And the dark, slimy, smelly mineral substance seemed like the most beautiful thing in the world.

Money was the one means at Mollie's disposal that might induce the indifferent white authorities to pursue a killer of Indians. After Lizzie died in July 1921, Mollie's brother-in-law, Bill Smith, had presented his suspicions to authorities that she'd been slowly poisoned, but by August they had still not looked into the case. Nor had any progress been made in the then-three-month-old probe of Anna's murder. To prod investigators, Mollie's family issued a statement saying that because of "the foulness of the crime" and "the dangers that exist to other people," they were offering a $2,000 cash reward for any information leading to the apprehension of those responsible. The Whitehorn family also offered a $2,500 reward to catch Charles's slayers. And William Hale, who campaigned for stamping out the criminal element from Osage County, promised his own reward to anyone who caught the killers, dead or alive. "We've got to stop this bloody business," he said.

But the situation with law enforcement continued to deteriorate. The Oklahoma attorney general soon charged Sheriff Freas with willfully "failing to enforce the law" by permitting bootlegging and gambling. Freas denied the allegations, and while the case awaited trial, these two powerful lawmen were pitted against each other. Given this turmoil, Hale announced that it was time to hire a private eye.

During much of the nineteenth and early twentieth centuries, private detective agencies had filled the vacuum left by decentralized, underfunded, incompetent, and corrupt sheriff and police departments. In literature and in the popular imagination, the all-seeing private eye—the gumshoe, the cinder dick, the sleuthhound, the shadow—displaced the crusading sheriff as the archetype of rough justice. He moved across the dangerous new frontiers of deep alleyways and roiling slums. His signature was not the smoking six-shooter; instead, like Sherlock Holmes, he relied upon the startling powers of reason and deduction, the ability to *observe* what the Watsons of the world merely saw. He found order in a scramble of clues and, as one author put it, "turned brutal crimes—the vestiges of the beast in man—into intellectual puzzles."

Yet from the outset the fascination with private detectives was mixed with aversion. They were untrained and unregulated and often had criminal records themselves. Beholden to paying clients, they were widely seen as surreptitious figures who burglarized people's secrets. (The term "to detect" derived from the Latin verb "to unroof," and because the devil, according to legend, allowed his henchmen to peer voyeuristically into houses by removing their roofs, detectives were known as "the devil's disciples.") In 1850, Allan Pinkerton founded the first American private detective agency; in advertisements, the company's motto, "We Never Sleep," was inscribed under a large, unblinking, Masonic-like eye, which gave rise to the term "private eye." In a manual of general principles and rules that served as a blueprint for the industry, Pinkerton admitted that the detective must at times "depart from the strict line of truth" and "resort to deception." Yet even many people who despised the profession deemed it a necessary evil. As one private eye put it, he might be a "miserable snake," but he was also "the silent, secret, and effective Avenger of the outraged Majesty of the Law when everything else fails."

Hale recruited a brooding private detective from Kansas City, who went by the name of Pike. To preserve his cover, Pike, who smoked a corn pipe and had a smudge of a mustache, met Hale at a concealed spot near Whizbang. (Civic leaders like Hale considered the name Whizbang undignified and instead called the town Denoya, after a prominent Osage family.) As smoke from the oil fields melted into the sky, Hale conferred with Pike. Then Pike slipped away to pursue his investigation.

At the direction of Mollie and her family, Anna's estate also hired private detectives. The estate was being administered by Scott Mathis, the Big Hill Trading Company owner, who had long managed the financial affairs of Anna and Lizzie as a guardian. The U.S. government, contending that many Osage were unable to handle their money, had required the Office of Indian Affairs to determine which members of the tribe it considered capable of managing their trust funds. Over the tribe's vehement objections, many Osage, including Lizzie and Anna, were deemed "incompetent," and were forced to have a local white guardian overseeing and authorizing all of their spending, down to the toothpaste they purchased at the corner store. One Osage who had served in World War I complained, "I fought in France for this country, and yet I am not allowed even to sign my own checks." The guardians were usually drawn from the ranks of the most prominent white citizens in Osage County.

Mathis put together a team of private eyes, as did the estate for Whitehorn. The private detectives investigating the Osage deaths had often worked for the William J. Burns International Detective Agency before venturing out on their own. Burns, a former Secret Service agent, had succeeded Pinkerton as the world's most celebrated private eye. A short, stout man, with a luxuriant mustache and a shock of red hair, Burns had once aspired to be an actor, and he cultivated a mystique, in part by writing pulp detective stories about his cases. In one such book, he declared, "My name is William J. Burns, and my address is New York, London, Paris, Mon-

~~~~ *The Big Hill Trading Company was run by Scott Mathis, who was a guardian of Anna and Lizzie.*

treal, Chicago, San Francisco, Los Angeles, Seattle, New Orleans, Boston, Philadelphia, Cleveland, and wherever else a law-abiding citizen may find need of men who know how to go quietly about throwing out of ambush a hidden assassin or drawing from cover criminals who prey upon those who walk straight." Though dubbed a "front-page detective" for his incessant self-promotion, he had an impressive track record, including catching those responsible for the 1910 bombing of the headquarters of the *Los Angeles Times,* which killed twenty people. The *New York Times* called Burns "perhaps the only really great detective, the only detective of genius, whom this country has produced," and Sir Arthur Conan Doyle gave him the moniker he longed for: "America's Sherlock Holmes."

Unlike Sherlock Holmes, though, Burns had rigged juries, and allegedly kidnapped a suspect, and he routinely used the sordid techniques of imperial spies. After being caught breaking in to a New York law office in an attempt to steal evidence, he said that such methods were sometimes needed to prove a conspiracy and

~~~~ *The private detective*
William J. Burns

that such lines had been crossed "a thousand times" by private investigators. Burns perfectly embodied the new profession.

That summer, the team of operatives hired by Mathis began to infiltrate Osage County. Each agent identified himself, in his daily reports, only by a coded number. At the outset, operative No. 10 asked Mathis, who'd been a juror on the inquest, to show him the crime scene. "Mathis and myself drove out to the place where the body was found," No. 10 wrote.

One of the investigators spoke to Anna's main servant. She revealed that after the body was found, she'd obtained a set of Anna's keys and had gone, with Anna's sister Rita Smith, to Anna's house. Incredibly, no one from the sheriff's office had searched the place yet. The women eased open the door and stepped through the silence. They could see Anna's jewelry and blankets and pictures, the accumulated treasures of her life, now resembling the ruins of a lost city. The servant, who had helped dress Anna the day she disappeared, recalled, "Everything was just as we left it"— except for one thing. Anna's alligator purse, which she had taken to Mollie's luncheon, was now lying on the floor, the servant said, with "everything torn out of it."

Nothing else in the house appeared to have been stolen, and the presence of the bag indicated that Anna had likely returned to her house at some point after the luncheon. Mollie's brother-in-law Bryan seemed to be telling the truth about having brought her home. But had he taken her back out? Or had she gone away with someone else?

No. 10 turned to another potentially rich vein of clues: the records of Anna's incoming and outgoing telephone calls. In those days, phone calls were manually patched through by an operator at a switchboard, with long-distance calls often relayed through multiple switchboards. These operators frequently kept a written record of the calls. According to the log of a Fairfax operator, at about 8:30, on the night Anna disappeared, someone had rung her house from a phone belonging to a business in Ralston, a town six miles southwest of Gray Horse. The records showed that someone, presumably Anna, had picked up. That meant that Anna was likely still in her house at 8:30—further evidence that Bryan had been truthful about taking her home.

The private detective, sensing that he was on the verge of a breakthrough, hurried to the Ralston business where the call originated. The proprietor insisted that he hadn't called Anna's house and that nobody else would have been allowed to make a long-distance call from his phone. Bolstering his claims, no Ralston operator had a record of the call being patched through to the Fairfax operator. "This call seems a mystery," No. 10 wrote. He suspected that the Ralston number was really a "blind"—that an operator had been paid to destroy the original log ticket, which revealed the true source of the call. Someone, it seemed, was covering his or her tracks.

No. 10 wanted to look closely at Oda Brown. "General suspicion points towards the divorced husband," he wrote. But it was getting late and he finished his report, saying, "Discontinued on case 11 P.M."

═══

A week later, another operative from the team—No. 46—was sent to locate Brown in Ponca City, twenty-five miles northwest of

Gray Horse. A savage storm blew across the prairie and turned the streets into rivers of mud, so the private detective didn't arrive in Ponca City until dark, only to discover that Brown wasn't there. He was said to be visiting Perry, Oklahoma, where his father lived. The next day, No. 46 took a train south to Perry, but Brown wasn't there, either; he was now said to be in Pawnee County. "Consequently I left Perry on the first train," No. 46 wrote in his report. This was what Sherlock Holmes stories left out—the tedium of real detective work, the false leads and the dead ends.

Back and forth No. 46 went until, in Pawnee County, he spied a slender, cigarette-smoking, shifty-looking man with rust-colored hair and flat gray eyes: Oda Brown. He was with a Pawnee woman whom he'd reportedly married after Anna's death. No. 46 stayed close, shadowing them. One day, No. 46 approached Brown, trying to befriend him. The Pinkerton manual advised, "The watchful Detective will seize the Criminal in his weakest moments and force from him, by his sympathy and the confidence which the Criminal has in him, the secret which devours him." No. 46 wormed his way deeper into Brown's confidence. When Brown mentioned that his ex-wife had been murdered, No. 46 tried to elicit from him where he'd been at the time of her death. Brown, perhaps suspecting his new friend was a professional snoop, said that he'd been away with another woman, though he wouldn't disclose the location. No. 46 studied Brown intently. According to the manual, a criminal's secret becomes an "enemy" within him and "weakens the whole fortress of his strength." But Brown didn't appear at all nervous.

While No. 46 was working on Brown, another operative, No. 28, learned a seemingly vital secret from a young Kaw Indian woman who lived near the western border of Osage County. In a signed statement, the woman claimed that Rose Osage, an Indian in Fairfax, had admitted to her that she'd killed Anna after Anna had tried to seduce her boyfriend, Joe Allen. Rose said that while the three were riding in a car she'd "shot her in the top of the head," then, with Joe's help, dumped the body by Three Mile Creek. Rose's clothes got splattered with Anna's blood, the story went, so she took them off and discarded them in the creek.

It was a grim tale, but operative No. 28 was buoyed by the discovery. In his daily report, he said that he'd spent hours with Mathis and Sheriff Freas, whose trial was still pending, pursuing this "clue that seems to be a lead on the case."

The private detectives, though, struggled to corroborate the informant's story. No one had spotted Anna with Rose or Joe. Nor were any clothes found in the stream by the body. Was it possible that the informant was simply lying to get the reward?

Sheriff Freas, his flesh unfolding from his voluminous neck and chest, urged the private detectives to discount Rose and her boyfriend as suspects. Then he offered a counter-rumor: two hard-boiled characters from the oil camps had purportedly been seen with Anna shortly before her death, and had afterward skipped town. The private detectives agreed to look into the sheriff's story. But concerning the allegations against Rose, No. 28 vowed, "We are going to follow out this theory."

———

The private detectives shared what they knew with Bill Smith, Mollie's brother-in-law, who was still conducting his own investigation. The twenty-nine-year-old Smith had been a horse thief before attaching himself to an Osage fortune: first by marrying Mollie's sister Minnie, and then—only months after Minnie's death from the mysterious "wasting illness" in 1918—by wedding Mollie's sister Rita. On more than one occasion when Bill drank, he'd raised his hand to Rita. A servant later recalled that after one row between Bill and Rita, "she came out kind of bruised up." Bill told the servant, "That was the only way to get along with them squaws." Rita often threatened to leave him, but she never did.

Rita had a keen mind, yet those close to her thought that her judgment was impaired by what one person described as "a love that

Mollie's sister Rita

was truly blind." Mollie had her doubts about Bill: Had he, in some way, been responsible for Minnie's death? Hale made it clear that he didn't trust Bill, either, and at least one local attorney speculated that Bill was "prostituting the sacred bond of marriage for sordid gain."

But since Anna's murder Bill had, by all appearances, vigorously sought to discover who the culprit was. When Bill learned that a tailor in town might have information, he went with a private detective to ask him questions, only to find that he was spreading the now-familiar rumor: that Rose Osage had killed Anna in a fury of jealousy.

Desperate for a break, the private detectives decided to install a listening device to eavesdrop on Rose and her boyfriend. At the time, statutes governing electronic surveillance were nebulous, and Burns was an avid user of a Dictograph—a primitive listening device that could be concealed in anything from a clock to a

chandelier. "Burns was the first American to see the immense possibilities of the instrument in detective work," the *Literary Digest*
reported in 1912. "He is so enamored with it that he always carries
one in his pocket." Just as Allan Pinkerton, in the nineteenth century, was known as "the eye," Burns, in the twentieth century, had
become "the ear."

The detectives, hiding in another room, began listening to the
staticky voices of Rose and her boyfriend through earphones. But,
as is so often the case with surveillance, the rush of excitement gave
way to the tediousness of other people's inner lives, and the private
detectives eventually stopped bothering to jot down the innocuous
details that they overheard.

Using more conventional means, however, the private detectives made a startling discovery. The cabdriver who'd taken Anna
to Mollie's house on the day she vanished told them that Anna had
asked him to stop first at the cemetery in Gray Horse. She had
climbed out and stumbled through the stones until she paused by
her father's tomb. For a moment, she stood near the spot where
she, too, would soon be buried, as if offering a mourning prayer to
herself. Then she returned to the car and asked the driver to send
someone to bring flowers to her father's tomb. She wanted his grave
to always be pretty.

While they continued to Mollie's house, Anna leaned toward
the driver. He could smell her liquored breath as she divulged a
secret: she was going to have "a little baby."

"My goodness, no," he replied.

"I am," she said.

"Is that so?"

"Yes."

Detectives later confirmed the story with two people close to
Anna. She had also confided to them the news of her pregnancy. Yet
no one knew who the father was.

One day that summer, a stranger with a Chaplinesque mustache showed up in Gray Horse to offer his assistance to the private eyes. The man, who was armed with a .44-caliber, snub-nosed English Bulldog, was named A. W. Comstock, and he was a local attorney and the guardian of several Osage Indians. Some locals thought that Comstock, with his aquiline nose and tan complexion, might be part American Indian—an impression that he did little to discourage as he built up his legal practice. "The fact he represented himself to be an Indian would make him get along pretty well with the Indians, wouldn't it?" another lawyer skeptically remarked. William Burns had once investigated Comstock for allegedly assisting an oil company in a scheme to bribe the Osage Tribal Council for a favorable lease, but the charge was never proven.

Given Comstock's numerous contacts among the Osage, the private eyes now took him up on his offer to help. While the detectives were trying to establish a connection between the slayings of Charles Whitehorn and Anna Brown, Comstock passed on tidbits that he collected from his network of informants. There was chatter that Whitehorn's widow, Hattie, had coveted her husband's money, chatter that she'd been jealous of his relationship with another woman. Was it possible that this woman was Anna Brown? Such a hypothesis led to the next logical question: Was Whitehorn the father of her baby?

The detectives began to follow Hattie Whitehorn around the clock, relishing being able to see without being seen: "Operative shadowed Mrs. Whitehorn to Okla. City from Pawhuska.... Left Okla. City with Mrs. Whitehorn for Guthrie.... Trailed Mrs. Whitehorn, Tulsa to Pawhuska." But there were no developments.

By February 1922, nine months after the murders of Whitehorn and Anna Brown, the investigations into the cases seemed to have reached a permanent impasse. Pike, the detective Hale had enlisted, had moved on. Sheriff Freas was also no longer leading the investigation; that February, he was expelled from office after a jury had found him guilty of failing to enforce the law.

Then, on a frigid night that month, William Stepson, a twenty-nine-year-old Osage champion steer roper, received a call that prompted him to leave his house in Fairfax. He returned home to his wife and two children several hours later, visibly ill. Stepson had always been in remarkable shape, but within hours he was dead. Authorities, upon examining the body, believed that someone he met during his excursion had slipped him a dose of poison, possibly strychnine—a bitter white alkaloid that, according to a nineteenth-century medical treatise, was "endowed with more destructive energy" than virtually any other poison. The treatise described how a lab animal injected with strychnine becomes "agitated and trembles, and is then seized with stiffness and starting of the limbs," adding, "These symptoms increase till at length it is attacked with a fit of violent general spasm, in which the head is bent back, the spine stiffened, the limbs extended and rigid, and the respiration checked by the fixing of the chest." Stepson's final hours would have been a hideous torment: his muscles convulsing, as if he were being jolted with electricity; his neck craning and his jaw tightening; his lungs constricting as he tried to breathe, until at last he suffocated.

William Stepson

By the time of Stepson's death, scientists had devised numerous tools to detect poison in a corpse. A sample of tissue could be extracted from the body and tested for the presence of an array of toxic substances—from strychnine to arsenic. Yet in much of the country these forensic methods were

applied even less consistently than fingerprint and ballistic techniques. In 1928, a survey by the National Research Council concluded that the coroner in most counties of the United States was
an "untrained and unskilled individual" and had "a small staff of
mediocre ability, and with inadequate equipment." In places like
Osage County, where there was no coroner trained in forensics and
no crime laboratory, poisoning was a perfect way to commit murder. Poisons were abundantly available in products found on the
shelves of apothecaries and grocery stores, and unlike a gunshot
they could be administered without a sound. And the symptoms
of many toxic substances mimicked natural ailments—the nausea
and diarrhea of cholera, or the seizure of a heart attack. During
Prohibition, there were so many accidental deaths caused from
wood alcohol and other toxic brews of bootleg whiskey that a killer
could also spike a person's glass of moonshine without ever arous-
ing suspicions.

On March 26, 1922, less than a month after Stepson's death, an
Osage woman died of a suspected poisoning. Once again, no thor-
ough toxicology exam was performed. Then, on July 28, Joe Bates,
an Osage man in his thirties, obtained from a stranger some whiskey, and after taking a sip, he began frothing at the mouth, before
collapsing. He, too, had died of what authorities described as some
strange poison. He left behind a wife and six children.

That August, as the number of suspicious deaths continued
to climb, many Osage prevailed upon Barney McBride, a wealthy
fifty-five-year-old white oilman, to go to Washington, D.C., and
ask federal authorities to investigate. McBride had been married
to a Creek Indian, now deceased, and was raising his stepdaughter.
He had taken a strong interest in Indian affairs in Oklahoma, and
he was trusted by the Osage; a reporter described him as a "kind-
hearted, white-haired man." Given that he also knew many officials
in Washington, he was considered an ideal messenger.

When McBride checked in to a rooming house in the capital, he
found a telegram from an associate waiting for him. "Be careful," it

said. McBride carried with him a Bible and a .45-caliber revolver. In the evening, he stopped at the Elks Club to play billiards. When he headed outside, someone seized him and tied a burlap sack tightly over his head. The next morning, McBride's body was found in a culvert in Maryland. He had been stabbed more than twenty times, his skull had been beaten in, and he had been stripped naked, except for his socks and shoes, in one of which had been left a card with his name. The forensic evidence suggested that there had been more than one assailant, and authorities suspected that his killers had shadowed him from Oklahoma.

News of the murder quickly reached Mollie and her family. The killing—which the *Washington Post* called "the most brutal in crime annals in the District"—appeared to be more than simply a murder. It had the hallmarks of a message, a warning. In a headline, the *Post* noted what seemed to be increasingly clear: CONSPIRACY BELIEVED TO KILL RICH INDIANS.

Even with the murders, they kept on coming, the greatest oil barons in the world. Every three months, at ten in the morning, these oilmen—including E. W. Marland and Bill Skelly and Harry Sinclair and Frank Phillips and his brothers—pulled in to the train station in Pawhuska, in their own luxurious railcars. The press would herald their approach with bulletins: "MILLIONAIRES' SPECIAL" DUE TO ARRIVE; PAWHUSKA GIVES CITY OVER TO OIL MEN TODAY; MEN OF MILLIONS AWAIT PSYCHOLOGICAL MOMENT.

The barons came for the auction of Osage leases, an event that was held about four times a year and that was overseen by the Department of the Interior. One historian dubbed it the "Osage Monte Carlo." Since the auctions had begun, in 1912, only a portion of Osage County's vast underground reservation had been opened to drilling, while the bidding for a single lease, which typically covered a 160-acre tract, had skyrocketed. In 1923, the *Daily Oklahoman* said, "Brewster, the hero of the story, 'Brewster's Millions,' was driven almost to nervous prostration in trying to spend $1,000,000 in one year. Had Brewster been in Oklahoma . . . he could have spent $1,000,000 with just one little nod of his head."

In good weather, the auctions were held outdoors, on a hilltop

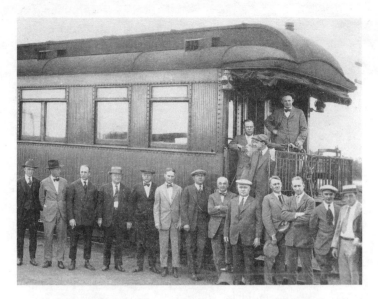

Frank Phillips (on bottom step) and other oilmen arrive in Osage territory in 1919.

in Pawhuska, in the shade of a large tree known as the Million Dollar Elm. Spectators would come from miles away. Ernest sometimes attended the events, and so did Mollie and other members of the tribe. "There is a touch of color in the audiences, too, for the Osage Indians...often are stoical but interested spectators," the Associated Press reported, deploying the usual stereotypes. Others in the community—including prominent settlers like Hale and Mathis, the Big Hill Trading Company owner—took a keen interest in the auctions. The money flowing into the community from the oil boom had helped to build their businesses and to realize their once seemingly fantastical dreams of turning the raw prairie into a beacon of commerce.

The auctioneer—a tall white man with thinning hair and a booming voice—would eventually step under the tree. He typically wore a gaudy striped shirt and a celluloid collar and a long flowing tie; a metal chain, connected to a timepiece, dangled from

Colonel Walters conducting an auction under the Million Dollar Elm

his pocket. He presided over all the Osage sales, and his moniker, Colonel, made him sound like a veteran of World War I. In fact, it was part of his christened name: Colonel Ellsworth E. Walters. A master showman, he urged bidders on with folksy sayings like "Come on boys, this old wildcat is liable to have a mess of kittens."

Because the least valued oil leases were offered first, the barons usually lingered in the back, leaving the initial bidding to upstarts. Jean Paul Getty, who attended several Osage auctions, recalled how one oil lease could change a man's fate: "It was not unusual for a penniless wildcatter, down to his last bit and without cash or credit with which to buy more, to ... bring in a well that made him a rich man." At the same time, a wrong bid could lead to ruin: "Fortunes were being made—and lost—daily."

The oilmen anxiously pored over geological maps and tried to glean intelligence about leases from men they employed as "rock hounds" and spies. After a break for lunch, the auction proceeded to more valuable leases, and the crowd's gaze inevitably turned toward the oil magnates, whose power rivaled, if not surpassed, that of the railroad and steel barons of the nineteenth century. Some of them had begun to use their clout to bend the course of history. In 1920, Sinclair, Marland, and other oilmen helped finance the successful presidential bid of Warren Harding. One oilman from Oklahoma told a friend that Harding's nomination had cost him and his interests $1 million. But with Harding in the White House, a historian noted, "the oil men licked their chops." Sinclair funneled, through the cover of a bogus company, more than $200,000 to the new secretary of the interior, Albert B. Fall; another oilman had his son deliver to the secretary $100,000 in a black bag.

In exchange, the secretary allowed the barons to tap the navy's invaluable strategic oil reserves. Sinclair received an exclusive lease to a reserve in Wyoming, which, because of the shape of a sandstone rock near it, was known as Teapot Dome. The head of Standard Oil warned a former Harding campaign aide, "I understand the Interior Department is just about to close a contract to lease Teapot Dome, and all through the industry it smells.... I *do* feel that you should tell the President that it *smells*."

The illicit payoffs were as yet unknown to the public, and as the barons moved toward the front of the Million Dollar Elm, they were treated as princes of capitalism, the crowd parting before them. During the bidding, tensions among the magnates sometimes boiled over. Once, Frank Phillips and Bill Skelly began to fight, rolling on the ground like rabid racoons, while Sinclair nodded at Colonel and walked off triumphantly with the lease. A reporter said, "Veterans of the New York Stock Exchange have witnessed no more thrilling scramble of humanity than the struggling group of oil men of state and national repute throw themselves into the fray to get at the choice tracts."

=====

On January 18, 1923, five months after the murder of McBride, many of the big oilmen gathered for another auction. Because it was winter, they met in the Constantine Theater, in Pawhuska.

Billed as "the finest building of its kind in Oklahoma," the theater had Greek columns and murals and a necklace of lights around the stage. As usual, Colonel started with the less valued leases. "What am I bid?" he called out. "Remember, no tracts sold for less than five hundred dollars."

A voice came out of the crowd: "Five hundred."

"I'm bid five hundred," Colonel boomed. "Who'll make it six hundred? Five going to six. Five-six, five-six—thank you—six, now seven, six-now-sev'n..." Colonel paused, then yelled, "Sold to this gentleman for six hundred dollars."

Throughout the day, bids for new tracts steadily grew in value: ten thousand...fifty thousand...a hundred thousand...

Colonel quipped, "Wall Street is waking up."

Tract 13 sold for more than $600,000, to Sinclair.

Colonel took a deep breath. "Tract 14," he said, which was in the middle of the rich Burbank field.

The crowd hushed. Then an unassuming voice rose from the middle of the room: "Half a million." It was a representative from Gypsy Oil Company, an affiliate of Gulf Oil, who was sitting with a map spread on his knees, not looking up as he spoke.

"Who'll make it six hundred thousand?" Colonel asked.

Colonel was known for his ability to detect even the slightest nod or gesture from bidders. At auctions, Frank Phillips and one of his brothers used almost imperceptible signals—a raised eyebrow or a flick of a cigar. Frank joked that his brother had once cost them $100,000 by swatting a fly.

Colonel knew his audience and pointed at a gray-haired man with an unlit cigar clamped between his teeth. He was representing a consortium of interests that included Frank Phillips and Skelly—the old adversaries now allies. The gray-haired man made an almost invisible nod.

"Seven hundred," cried Colonel, quickly pointing to the first bidder. Another nod.

"Eight hundred," Colonel said.

Downtown Pawhuska in 1906, before the oil boom

Pawhuska was transformed during the oil rush.

He returned to the first bidder, the man with the map, who said, "Nine hundred."

Another nod from the gray-haired man with the unlit cigar. Colonel belted out the words: "One million dollars."

Still, the bids kept climbing. "Eleven hundred thousand now twelve," Colonel said. "Eleven—now twelve—now twelve."

Finally, no one spoke. Colonel stared at the gray-haired man, who was still chewing on his unlit cigar. A reporter in the room remarked, "One wishes for more air."

Colonel said, "This is Burbank, men. Don't overlook your hands."

No one moved or uttered a word.

"Sold!" Colonel shouted. "For one million one hundred thousand dollars."

Each new auction seemed to surpass the previous one for the record of the highest single bid and the total of millions collected. One lease sold for nearly $2 million, while the highest total collected at an auction climbed to nearly $14 million. A reporter from *Harper's Monthly Magazine* wrote, "Where will it end? Every time a new well is drilled the Indians are that much richer." The reporter added, "The Osage Indians are becoming so rich that something will have to be done about it."

———

A growing number of white Americans expressed alarm over the Osage's wealth—outrage that was stoked by the press. Journalists told stories, often wildly embroidered, of Osage who discarded grand pianos on their lawns or replaced old cars with new ones after getting a flat tire. *Travel* magazine wrote, "The Osage Indian is today the prince of spendthrifts. Judged by his improvidence, the Prodigal Son was simply a frugal person with an inherent fondness for husks." A letter to the editor in the *Independent*, a weekly magazine, echoed the sentiment, referring to the typical Osage as a good-for-nothing who had attained wealth "merely because the Government unfortunately located him upon oil land which we white folks have developed for him." John Joseph Mathews bitterly recalled reporters "enjoying the bizarre impact of wealth on the Neolithic men, with the usual smugness and wisdom of the unlearned."

The accounts rarely, if ever, mentioned that numerous Osage had skillfully invested their money or that some of the spending by the Osage might have reflected ancestral customs that linked grand displays of generosity with tribal stature. Certainly during the Roaring Twenties, a time marked by what F. Scott Fitzgerald called "the greatest, gaudiest spree in history," the Osage were not alone in their profligacy. Marland, the oil baron who found the Burbank field, had built a twenty-two-room mansion in Ponca City, then abandoned it for an even bigger one. With an interior modeled after the fourteenth-century Palazzo Davanzati in Florence, the house had fifty-five rooms (including a ballroom with a gold-leaf ceiling and Waterford crystal chandeliers), twelve bathrooms, seven fireplaces, three kitchens, and an elevator lined with buffalo skin. The grounds contained a swimming pool and polo fields and a

The press claimed that whereas one out of every eleven Americans owned a car, virtually every Osage had eleven of them.

golf course and five lakes with islands. When questioned about this excess, Marland was unapologetic: "To me, the purpose of money was to buy, and to build. And that's what I've done. And if that's what they mean, then I'm guilty." Yet in only a few years, he would be so broke that he couldn't afford his lighting bill and had to vacate his mansion. After a stint in politics, he tried to discover another gusher but failed. His architect recalled, "The last time I saw him, I think he was just sitting on a nail keg of some kind out there northeast of town. It was raining and he had on a raincoat and rain hat but he was just sitting there kind of dejected. Two or three men were working his portable drilling rig and hoping they might find oil. So I just walked off with a lump in my throat and tears in my eyes." Another famed oilman in Oklahoma quickly burned through $50 million and ended up destitute.

Many Osage, unlike other wealthy Americans, could not spend their money as they pleased because of the federally imposed system of financial guardians. (One guardian claimed that an Osage adult was "like a child six or eight years old, and when he sees a new toy he wants to buy it.") The law mandated that guardians be assigned to any American Indians whom the Department of the Interior deemed "incompetent." In practice, the decision to appoint a guardian—to render an American Indian, in effect, a half citizen—was nearly always based on the quantum of Indian blood in the property holder, or what a state supreme court justice referred to as "racial weakness." A full-blooded American Indian was invariably appointed a guardian, whereas a mixed-blood person rarely was. John Palmer, the part-Sioux orphan who had been adopted by an Osage family and who played such an instrumental role in preserving the tribe's mineral rights, pleaded to members of Congress, "Let not that quantum of white blood or Indian determine the amount that you take over from the members of this tribe. It matters not about the quantum of Indian blood. You gentlemen do not deal with things of that kind."

Such pleas, inevitably, were ignored, and members of Congress would gather in wood-paneled committee rooms and spend hours examining in minute detail the Osage's expenditures, as if the country's security were at stake. At a House subcommittee hearing in 1920, lawmakers combed through a report from a government inspector who had been sent to investigate the tribe's spending habits, including those of Mollie's family. The investigator cited with displeasure "Exhibit Q": a bill for $319.05 that Mollie's mother, Lizzie, had racked up at a butcher shop before her death.

The investigator insisted that the devil had been in control of the government when it negotiated the oil-rights agreement with the tribe. Full of fire and brimstone, he declared, "I have visited and worked in and about most of the cities of our country, and am more or less familiar with their filthy sores and iniquitous cesspools. Yet I never wholly appreciated the story of Sodom and Gomorrah, whose sins and vices proved their undoing and their downfall, until I visited this Indian nation."

He implored Congress to take greater action. "Every white man in Osage County will tell you that the Indians are now running wild," he said, adding, "The day has come when we must begin our restriction of these moneys or dismiss from our hearts and conscience any hope we have of building the Osage Indian into a true citizen."

A few congressmen and witnesses tried to mitigate the scapegoating of the Osage. At a subsequent hearing, even a judge who served as a guardian acknowledged that rich Indians spent their wealth no differently than white people with money did. "There is a great deal of humanity about these Osages," he said. Hale also argued that the government should not be dictating the Osage's financial decisions.

But in 1921, just as the government had once adopted a ration system to pay the Osage for seized land—just as it always seemed to turn its gospel of enlightenment into a hammer of coercion—Congress implemented even more draconian legislation controlling how the Osage could spend their money. Guardians would not only continue to oversee their wards' finances; under the new law, these Osage Indians with guardians were also "restricted," which meant that each of them could withdraw no more than a few thousand dollars annually from his or her trust fund. It didn't matter if these Osage needed their money to pay for education or a sick child's hospital bills. "We have many little children," the last hereditary chief of the tribe, who was in his eighties, explained in a statement issued to the press. "We want to raise them and educate them. We want them to be comfortable, and we do not want our money held up from us by somebody who cares nothing for us." He went on, "We want our money now. We have it. It is ours, and we don't want some autocratic man to hold it up so we can't use it.... It is an injustice to us all. We do not want to be treated like a lot of little children. We are men and able to take care of ourselves." As a full-blooded Osage, Mollie was among those whose funds were restricted, though at least her husband, Ernest, was her guardian.

It wasn't only the federal government that was meddling in the tribe's financial affairs. The Osage found themselves surrounded by predators—"a flock of buzzards," as one member of the tribe complained at a council meeting. Venal local officials sought to devour the Osage's fortunes. Stickup men were out to rob their bank accounts. Merchants demanded that the Osage pay "special"—that is, inflated—prices. Unscrupulous accountants and lawyers tried to exploit full-blooded Osage's ill-defined legal status. There was even a thirty-year-old white woman in Oregon who sent a letter to the tribe, seeking a wealthy Osage to marry: "Will you please tell the richest Indian you know of, and he will find me as good and true as any human being can be."

At one congressional hearing, another Osage chief named Bacon Rind testified that the whites had "bunched us down here in the backwoods, the roughest part of the United States, thinking 'we will drive these Indians down to where there is a big pile of rocks and put them there in that corner.'" Now that the pile of rocks had turned out to be worth millions of dollars, he said, "everybody wants to get in here and get some of this money."

In the first days of February 1923, the weather turned violently cold. Icy winds cut across the plains and howled through the ravines and rattled tree branches. The prairie became as hard as stone, birds disappeared from the sky, and the Grandfather sun looked pale and distant.

One day, two men were out hunting four miles northwest of Fairfax when they spotted a car at the bottom of a rocky swale. Rather than approaching it, the hunters returned to Fairfax and informed authorities, and a deputy sheriff and the town marshal went to investigate. In the dying light, they walked down a steep slope toward the vehicle. Curtains, as vehicles often had back then, obscured the windows, and the car, a Buick, resembled a black coffin. On the driver's side, there was a small opening in the curtain, and the deputy peered through it. A man was slumped behind the steering wheel. "He must be drunk," the deputy said. But as he yanked open the driver's door, he saw blood, on the seat and on the floor. The man had been fatally shot in the back of the head. The angle of the shot, along with the fact that there was no gun present, ruled out suicide. "I seen he had been murdered," the deputy later recalled.

Since the brutal slaying of the oilman McBride, nearly six months had passed without the discovery of another suspicious death. Yet as the two lawmen stared at the man in the car, they realized that the killing hadn't stopped after all. The corpse was mummified by the cold, and this time the lawmen had no trouble identifying the victim: Henry Roan, a forty-year-old Osage Indian who was married with two children. He'd once worn his hair in two long braids before being forced to cut them off at boarding school, just as he'd been made to change his name from Roan Horse. Even without the braids—even entombed in the car—his long, handsome face and tall, lean body evoked those of an Osage warrior.

The lawmen returned to Fairfax, where they notified the justice of the peace. They also made sure that Hale was informed; as the mayor of Fairfax recalled, "Roan considered W. K. Hale his best friend." Roan was one of the full-bloods whose financial allowance had been officially curtailed, and he had often asked Hale to advance him cash. "We were good friends and he sought my aid when in trouble," Hale later recalled, adding that he'd given his friend so many loans that Roan had listed him as the beneficiary on his $25,000 life-insurance policy.

Henry Roan

A couple of weeks before his death, Roan had phoned Hale, distraught. Roan had learned that his wife was having an affair with a man named Roy Bunch. Hale went to visit with Roan and tried to console him.

Several days later, Hale bumped into Roan at the bank in downtown Fairfax. Roan asked him if he could borrow a few dollars; he was still morose about his wife, and he wanted to get a drink of moon liquor. Hale advised him not to buy any whiskey: "Henry, you better quit that. It's hurting you." And he warned him that the Prohibition men were "going to get" him.

"I am not going to bring any to town," Roan said. "I will hide it out."

Roan then disappeared, until his body turned up.

Once more, the macabre rituals began. The deputy and the marshal returned to the ravine, and Hale went with them. By then, darkness had enshrouded the crime scene, and the men lined up their vehicles on the hill and shone their headlights down into the depths below—into what one law-enforcement official called "truly a valley of death."

Hale remained on top of the hill and watched as the coroner's inquest began, the men bobbing in and out of the silhouetted Buick. One of the Shoun brother doctors concluded that the time of death was around ten days earlier. The lawmen noted the position of Roan's body—"his hands folded across his breast and his head on the seat"—and how the bullet had exited through his right eye and then shattered the windshield. They noted the broken glass strewn on the hood and on the ground beyond. They noted the things he carried: "$20 in greenback, two silver dollars, and . . . a gold watch." And the lawmen noted nearby tread marks in the frozen mud from another car—presumably the assassin's.

Word of the murder rekindled the sense of prickly dread. The *Osage Chief*—which, in the same issue, happened to carry a tribute to Abraham Lincoln as an inspiration to Americans—stated on its front page, HENRY ROAN SHOT BY UNKNOWN HAND.

The news jolted Mollie. In 1902, more than a decade before

meeting Ernest, she and Roan had been briefly married. There
are few surviving accounts detailing the relationship, but it was
likely an arranged marriage: youths—Mollie was only fifteen at
the time—pressed together to preserve a vanishing way of life.
Because the marriage had been contracted according to Osage cus-
tom, there was no need for a legal divorce, and they simply went
their own ways. Still, they remained bound by a memory of a fleet-
ing intimacy that had apparently ended with no bitterness and perhaps even some hidden warmth.

Many people in the county turned out for Roan's funeral. The
Osage elders sang the traditional songs for the dead, only now the
songs seemed for the living, for those who had to endure this world
of killing. Hale served again as a pallbearer, holding aloft the casket
of his friend. One of Hale's favorite poems echoed Jesus's command
in the Sermon on the Mount:

> Man's judgment errs, but there is One who "doeth all things well."
> Ever, throughout the voyage of life, this precept keep in view:
> "Do unto others as thou wouldst that they should do to you."

Mollie had always assisted the authorities, but as they began
looking into Roan's death, she became uneasy. She was, in her own
way, a product of the spirit of American self-construction. She
arranged the details of her past the way she tidied up her house,
and she had never told Ernest, her instinctively jealous second husband, about her Osage wedding with Roan. Ernest had provided
Mollie support during these terrible times, and they had recently
had a third child, a girl whom they had named Anna. If Mollie were
to let the authorities know of her connection to Roan, she would
have to admit to Ernest that she'd deceived him all these years. And
so she decided not to say a word, not to her husband or the authorities. Mollie had her secrets, too.

After Roan's death, electric lightbulbs began to appear on the outside of Osage houses, dangling from rooftops and windowsills and over back doors, their collective glow hollowing the dark. An Oklahoma reporter observed, "Travel in any direction that you will from Pawhuska and you will notice at night Osage Indian homes outlined with electric lights, which a stranger in the country might conclude to be an ostentatious display of oil wealth. But the lights are burned, as every Osage knows, as protection against the stealthy approach of a grim specter—an unseen hand—that has laid a blight upon the Osage land and converted the broad acres, which other Indian tribes enviously regard as a demi-paradise, into a Golgotha and field of dead men's skulls.... The perennial question in the Osage land is, 'who will be next?'"

The murders had created a climate of terror that ate at the community. People suspected neighbors, suspected friends. Charles Whitehorn's widow said she was sure that the same parties who had murdered her husband would soon "do away with her." A visitor staying in Fairfax later recalled that people were overcome by "paralyzing fear," and a reporter observed that a "dark cloak of mystery and dread...covered the oil-bespattered valleys of the Osage hills."

In spite of the growing risks, Mollie and her family pressed on with their search for the killers. Bill Smith confided in several people that he was getting "warm" with his detective work. One night, he was with Rita at their house, in an isolated area outside Fairfax, when they thought that they heard something moving around the perimeter of the house. Then the noise stopped; whatever, whoever, it was had disappeared. A few nights later, Bill and Rita heard the jostling again. Intruders—yes, they had to be—were outside, rattling objects, probing, then vanishing. Bill told a friend, "Rita's scared," and Bill seemed to have lost his bruising confidence.

Less than a month after Roan's death, Bill and Rita fled their home, leaving behind most of their belongings. They moved into an elegant, two-story house, with a porch and a garage, near the center of Fairfax. (They'd bought the house from the doctor James Shoun, who was a close friend of Bill's.) Several of the neighbors had watchdogs, which barked at the slightest disturbance; surely, these animals would signal if the intruders returned. "Now that we've moved," Bill told a friend, "maybe they'll leave us alone."

Not long afterward, a man appeared at the Smiths' door. He told Bill that he'd heard he was selling some farmland. Bill told him that he was mistaken. The man, Bill noticed, had a wild look about him, the look of an outlaw, and he kept glancing around the house as if he were casing it.

In early March, the dogs in the neighborhood began to die, one after the other; their bodies were found slumped on doorsteps and on the streets. Bill was certain that they'd been poisoned. He and Rita found themselves in the grip of tense silence. He confided in a friend that he didn't "expect to live very long."

On March 9, a day of swirling winds, Bill drove with a friend to the bootlegger Henry Grammer's ranch, which was on the western edge of the reservation. Bill told his friend that he needed a drink. But Bill knew that Grammer, whom the *Osage Chief* called the "county's most notorious character," possessed secrets and controlled an unseen world. The Roan investigation had produced one revelation: before disappearing, Roan had said that he was going to get whiskey at Grammer's ranch—the same place, coincidentally or not, where Mollie's sister Anna often got her whiskey, too.

Grammer was a rodeo star who had performed at Madison Square Garden and been crowned the steer-roping champion of the world. He was also an alleged train robber, a kingpin bootlegger with connections to the Kansas City Mob, and a blazing gunman. The porous legal system seemed unable to contain him. In 1904, in Montana, he gunned down a sheepshearer, yet he received only a three-year sentence. In a later incident, in Osage County, a man came into a hospital bleeding profusely from a gunshot wound, moaning, "I'm going to die, I'm going to die." He fingered

Grammer as his shooter, then passed out. But when the victim woke up the next day and realized that he wasn't going to the heavenly Lord—at least not anytime soon—he insisted that he had no idea who had pulled the trigger. As Grammer's bootlegging empire grew, he held sway over an army of bandits. They included Asa Kirby, a stickup man who had glimmering gold front teeth, and John Ramsey, a cow rustler who seemed the least bad of Grammer's bad men.

Henry Grammer received a three-year sentence after he killed a man in Montana.

Bill and his friend arrived at Grammer's ranch in the gathering dusk. A large wooden house and a barn loomed before them, and hidden in the surrounding woods were five-hundred-gallon copper stills. Grammer had set up his own private power plant so that his gangs could work all day and all night—the furtive light of the moon no longer needed to manufacture moonshine.

Finding that Grammer was away, Bill asked one of the workers for several jars of whiskey. He took a swig. In a nearby pasture, Grammer's prized horses often roamed. How easy it would have been for Bill, the old horse thief, to mount one and disappear. Bill drank some more. Then he and his friend drove back to Fairfax, passing the strings of lightbulbs—the 'fraid lights, as they were called—that shivered in the wind.

Bill dropped his friend off, and when he got home, he pulled his Studebaker in to the garage. Rita was in the house with Nettie Brookshire, a nineteen-year-old white servant who often stayed over.

Rita Smith and her servant Nettie Brookshire at a summer retreat

They soon went to bed. Just before three in the morning, a man who lived nearby heard a loud explosion. The force of the blast radiated through the neighborhood, bending trees and signposts and blowing out windows. In a Fairfax hotel, a night watchman sitting by a window was showered with broken glass and thrown to the floor. In another room of the hotel, a guest was hurled backward. Closer to the blast, doors on houses were smashed and torn asunder; wooden beams cracked like bones. A witness who had been a boy at the time later wrote, "It seemed that the night would never stop trembling." Mollie and Ernest felt the explosion, too. "It shook everything," Ernest later recalled. "At first I thought it was thunder." Mollie, frightened, got up and went to the window and could see something burning in the distant sky, as if the sun had burst violently into the night. Ernest went to the window and stood there with her, the two of them looking out at the eerie glow.

Ernest slipped on his trousers and ran outside. People were stumbling from their houses, groggy and terrified, carrying lanterns and firing guns in the air, a warning signal and a call for others to join what was a growing procession—a rush of people moving, on foot and in cars, toward the site of the blast. As people got closer, they cried out, "It's Bill Smith's house! It's Bill Smith's house!" Only there was no longer a house. Nothing but heaps of charred sticks and twisted metal and shredded furniture, which Bill and Rita had purchased just days earlier from the Big Hill Trading Company, and strips of bedding hanging from telephone wires and pulverized debris floating through the black toxic air. Even the Studebaker had been demolished. A witness struggled for words: "It just looked like, I don't know what." Clearly, someone had planted a bomb under the house and detonated it.

The flames amid the rubble consumed the remaining fragments of the house and gusted into the sky, a nimbus of fire. Volunteer firemen were carrying water from wells and trying to put out the blaze. And people were looking for Bill and Rita and Nettie. "Come on men, there's a woman in there," one rescuer cried out.

The justice of the peace had joined the search, and so had Mathis and the Shoun brothers. Even before remains were found, the Big Hill Trading Company undertaker had arrived with his hearse; a rival undertaker showed up as well, the two hovering like predatory birds.

The searchers scoured the ruins. James Shoun, having once owned the house, knew where the main bedroom had been situated. He combed in the vicinity, and that's when he heard a voice calling out. Others could hear it, too, faint but distinct: "Help!… Help!" A searcher pointed to a smoldering mound above the voice. Firemen doused the area with water, and amid the steaming smoke everyone began clawing the rubble away. As they worked, the voice grew louder, rising over the sound of the heaving, creaking wreckage. Finally, a face began to take shape, blackened and tormented. It was Bill Smith. He was writhing by his bed. His legs were seared beyond recognition. So were his back and hands. David Shoun later recalled that in all his years as a doctor he'd never seen a man in such agony: "He was halloing and was in awful misery." James Shoun tried to comfort Bill, telling him, "I won't let you suffer."

As the group of men cleared the debris, they could see that Rita was lying beside him in her nightgown. Her face was unmarred, and she looked as if she were still peacefully sleeping, in a dream. But when they lifted her up, they saw that the back of her head was crushed. She had no more life in her. When Bill realized that she was dead, he let out a torturous cry. "Rita's gone," he repeated. He told a friend who was there, "If you've got a pistol ..."

Ernest, wearing a bathrobe that someone had handed him to cover himself, was looking on. He was unable to turn away from the horror, and he kept muttering, "Some fire." The Big Hill undertaker asked him for permission to remove Rita's remains, and Ernest consented. Someone had to embalm her before Mollie saw her. What would she say when she learned that another sister had been murdered? Now Mollie, once expected to die first because of her diabetes, was the only one left.

The searchers couldn't find Nettie. The justice of the peace determined that the young woman, who was married and had a child, had been "blown to pieces." There weren't even sufficient remains for an inquest, though the rival undertaker found enough to claim the fee for a burial. "I figured on getting back and getting the hired girl with the hearse, but he beat me," the Big Hill undertaker said.

The doctors and the others lifted Bill Smith up as he grabbed for breath. They carried him toward an ambulance and took him to the Fairfax Hospital, where David Shoun injected him multiple times with morphine. He was the lone survivor, but before he could be questioned, he lost consciousness.

It had taken a while for local lawmen to arrive at the hospital. The town marshal and other officers had been in Oklahoma City for a court case. "The time of the deed was also deliberate," an

~~~ *Rita and Bill Smith's house before the blast—and then after*

investigator later noted, because it was done when officers "were all away." After hearing the news and rushing back to Fairfax, lawmen set up floodlights at the front and rear exits of the hospital, in case the killers planned to finish off Bill there. Armed guards kept watch, too.

In a state of delirium, wavering between life and death, Bill would sometimes mutter, "They got Rita and now it looks like they've got me." The friend who had accompanied him to Grammer's ranch came to see him. "He just kind a jabbered," the friend recalled. "I couldn't understand anything he said."

After nearly two days, Bill regained consciousness. He asked about Rita. He wanted to know where she was buried. David Shoun said he thought that Bill, fearing he might die, was about to make a declaration—to reveal what he knew about the bombing and the killers. "I tried to get it out of him," the doctor later told authorities. "I said, 'Bill, have you any idea who did it?' I was anxious to know." But the doctor said Bill never did disclose anything relevant. On March 14, four days after the bombing, Bill Smith died—another victim of what had become known as the Osage Reign of Terror.

———

A Fairfax newspaper published an editorial arguing that the bombing was beyond comprehension—"beyond our power to realize that humans would stoop so low." The paper demanded that the law "leave no stone unturned to ferret out the perpetrators and bring them to justice." A firefighter at the scene had told Ernest that those responsible for this "should be thrown in the fire and burned."

In April 1923, Governor Jack C. Walton of Oklahoma dispatched his top state investigator, Herman Fox Davis, to Osage County. A lawyer and a former private detective with the Burns agency, Davis had a groomed sleekness. He puffed on cigars, his eyes shining through a veil of blue smoke. A law-enforcement official called him the epitome of a "dime-novel detective."

Many Osage had come to believe that local authorities were colluding with the killers and that only an outside force like Davis could cut through the corruption and solve the growing number of cases. Yet within days Davis was spotted consorting with some of the county's notorious criminals. Another investigator then caught Davis taking a bribe from the head of a local gambling syndicate in exchange for letting him operate his illicit businesses. And it soon became clear that the state's special investigator in charge of solving the Osage murder cases was himself a crook.

In June 1923, Davis pleaded guilty to bribery and received a two-year sentence, but a few months later he was pardoned by the governor. Then Davis and several conspirators proceeded to rob— and murder—a prominent attorney; this time, Davis received a life sentence. In November, Governor Walton was impeached and removed from office, partly for having abused the system of pardons and paroles (and having turned "loose upon the honest citizens of the state a horde of murderers and criminals") and partly for having received illicit contributions from the oilman E. W. Marland that were used to build a lavish home.

Amid this garish corruption, W. W. Vaughan, a fifty-four-year-old attorney who lived in Pawhuska, tried to act with decency. A former prosecutor who vowed to eliminate the criminal element that was a "parasite upon those who make their living by honest means," he had worked closely with the private investigators struggling to solve the Osage murder cases. One day in June 1923, Vaughan received an urgent call. It was from a friend of George Bigheart, who was a nephew of the legendary chief James Bigheart. Suffering from suspected poisoning, Bigheart—who was forty-six and who had once written on a school application that he hoped to "help the needy, feed the hungry and clothe the naked"—had been rushed to a hospital in Oklahoma City. His friend said that he had information about the murders of the Osage but would speak only to Vaughan, whom he trusted. When Vaughan asked about Bigheart's condition, he was told to hurry.

Before leaving, Vaughan informed his wife, who had recently given birth to their tenth child, about a hiding spot where he had stashed evidence that he had been gathering on the murders. If anything should happen to him, he said, she should take it out immediately and turn it over to the authorities. She would also find money there for her and the children.

When Vaughan got to the hospital, Bigheart was still conscious. There were others in the room, and Bigheart motioned for them to leave. Bigheart then apparently shared his information, including incriminating documents. Vaughan remained at Bigheart's side for several hours, until he was pronounced dead. Then Vaughan telephoned the new Osage County sheriff to say that he had all the information he needed and that he was rushing back on the first train. The sheriff pressed him if he knew who had killed Bigheart. Oh, he knew more than that, Vaughan said.

He hung up and went to the station where he was seen boarding an overnight train. When the train pulled in to the station the next day, though, there was no sign of him. OWNER VANISHES LEAVING CLOTHES IN PULLMAN CAR, the *Tulsa Daily World* reported. MYSTERY CLOAKS DISAPPEARANCE OF W. W. VAUGHAN OF PAWHUSKA.

The Boy Scouts, whose first troop in the United States was organized in Pawhuska, in 1909, joined the search for Vaughan. Bloodhounds hunted for his scent. Thirty-six hours later, Vaughan's body was spotted lying by the railroad tracks, thirty miles north of Oklahoma City. He'd been thrown from the train; his neck was broken, and he'd been stripped virtually naked, just like the oilman McBride. The documents Bigheart had given him were gone, and when Vaughan's widow went to the designated hiding spot, it had been cleaned out.

The justice of the peace was asked by a prosecutor if he thought that Vaughan had known too much. The justice replied, "Yes, sir, and had valuable papers on his person."

The official death toll of the Osage Reign of Terror had climbed to at least twenty-four members of the tribe. Among the victims were two more men who had tried to assist the investigation: one, a prominent Osage rancher, plunged down a flight of stairs after being drugged; the other was gunned down in Oklahoma City on his way to brief state officials about the case. News of the murders began to spread. In an article titled "The 'Black Curse' of the Osages," the *Literary Digest*, a national publication, reported that members of the

~~~~ *W. W. Vaughan with his wife and several of their children*

tribe had been "shot in lonely pastures, bored by steel as they sat
in their automobiles, poisoned to die slowly, and dynamited as they
slept in their homes." The article went on, "In the meantime the
curse goes on. Where it will end, no one knows." The world's richest people per capita were becoming the world's most murdered.

The press later described the killings as being as "dark and sordid as any murder story of the century" and the "bloodiest chapter in American crime history."

All efforts to solve the mystery had faltered. Because of anonymous threats, the justice of the peace was forced to stop convening inquests into the latest murders. He was so terrified that merely to discuss the cases, he would retreat into a back room and bolt the door. The new county sheriff dropped even a pretense of investigating the crimes. "I didn't want to get mixed up in it," he later admitted, adding cryptically, "There is an undercurrent like a spring at the head of the hollow. Now there is no spring, it is gone dry, but it is broke way down to the bottom." Of solving the cases, he said, "It is a big doings and the sheriff and a few men couldn't do it. It takes the government to do it."

In 1923, after the Smith bombing, the Osage tribe began to urge the federal government to send investigators who, unlike the sheriff or Davis, had no ties to the county or to state officials. The Tribal Council adopted a formal resolution that stated:

> WHEREAS, in no case have the criminals been apprehended and brought to justice, and,
> WHEREAS, the Osage Tribal Council deems it essential for the preservation of the lives and property of members of the tribe that prompt and strenuous action be taken to capture and punish the criminals...
> BE IT FURTHER RESOLVED, that the Honorable Secretary of the Interior be requested to obtain the services of the Department of Justice in capturing and prosecuting the murderers of the members of the Osage Tribe.

Later, John Palmer, the half-Sioux lawyer, sent a letter to Charles Curtis, a U.S. senator from Kansas; part-Kaw, part-Osage, Curtis was then the highest official with acknowledged Indian ancestry ever elected to office. Palmer told Curtis that the situation was more dire than anyone could possibly imagine and that unless he and other men of influence got the Department of Justice to act, the "Demons" behind the "most foul series of crimes ever committed in this country" would escape justice.

———

While the tribe waited for the federal government to respond, Mollie lived in dread, knowing that she was the likely next target in the apparent plot to eliminate her family. She couldn't forget the night, several months before the explosion, when she had been in bed with Ernest and heard a noise outside her house. Someone was breaking into their car. Ernest comforted Mollie, whispering, "Lie still," as the perpetrator roared away in the stolen vehicle.

When the bombing occurred, Hale had been in Texas, and he now saw the charred detritus of the house, which resembled

Mollie with her sisters Rita (left), Anna (second from left), and Minnie (far right)

a wreckage of war—"a horrible monument," as one investigator called it. Hale promised Mollie that somehow he'd avenge her family's blood. When Hale heard that a band of outlaws—perhaps the same band responsible for the Reign of Terror—was planning to rob a store owner who kept diamonds in a safe, he handled the matter himself. He alerted the shopkeeper, who lay in wait; sure enough, that night the shopkeeper saw the intruders breaking in and blew one of them away with his single-barreled, 12-gauge shotgun. After the other outlaws fled, authorities went to inspect the dead man and saw his gold front teeth. It was Asa Kirby, Henry Grammer's associate.

One day, Hale's pastures were set on fire, the blaze spreading for miles, the blackened earth strewn with the carcasses of cattle. To Mollie, even the King of the Osage Hills seemed vulnerable, and after pursuing justice for so long, she retreated behind the closed doors and the shuttered windows of her house. She stopped entertaining guests or attending church; it was as if the murders had shattered even her faith in God. Among residents of the county, there were whispers that she'd locked herself away lest she go mad or that her mind was already unraveling under the strain. Her diabetes also appeared to be worsening. The Office of Indian Affairs received a note from someone who knew Mollie, saying that she was "in failing health and is not expected to live very long." Consumed by fear and ill health, she gave her third child, Anna, to a relative to be raised.

Time ground on. There are few records, at least authoritative ones, of Mollie's existence during this period. No record of how she felt when agents from the Bureau of Investigation—an obscure branch of the Justice Department that in 1935, would be renamed the Federal Bureau of Investigation—finally arrived in town. No record of what she thought of physicians like the Shoun brothers, who were constantly coming and going, injecting her with what was said to be a new miracle drug: insulin. It was as if, after being forced to play a tragic hand, she'd dealt herself out of history.

Then, in late 1925, the local priest received a secret message from Mollie. Her life, she said, was in danger. An agent from the Office of Indian Affairs soon picked up another report: Mollie wasn't dying of diabetes at all; she, too, was being poisoned.

CHRONICLE TWO

THE
EVIDENCE MAN

◥◥◥◥

A conspiracy is everything that ordinary life is not.
It's the inside game, cold, sure, undistracted, forever
closed off to us. We are the flawed ones, the inno-
cents, trying to make some rough sense of the daily
jostle. Conspirators have a logic and a daring beyond
our reach. All conspiracies are the same taut story of
men who find coherence in some criminal act.

—Don DeLillo, *Libra*

One day in the summer of 1925, Tom White, the special agent in charge of the Bureau of Investigation's field office in Houston, received an urgent order from headquarters in Washington, D.C. The new boss man, J. Edgar Hoover, asked to speak to him right away—in person. White quickly packed. Hoover demanded that his staff wear dark suits and sober neckties and black shoes polished to a gloss. He wanted his agents to be a specific American type: Caucasian, lawyerly, professional. Every day, he seemed to issue a new directive—a new Thou Shall Not—and White put on his big cowboy hat with an air of defiance.

He bade his wife and two young boys good-bye and boarded a train the way he had years earlier when he served as a railroad detective, riding from station to station in pursuit of criminals. Now he wasn't chasing anything but his own fate. When he arrived in the nation's capital, he made his way through the noise and lights to headquarters. He'd been told that Hoover had an "important message" for him, but he had no idea what it was.

White was an old-style lawman. He had served in the Texas Rangers near the turn of the century, and he had spent much of his life roaming on horseback across the southwestern frontier, a

Winchester rifle or a pearl-handled six-shooter in hand, tracking fugitives and murderers and stickup men. He was six feet four and had the sinewy limbs and the eerie composure of a gunslinger. Even when dressed in a stiff suit, like a door-to-door salesman, he seemed to have sprung from a mythic age. Years later, a bureau agent who had worked for White wrote that he was "as God-fearing as the mighty defenders of the Alamo," adding, "He was an impressive sight in his large, suede Stetson, and a plumb-line running from head to heel would touch every part of the rear of his body. He had a majestic tread, as soft and silent as a cat. He talked like he looked and shot—right on target. He commanded the utmost in respect and scared the daylights out of young Easterners like me who looked upon him with a mixed feeling of reverence and fear, albeit if one looked intently enough into his steel-gray eyes he could see a kindly and understanding gleam."

White had joined the Bureau of Investigation in 1917. He had wanted to enlist in the army, to fight in World War I, but he had

Tom White

been barred because of a recent surgery. Becoming a special agent was his way of serving his country, he said. But that was only part of it. Truth was, he knew that the tribe of old frontier lawmen to which he belonged was vanishing. Though he wasn't yet forty, he was in danger of becoming a relic in a Wild West traveling show, living but dead.

President Theodore Roosevelt had created the bureau in 1908, hoping to fill the void in federal law enforcement. (Because of lingering opposition to a national police force, Roosevelt's attorney general had acted without legislative approval, leading one congressman to label the new organization a "bureaucratic bastard.") When White entered the bureau, it still had only a few hundred agents and only a smattering of field offices. Its jurisdiction over crimes was limited, and agents handled a hodgepodge of cases: they investigated antitrust and banking violations; the interstate shipment of stolen cars, contraceptives, prizefighting films, and smutty books; escapes by federal prisoners; and crimes committed on Indian reservations.

Like other agents, White was supposed to be strictly a fact-gatherer. "In those days we had no power of arrest," White later recalled. Agents were also not authorized to carry guns. White had seen plenty of lawmen killed on the frontier, and though he didn't talk much about these deaths, they had nearly caused him to abandon his calling. He didn't want to leave this world for some posthumous glory. Dead was dead. And so when he was on a dangerous bureau assignment, he sometimes tucked a six-shooter in his belt. To heck with the Thou Shall Nots.

His younger brother J. C. "Doc" White was also a former Texas Ranger who had joined the bureau. A gruff, hard-drinking man who often carried a bone-handled six-shooter and, for good measure, a knife slipped into his leather boot, he was brasher than Tom—"rough and ready," as a relative described him. The White brothers were part of a small contingent of frontier lawmen who were known inside the bureau as the Cowboys.

Tom White had no formal training as a law-enforcement officer, and he struggled to master new scientific methods, such as decoding the mystifying whorls and loops of fingerprints. Yet he had been upholding the law since he was a young man, and he had honed his skills as an investigator—the ability to discern underlying patterns and turn a scattering of facts into a taut narrative. Despite his sensitivity to danger, he had experienced wild gunfights, but unlike his brother Doc—who, as one agent said, had a "bullet-spattered career"—Tom had an almost perverse habit of *not* wanting to shoot, and he was proud of the fact that he'd never put anyone into the ground. It was as if he were afraid of his own dark instincts. There was a thin line, he felt, between a good man and a bad one.

Tom White had witnessed many of his colleagues at the bureau cross that line. During the Harding administration, in the early 1920s, the Justice Department had been packed with political cronies and unscrupulous officials, among them the head of the bureau: William Burns, the infamous private eye. After being appointed director, in 1921, Burns had bent laws and hired crooked agents, including a confidence man who peddled protection and pardons to members of the underworld. The Department of Justice had become known as the Department of Easy Virtue.

In 1924, after a congressional committee revealed that the oil baron Harry Sinclair had bribed the secretary of the interior Albert Fall to drill in the Teapot Dome federal petroleum reserve—the name that would forever be associated with the scandal—the ensuing investigation lay bare just how rotten the system of justice was in the United States. When Congress began looking into the Justice Department, Burns and the attorney general used all their power, all the tools of law enforcement, to thwart the inquiry and obstruct justice. Members of Congress were shadowed. Their offices were broken in to and their phones tapped. One senator denounced the various "illegal plots, counterplots, espionage, decoys, dictographs" that were being used not to "detect and prosecute crime but...to shield profiteers, bribe takers and favorites."

By the summer of 1924, Harding's successor, Calvin Coolidge, had gotten rid of Burns and appointed a new attorney general, Harlan Fiske Stone. Given the growth of the country and the profusion of federal laws, Stone concluded that a national police force was indispensable, but in order to serve this need, the bureau had to be transformed from top to bottom.

To the surprise of many of the department's critics, Stone selected J. Edgar Hoover, the twenty-nine-year-old deputy director of the bureau, to serve as acting director while he searched for a permanent replacement. Though Hoover had avoided the stain of Teapot Dome, he had overseen the bureau's rogue intelligence division, which had spied on individuals merely because of their political beliefs. Hoover had also never been a detective. Never been in a shoot-out or made an arrest. His grandfather and his father, who were deceased, had worked for the federal government, and Hoover, who still lived with his mother, was a creature of the bureaucracy—its gossip, its lingo, its unspoken deals, its bloodless but vicious territorial wars.

Coveting the directorship as a way to build his own bureaucratic empire, Hoover concealed from Stone the extent of his role in domestic surveillance operations and promised to disband the intelligence division. He zealously implemented the reforms requested by Stone that furthered his own desire to remake the bureau into a modern force. In a memo, Hoover informed Stone that he had begun combing through personnel files and identifying incompetent or crooked agents who should be fired. Hoover also told Stone that per his wishes he had raised the employment qualifications for new agents, requiring them to have some legal training or knowledge of accounting. "Every effort will be made by employees of the Bureau to strengthen the morale," Hoover wrote, "and to carry out to the letter your policies."

In December 1924, Stone gave Hoover the job he longed for. Hoover would rapidly reshape the bureau into a monolithic force— one that, during his nearly five-decade reign as director, he would deploy not only to combat crime but also to commit egregious abuses of power.

========

Hoover had already assigned White to investigate one of the first law-enforcement corruption cases to be pursued in the wake of Teapot Dome. White took over as the warden of the federal penitentiary in Atlanta, where he led an undercover operation to catch officials who, in exchange for bribes, were granting prisoners nicer living conditions and early releases. One day during the investigation, White came across guards pummeling a pair of prisoners. White threatened to fire the guards if they ever abused an inmate again. Afterward, one of the prisoners asked to see White privately. As if to express his gratitude, the prisoner showed White a Bible, then began to lightly rub a mixture of iodine and water over its blank fly page. Words magically began to appear. Written in invisible ink, they revealed the address where a bank robber—who had escaped before White became warden—was hiding out. The secret message helped lead to the bank robber's capture. Other prisoners, meanwhile, began to share information, allowing White to uncover what was described as a system of "gilded favoritism and millionaire immunity." White gathered enough evidence to convict the former warden, who became prisoner No. 24207 in the same penitentiary. A bureau official who visited the prison wrote in a report, "I was very much struck with the feeling among the inmates relative to the action and conduct of Tom White. There seems to be a general feeling of satisfaction and confidence, a feeling that they are now going to get a square deal." After the investigation, Hoover sent a letter of commendation to White that said, "You brought credit and distinction not only to yourself but to the service we all have at heart."

White now arrived at headquarters, which was then situated on two leased floors in a building on the corner of K Street and Vermont Avenue. Hoover had been purging many of the frontier lawmen from the bureau, and as White headed to Hoover's office, he could see the new breed of agents—the college boys who typed faster than they shot. Old-timers mocked them as "Boy Scouts" who had "college-trained flat feet," and this was not untrue; as one agent later admitted, "We were a bunch of greenhorns who had no idea what we were doing."

White was led into Hoover's immaculate office, where there was an imposing wooden desk and a map on the wall showing the locations of the bureau's field offices. And there, before White, was the boss man himself. Hoover was then remarkably slim and boy-ish looking. In a photograph taken of him several months earlier, he is wearing a stylish dark suit. His hair is thick and wavy, his jaw is held tight, and his lips are pressed together sternly. His brown eyes have a watchful gaze, as if he were the one looking through a camera.

Hoover at the Bureau of Investigation in December 1924

White and his cowboy hat loomed over the diminutive Hoover, who was so sensitive about his modest stature that he rarely promoted taller agents to headquarters and later installed a raised dais behind his desk to stand on. If Hoover was intimidated by the sight of this monstrous Texan, he didn't show it: he told White that he needed to discuss a matter of the utmost urgency with him. It had to do with the murders of the Osage. White knew that the sensational case was one of the bureau's first major homicide investigations, but he was unfamiliar with its details, and he listened as Hoover spoke in staccato bursts—a strategy that Hoover had devised in his youth to overcome a bad stutter.

In the spring of 1923, after the Osage Tribal Council had passed the resolution seeking the Justice Department's help, the then director, Burns, had dispatched an agent from the bureau to investigate the murders, which by then totaled at least twenty-four Osage. The agent spent a few weeks in Osage County before concluding that "any continued investigation is useless." Other agents were subsequently dispatched to investigate, all to no avail. The Osage had been forced to finance part of the federal investigation with their own money—an amount that would eventually reach $20,000, the equivalent today of nearly $300,000. Despite this expenditure, Hoover had decided, after assuming command of the bureau, to dump the case back on state authorities in order to evade responsibility for the failure. The FBI agent who was in charge of the Oklahoma field office had assured Hoover that the transfer could be handled without any "unfavorable comment" in the press. Yet that was before the bureau, Hoover's bureau, had blood on its hands. A few months earlier, agents had persuaded the new governor of Oklahoma to release the outlaw Blackie Thompson, who'd been captured and convicted of bank robbery, so that he could work undercover for the bureau to gather evidence on the Osage killings. In field reports, the agents noted excitedly that their "undercover man" had begun to work among "the crooks in the oil fields and get the evidence he has promised us." The agents proclaimed, "We expect splendid results."

But while the agents were supposed to be keeping Blackie under close surveillance, they'd lost him in the Osage Hills. He then proceeded to rob a bank. And kill a police officer. It took months for authorities to apprehend Blackie, and, as Hoover noted, "a number of officers had to take their lives in their hands to correct this mistake." So far, Hoover had managed to keep the bureau's role in the affair out of the press. But behind the scenes there was a growing political uproar. The state attorney general had sent Hoover a telegram indicating that he held the bureau "responsible for failure" of the investigation. John Palmer, the tribe's well-known advocate, sent an angry letter to Charles Curtis, the Kansas senator, insinuating that the bureau's investigation had been tainted by corruption: "I join in the general belief that the murderers have been shrewd enough and politically and financially able enough to have honest and capable officers removed or sent to other parts, and also to quiet dishonest officials whose duty it was and is to hunt the perpetrators of these awful crimes." Comstock, the Oklahoma lawyer who had served as the guardian to several Osage, had personally briefed Senator Curtis on the bureau's catastrophic bungling.

When Hoover met with White, his grip on power remained tenuous, and he was suddenly confronting the one thing that he'd done everything to avoid since becoming director: a scandal. The situation in Oklahoma, Hoover believed, was "acute and delicate." Even a whiff of misconduct coming so soon after Teapot Dome could end his career. Only weeks earlier, he'd sent a "confidential" memo to White and other special agents, stating, "This Bureau cannot afford to have a public scandal visited upon it."

As White listened to Hoover, it became evident why he'd been summoned. Hoover needed White—one of his few experienced agents, one of the Cowboys—to resolve the case of the Osage murders and thereby protect Hoover's job. "I want you," Hoover said, to "direct the investigation."

He ordered White to set out for Oklahoma City and assume command of the field office there. Later, Hoover pointed out to White that because of the region's lawlessness, the field "office is probably turning out more work than any other office in the country and, consequently, has to have in charge of it a thoroughly competent and experienced investigator and one who can handle men." White knew that relocating to Oklahoma would be a great burden to his family. But he understood the stakes of the mission, and he told Hoover, "I am human enough and ambitious enough to want it."

White had no doubt what would happen if he didn't succeed: previous agents on the case had been banished to distant outposts or cast out from the bureau entirely. Hoover had said, "There can be no excuse offered for . . . failure." White was also aware that several of those who had tried to catch the killers had themselves been killed. From the moment he walked out of Hoover's office, he was a marked man.

After taking over the Oklahoma City field office in July 1925, White reviewed the bureau's voluminous files on the Osage murders, which had been amassed over the previous two years. Murder cases that are not solved quickly are often never solved. Evidence dries up; memories fade. More than four years had elapsed since the killings of Anna Brown and Charles Whitehorn, and frequently the only way to crack such cases is to find an overlooked clue submerged within the original cache of records.

The files on the murders of the Osage contained history in its rawest form: bits of data vacuumed up without any chronology or narrative, like a novel whose pages were out of order. White scoured this randomness for a hidden design. Though he was accustomed on the frontier to dealing with violent death, the brutality detailed in the reports was breathtaking. An agent wrote of the bombing of the Smiths' house, "The two women perished instantly, their bodies being blown asunder, and pieces of their flesh being later found plastered on a house 300 feet away." Previous agents had concentrated on the six cases that seemed most likely to be solved: the bombing deaths of Rita Smith and her husband, Bill Smith, and their servant Nettie Brookshire, and the fatal shootings of Anna Brown, Henry Roan, and Charles Whitehorn.

White struggled to find links among all the two dozen murders, but a few things were evident: rich Osage Indians were being targeted, and three of the victims—Anna Brown, Rita Smith, and their mother, Lizzie—were blood related. Surprisingly, agents hadn't spoken to Lizzie's surviving daughter, Mollie Burkhart. Investigators were taught to see the world through the eyes of others. But how could White fathom what this woman had seen—from being born in a lodge on the wild prairie to being catapulted into a fortune to being terrorized as her family and other Osage were picked off one by one? The files offered few insights about Mollie's life, mentioning only that she was ill with diabetes and had secluded herself in her house.

A few details in the files seemed telling. Repeat killers tend to rigidly adhere to a routine, yet the Osage murders were carried out in a bewildering array of methods. There was no signature. This, along with the fact that bodies turned up in different parts of the state and country, suggested that this was not the work of a single killer. Instead, whoever was behind the crimes must have employed henchmen. The nature of the murders also gave some insight into the mastermind: the person was not an impulsive killer but a connoisseur of plots who was intelligent enough to understand toxic substances and calculating enough to carry out his diabolical vision over years.

As White scrutinized the data in reports, one plausible story line after another seemed to cohere. But upon close inspection, the information invariably traced back to the same dubious sources: private eyes and local lawmen, whose opinions were based on little more than hearsay. Given that corruption seemed to permeate every institution in Osage County, these sources might be intentionally spreading disinformation in order to conceal the real plot. White realized that the greatest problem with the earlier investigations was not that agents had failed to uncover any leads; it was that there were *too* many. Agents would develop one, then simply drop it, or fail to corroborate it or to conclusively disprove it. Even when agents seemed to be moving on the right track, they had not managed to produce any evidence that would be admissible in a court of law.

As White strove to be a modern evidence man, he had to learn many new techniques, but the most useful one was timeless: coldly, methodically separating hearsay from facts that he could prove. He didn't want to hang a man simply because he had constructed a seductive tale. And after years of bumbling, potentially crooked investigations into the Osage murders, White needed to weed out half facts and build an indubitable narrative based on what he called an "unbroken chain of evidence."

White preferred to investigate his cases alone, but given the number of murders and leads to follow, he realized that he would need to assemble a team. Yet even a team wouldn't overcome one of the main obstacles that had stymied previous investigators: the refusal of witnesses to cooperate because of prejudice, corruption, or, as an agent put it, an "almost universal fear of being 'bumped off.'" So White decided that he would be the public face of the investigation, while most of the agents operated undercover.

Hoover promised him, "I'll assign as many men as you need." Recognizing the limits of his college boys, Hoover had kept on the rolls a handful of other Cowboys, including White's brother Doc. These agents were still learning scientific sleuthing, still adjusting to completing their reports on a typewriter. But White decided that these men were the only candidates who could handle such an assignment: infiltrating wild country, dealing with outlawry, shadowing suspects, going days without sleep, maintaining cover under duress, and handling deadly weapons if necessary. White began putting together a squad of Cowboys, but he didn't include Doc: since serving in the Rangers, he and his brother had avoided being assigned to the same cases, in order to protect their family from potentially losing two members at once.

White first recruited a former New Mexico sheriff, who, at fifty-six, became the oldest member of the team. Though reserved to the point of being shy, the sheriff was adept at assuming under-cover identities, having pretended to be everything from a cow rustler to a counterfeiter. White then enlisted a stocky, garrulous, and blond-haired former Texas Ranger who, according to a supe-rior, was best suited for situations "where there is any element of danger." In addition, White brought on an experienced deep-cover operative who looked more like an insurance salesman—perhaps because it was his former profession.

One agent from the previous investigation, White decided, should be retained: John Burger. He had a comprehensive knowl-edge of the case—from the suspects to the trails of evidence—and he had developed an extensive network of informants that included many outlaws. Because Burger was already well known in Osage County, he would work openly with White. So would another agent, Frank Smith, a Texan who listed his interests thus: "Pistol and rifle practice—Big game hunting—Game fishing—Mountain climbing—Adventures—Man hunting." In Hoover's bureau, Smith was classified as one of "the older type of uneducated Agents."

Finally, White brought in the singular John Wren. A onetime spy for the revolutionary leaders in Mexico, Wren was a rarity in the bureau: an American Indian. (Quite possibly, he was the only one.) Wren was part Ute—a tribe that had flourished in what is today Colorado and Utah—and he had a twirled mustache and black eyes. He was a gifted investigator, but he'd recently washed out of the bureau for failing to file reports and meet regulations. A special agent in charge had said of him with exasperation, "He is exceedingly skilled in handling cases, and some of his work can only be described as brilliant. But of what avail are many nights and days of hard application to duty if the results are not embodied in written reports? He has all the information in his head but will not

~~~~ *White's team included a former Texas Ranger who*
was said to be suited for "any element of danger."

commit it to paper." In March 1925, Hoover had reinstated Wren but
only after warning him, "Unless you measure up to the standards
that are now in effect in this Bureau, I will be compelled to request
your resignation." White knew that Wren would bring an essential
perspective to the team. Some of the previous agents on the case,
including Burger, had betrayed the kind of casual prejudice toward
the Osage that was then commonplace. In a joint report, Burger
and another agent had stated, "The Indians, in general, are lazy,
pathetic, cowardly, dissipated," and Burger's colleague insisted that
the only way to make "any of these dissolute, stubborn Osage Indians talk and tell what they know is to cut off their allowance ... and

if necessary, throw them in jail." Such contempt had deepened the Osage's distrust of the federal agents and hindered the investigation. But Wren, who referred to himself as one of Hoover's "braves," had capably handled many delicate cases on reservations.

White relayed to Hoover which men he wanted, and those not already assigned to the Oklahoma office received urgent orders, in code, from headquarters: "PROCEED UNDER COVER IMMEDIATELY REPORTING TO AGENT IN CHARGE TOM WHITE." Once the team had been assembled, White grabbed his gun and set out for Osage County—another traveler in the mist.

10 ~~~ ELIMINATING THE IMPOSSIBLE

One after the other, the strangers slipped into Osage County. The former sheriff showed up, in the guise of an elderly, quiet cattleman from Texas. Then the talkative former Texas Ranger appeared, also presenting himself as a rancher. Not long afterward, the onetime insurance salesman opened a business in downtown Fairfax, peddling bona fide policies. Finally, Agent Wren arrived as an Indian medicine man who claimed to be searching for his relatives.

White had counseled his men to keep their covers simple so they didn't betray themselves. The two operatives acting as cattlemen soon ingratiated themselves with William Hale, who considered them fellow Texas cowboys and who introduced them to many of the leading townsfolk. The insurance salesman dropped by the houses of various suspects, under the pretense of hawking policies. Agent Wren made his own inroads, attending tribal gatherings and gleaning information from Osage who might not otherwise talk to a white lawman. "Wren had lived among the Indians . . . and had gotten away with it in remarkable shape," White told Hoover, adding that his undercover men seemed to be able to "withstand the rigor of the life."

It was hard for White to know where to begin the investigation. The records from the coroner's inquest into the death of Anna Brown had mysteriously vanished. "My desk was broken into and the testimony disappeared," the justice of the peace in Fairfax said.

Virtually no evidence had been preserved from the various crime scenes, but in the case of Anna, the undertaker had secretly kept one object: her skull. About the size of a melon, the hollow chamber felt unnervingly light in one's hand, air blowing through as though it were a sun-bleached shell. White examined the skull and could see the hole in the back where the bullet had entered. He concluded, as earlier investigators had, that the bullet must have come from a small-caliber gun—a .32 or perhaps a .38 pistol. He, too, noticed the oddity that there was no exit wound in the front of Anna's skull, which meant that the bullet had lodged inside her head. The bullet would've been impossible to miss during the autopsy. Someone on the scene—a conspirator or even the killer—must have swiped it.

The justice of the peace admitted that he had harbored such suspicions as well. He was pressed on the matter: Was it possible that, say, the two doctors, David and James Shoun, had taken it? "I don't know," he said.

When David Shoun was questioned, he conceded that there was no exit wound, but he insisted that he and his brother had "made a diligent search" for the bullet. James Shoun protested similarly. White was convinced that somebody had altered the crime scene. But, given the number of people present during the autopsy—including the local lawmen, the undertaker, and Mathis, the Big Hill Trading Company owner—it seemed impossible to say who the culprit was.

=====

To separate the facts from the hearsay contained in the bureau's case files, White settled upon a simple but elegant approach: he would methodically try to corroborate each suspect's alibi. As Sherlock Holmes famously said, "When you have eliminated the impossible, whatever remains, however improbable, must be the truth."

White relied upon Agent Burger to guide him through the murk of the previous federal investigation. Agent Burger had worked on the case for a year and a half, and during that time he had pursued many of the same leads as the private eyes hired by Hale and Mathis and Mollie's family. By drawing on Agent Burger's findings, White was able to quickly rule out many of the suspects, including Anna's ex-husband, Oda Brown. His alibi—that he was with another woman—checked out, and it became clear that the forger who had implicated Brown had fabricated his story hoping to bargain with prosecutors for better prison conditions. Further investigation eliminated other suspects, like the ruffian oil workers who had been pinpointed by Harve Freas, the ousted sheriff.

White then explored the rumor that Rose Osage had killed Anna because Anna had tried to seduce her boyfriend, Joe Allen. (Rose and Joe had since married.) White learned of the statement that private investigator No. 28 had obtained from the Kaw Indian woman, in which Rose had confessed to being the murderer. In a field report, an agent from the bureau observed, "It is a matter of common knowledge that Rose ... was of a violent and jealous disposition." The Fairfax town marshal also shared with

Agent John Burger

agents a disturbing detail: around the time of Anna's murder, he had found a dark stain on the backseat of Rose's car. It looked like blood, he said.

Agent Burger informed White that he had once brought Rose Osage and Joe to the sheriff's office for questioning. The two suspects were placed in separate rooms and left to stir. When Agent Burger interrogated Rose, she insisted that she'd nothing to do with Anna's killing. "I never had a quarrel or fight with Anna," she stated. Agent Burger then confronted Joe, who, in the agent's words, was "very self-contained, sullen and wicked appearing." Another investigator had separately asked Joe, "Were you thick with Annie?"

"No, I was never," he said.

Joe gave the same alibi Rose did: on the night of May 21, 1921, they had been together in Pawnee, seventeen miles southwest of Gray Horse, and had stopped at a rooming house. The owner of the rooming house—which was one of those seething places that often reeked of sex and moonshine—supported Joe and Rose's claims. The investigators noticed, however, that the stories told by Rose and Joe were almost verbatim, as if they had rehearsed them.

Rose and Joe were released, and afterward Agent Burger sought the help of an informant—the bootlegger and dope peddler Kelsie Morrison, who seemed an ideal source of intelligence. He'd once been married to an Osage woman, and was close to Rose and other suspects. Before Agent Burger could recruit Morrison, though, he needed to find him: Morrison had fled Osage County after assaulting a local Prohibition officer. Burger and other agents made inquiries and learned that Morrison was in Dallas, Texas, using the alias Lloyd Miller. The agents sprang a trap. They had a registered letter sent to the P.O. box listed under Miller's name, then they nabbed Morrison when he went to retrieve it. "We interviewed 'Lloyd Miller' who for about an hour denied that he was Kelsie Morrison but finally admitted that he was," Agent Burger reported.

Morrison, whom Agent Burger described as an "unusually

shrewd and reckless and self-confessed criminal," dressed like a dance-hall hustler. Tall, bullet scarred, small-eyed, and jittery, he seemed to be wasting away from within—hence his nickname, Slim. "Talks and smokes cigarettes a lot," Agent Burger noted in a report. "Sniffs nose and works mouth and nose like rabbit almost continuously, especially when excited."

The feds cut a deal with Morrison: in return for getting his arrest warrant for assault quashed, he would work as an informant on the Osage murder cases. Agent Burger told headquarters, "This arrangement is strictly confidential and not to be divulged outside of this Bureau to anyone, under any circumstances."

There was a risk that Morrison might slip away, and before releasing him, Agent Burger made sure that he'd gone through a rigorous process known as Bertillonage. Devised by the French criminologist Alphonse Bertillon in 1879, it was the first scientific method for identifying repeat criminals. Using a caliper and other special tools, Agent Burger, with the help of the Dallas police, took eleven of Morrison's body measurements. Among them were the length of his left foot, the width and length of his head, and the diameter of his right ear.

After Agent Burger informed Morrison of the purpose of these measurements, he also commissioned a mug shot, another of Bertillon's innovations. In 1894, Ida Tarbell, the muckraking journalist, wrote that any prisoner who passed through Bertillon's system would be forever "spotted": "He may efface his tattooing, compress his chest, dye his hair, extract his teeth, scar his body, dissimulate his height. It is useless."

But Bertillonage was already being displaced by a more efficient method of identification that was revolutionizing the world of scientific detection: fingerprinting. In some cases, a suspect could now be placed at the scene of a crime even without a witness present. When Hoover became the bureau's acting director, he created the Identification Division, a central repository for the fingerprints of arrested criminals from around the country. Such scientific

methods, Hoover proclaimed, would assist "the guardians of civilization in the face of the common danger."

Agent Burger had Morrison's fingertips dabbed in ink. "We
have his picture, description, measurements and fingerprints in the
event we have cause to apprehend him," he informed headquarters.

He then gave Morrison some spending money. Morrison promised to visit Rose Osage and Joe Allen as well as members of the
underworld, to see what he could learn about the murders. Morrison warned that if anyone discovered he was working for the feds,
it would mean his death.

He reported back that he had asked Rose, regarding Anna's
murder, "Why'd you do it?" And she replied, "You don't know a god
damn thing about it, Slim, I did not kill Anna." In a memo, Agent
Burger noted of his prized informant, "If he is not bumped off too
soon he can do us a lot of good."

———

White now reviewed all the information that had been gathered
by Morrison and the agents regarding Rose Osage and Joe Allen. In
light of Rose's statement to Morrison and the fact that the rooming
house owner had confirmed Rose and Joe's alibi, the Kaw Indian's
statement that Rose had confessed to her seemed puzzling. One
detail, in particular, was curious. According to the Kaw Indian's
account of Rose's confession, Anna was in the car when Rose shot
her, and her body was then dumped at Three Mile Creek, where
Rose also discarded her own bloodstained clothes.

The autopsy findings were telling. Criminologists had come
to understand that blood coagulates at the lowest point of a body
after death, producing dark splotches on the skin. If, when one finds
a corpse, these splotches appear on the higher regions, it is a sign
that someone has moved the body. In Anna's case, the doctors had
not reported any indications of this, and from all the descriptions of
the crime scene there had been no trail of blood from the car down
to the creek.

It seemed that the witness must be lying and that Rose and Joe were innocent. This would explain why the Dictograph set up by the private detectives working for Mollie Burkhart's family had never picked up any incriminating statements, and why Rose's clothes had never been found in the creek. When agents interrogated the Kaw Indian, it didn't take much for her to crack. She admitted that Rose had never told her any such story about the killing. In fact, a strange white man had come to her house, written up the statement, and forced her to sign it, even though none of it was true. White realized that the conspirators were not only erasing evidence—they were manufacturing it.

Hoover immediately began pestering White for updates. Once, when White was in the field and did not respond immediately, Hoover chastised him, saying, "I do not understand why, at the end of the day, you could not have wired me fully as to the developments and general situation." Hoover's attention to the case had waxed and waned over the years, but he had become so agitated about the growing criticism he was receiving in Oklahoma that prior to White's arrival he had started to investigate matters himself. Though he was not one to venture into the muck of the field (he had a phobia of germs and had installed in his home a special filtration system to purify the air), he would sit in his office, poring over incoming reports from agents—his eyes and ears on the menacing world.

As Hoover studied the reports on the Osage murders, he found it an "interesting observation" that Anna Brown and Roan were both killed with a bullet to the back of the head, and "after carefully going over all of the angles," he came to believe that a white woman, Necia Kenny, who was married to an Osage man, might hold the key to the case. Kenny had told agents that A. W. Comstock, the attorney who served as a guardian for several Osage, was

A. W. Comstock with an Osage Indian

likely part of the conspiracy. Hoover hadn't forgotten that Comstock had criticized the bureau and had threatened to turn Senator Curtis against him—which made Comstock, in Hoover's eyes, a malicious rat. "I am convinced that Mrs. Kenny is pretty well on the right track," Hoover had told one of his agents.

Kenny had a history of mental instability—she claimed to be possessed by spells—and she had once even attempted to murder another local attorney. Still, Hoover himself had interviewed her in Washington, not once, but twice, and he arranged for a government expert on "mental diseases" to evaluate her. The doctor concluded that she was paranoid, but noted, as Hoover put it, that she "perceives items which would escape the observation of the average individual." As a result, Hoover said, Kenny "is of greater value to us in furnishing leads than she would be possibly as a witness."

White hadn't been able to substantiate Kenny's allegations, but he wasn't sure what to make of Comstock, either. Armed with his English Bulldog revolver, Comstock was one of the few prominent white citizens in Osage County who seemed willing to assist investigators. He had told agents that he was sure he could secure critical evidence—if only he could have access to the bureau's files. White refused to share any confidential records. Still, Comstock would routinely come to see White, sharing helpful tidbits of information and checking on the progress of the investigation. Then he would disappear into the streets with his gleaming English Bulldog.

═══

By the end of July 1925, White had turned his full attention to the last of the listed suspects in Anna Brown's murder: Bryan Burkhart, Mollie's brother-in-law. White learned that during the inquest, in 1921, Bryan had stated that on the night Anna disappeared he'd taken her straight home from Ernest and Mollie's house, dropping her off between 4:30 and 5:00 p.m.; Bryan then headed into Fairfax, where he was seen with Hale, Ernest, and his visiting uncle and aunt, who went with him to watch the musical *Bringing Up Father.* There wouldn't have been time for him to go to the creek, shoot Anna, and return to town before the show started. His alibi seemed airtight.

To corroborate it, Agent Burger and a colleague had earlier traveled to Campbell, a town in northern Texas, where Ernest and Bryan's aunt and uncle lived. The agents sped past the old trails that cowboys had once followed—trails that were now supplanted by cattle cars pulled by shrieking locomotives. Agents discovered that Hale had grown up in a wooded grove only a few miles from Campbell. His mother had died when he was three years old—the King of the Osage Hills, too, burdened by a past.

In Campbell, agents stopped at the austere house of Bryan's

uncle and aunt. The uncle was away, but the aunt invited the investigators inside and launched into a venomous rant about how Ernest had married one of those red millionaires. Burger asked her about the night Anna disappeared. Oh, she'd heard the whispers about how Bryan was responsible for killing that drunken Indian, she said. But none of it was true. After dropping Anna off, Bryan had joined the rest of the party in Fairfax.

The uncle suddenly appeared at the front door. He seemed displeased to find a pair of federal agents inside his home. He was reluctant to speak, but he confirmed that Bryan had met them in Fairfax after dropping Anna off. He added that after the show he and his wife had spent the evening in the same house with Bryan and that Bryan was there the whole time; he simply couldn't have been the murderer. The uncle then made it clear that he wanted the agents to get the hell out.

———

In August 1925, White sent his undercover operatives to infiltrate the town of Ralston. White wanted his team to investigate a lead that had not been properly followed up: on the night Anna Brown disappeared, case records showed, she might have been spotted in a car by a group of white men who were sitting in front of a hotel on Ralston's main street. Previous investigators, including local lawmen and the private eyes, had spoken to these valuable witnesses and then seemingly buried what they had learned. At least one of the witnesses had since vanished, and White was convinced that, as one agent had noted in a report, such people were being "paid by suspects to go away and stay away."

White and his men tried to track down some of the witnesses outside the hotel, including an elderly farmer who had been questioned earlier by an agent. During that initial interview, the farmer had seemed to be suffering from dementia: he had stared at the agent blankly. After a while, though, he had perked up. His memory was just fine, he explained; he'd simply wanted to make sure that the investigators were who they said they were. Talking to the wrong person about these murders was liable to get one planted in the ground.

The farmer now spoke to White and his men. According to testimony that the farmer subsequently gave under oath, he remembered that evening well, because he'd often discussed it with friends of his who gathered regularly at the hotel. "We old fellows have a lot of time in town and that is where we sit down," he said. He recalled that the car had stopped by the curb and through its open window he could see Anna—she was right there in front of him. She said hello, and someone in the group said back, "Hello, Annie."

The farmer's wife, who had been with him in Ralston that night, was also certain that the woman in the car was Anna, though she didn't talk to her. "There was Indians so much around there," she testified. "Sometimes I spoke to one, and sometimes I didn't. Sometimes when I spoke to one they didn't speak." Asked if Anna had been slumped over from drinking, she said, "Just sitting like they all sit, just about like this." She posed herself straight and rigid, like a statue, her rendition of a stoic Indian.

At one point, she was asked if anyone had been with Anna in the car.

"Yes, sir," the farmer's wife said.

"Who?"

"Bryan Burkhart."

Bryan, she said, had been driving the car and wearing a cowboy hat. Another witness said that he also saw Bryan with Anna in the car. "They went straight west from there right on through town and I don't know where they went from there," the witness recalled.

It was the first proven crack in Bryan's alibi. He might have taken Anna home, but he'd eventually gone back out with her. As an agent wrote in a report, Bryan "perjured himself when he swore before the coroner's inquest at Fairfax…that he had left Anna safely at her home in Fairfax between 4:30 and 5 p.m."

White needed to establish where the two had gone after leaving Ralston. Piecing together details from Agent Burger's previous informants as well as from witnesses located by the undercover team, White was able to create a time line. Bryan and Anna had stopped at a nearby speakeasy and stayed there until about 10:00 p.m. Then they headed to another hell joint, several miles north of Fairfax. Bryan's uncle was spotted with them, so perhaps the uncle had been lying to Agent Burger, to cover not only for Bryan but for himself as well. The owner of the place told agents that Bryan and Anna had been drinking there until about 1:00 a.m.

Accounts of where Bryan and Anna went after that grew murkier. One witness said that they'd stopped, alone, at another speakeasy closer to Fairfax. Others reported seeing Bryan and Anna leave the speakeasy in the company of a "third man" who wasn't the

Bryan Burkhart

uncle. "Third man is said to have been present with Anna Brown and Bryan Burkhart," Agent Burger noted. The last sighting of Anna and Bryan together that the investigators heard about had been at approximately 3:00 a.m. A witness who knew them both said that she'd heard a car stop near her house in Fairfax. A man whom she believed to be Bryan shouted, "Stop your foolishness, Annie, and get into this car."

After that, there was no trace of Anna—she'd been ghosted. Bryan's neighbor, though, spotted him returning home at sunrise. Bryan later told the neighbor not to say a word to anybody, and gave him money to keep quiet.

White had homed in on a prime suspect. But, as with many mysteries, each answer to a question opened up another question. If Bryan had killed Anna, what was his motive? Was he involved in the other murders? And who was the third man?

By the end of that summer, White began to suspect that there was a mole inside the investigation. When one of his agents was questioning a seedy local attorney—who, according to an informant, was trying to "strangle" the government's probe—the attorney betrayed a shocking knowledge of the inner workings of the case. Finally, he admitted that he'd "seen part of the reports made by the Bureau . . . and had an opportunity to see more of them."

The bureau's probe had long been plagued by leaks and sabotage. One agent complained that "information contained in reports immediately gets into the possession of unauthorized and unscrupulous persons." A U.S. attorney also discovered that the reports furnished to him by the bureau had vanished from his office. The breaches threatened the lives of agents and created insidious doubts, with officials questioning each other's loyalty. One federal prosecutor demanded that no copy of his report be "handed to any representative of the State of Oklahoma."

Perhaps most damagingly, two private eyes, including one from the Burns agency, tried to expose the bureau's main informant, Kelsie Morrison. These private eyes leaked to several local officials that Morrison was working with the bureau, then went so far as to detain him on a trumped-up robbery charge. Agent Burger said that the conduct of one of these private detectives was "reprehensible" and was "certainly hurting our investigation." Obstruction, he noted, appeared to be these private detectives' "sole object," adding, "Someone must be paying them to do this." An agent reported that Morrison, after being released from jail, seemed "frightened out of his wits." During one of their meetings, Morrison beseeched agents to get the "son-of-bitches" who did the killings before they got him. Agent Burger warned Morrison, "Look out for double crossing and traps."

At night, White sometimes met with his team in the countryside, the men huddling in the dark like fugitives. Agents in the past had sensed that they were being followed, and White gave his men advice in case their cover was blown: "Keep your balance, avoid

The former New Mexico sheriff who played the role of a cattleman on White's team

any rough stuff if possible." Making it clear that they should carry weapons, he added, "But if you have to fight to survive, do a good job."

———

White found himself wandering through a wilderness of mirrors—his work more akin to espionage than to criminal investigation. There were moles and double agents and possibly triple agents. No one had aroused more suspicion than the private eye called Pike. A gentleman in Osage County had once approached Agent Burger and introduced himself as an intermediary, a go-between, for Pike. Agents were aware that Pike had been hired by William Hale back in 1921 to solve the Osage murders but had abandoned the case after failing to make any progress.

The intermediary, however, said that Pike had actually withheld a crucial piece of information that he had discovered during his investigation: he knew the identity of the third man who'd been spotted with Bryan and Anna around the time that she was killed. Agent Burger wrote that Pike apparently "has known and talked with this third man." But the intermediary made it clear that Pike would share this information under one condition: that he be paid a king's ransom. "It is quite apparent there is some crooked work afoot," Agent Burger wrote in a report.

Agents demanded, through the intermediary, that Pike come forward. But again he didn't comply, evidently determined to extort money and obstruct justice. Agents launched a manhunt for Pike, whose last known address was in Kansas City. "Pike will have to be located and apprehended," Agent Burger wrote. "He changed his Kansas City address soon after it became known that we were working on him. We feel sure he has been paid to skip."

Not long after, Pike was caught allegedly committing highway robbery in Tulsa. Out of angles to play, he gave up a name of a local gambler. Agents could confirm that the gambler had been at one of the speakeasies drinking with Bryan and Anna on the night of

May 21. But further investigation proved that the gambler had gone home too early to be the third man.

It seemed as if the agents had once more been duped. But they continued to work on Pike, to pressure him, and over time he began to reveal, little by little, a hidden dimension to the case. He disclosed that he'd never really been hired to solve the murder of Anna Brown; in fact, he'd been asked to conceal Bryan's whereabouts on the night of the crime.

Pike told agents that he was supposed to manufacture evidence and to generate false witnesses—to "shape an alibi," as he put it. What's more, he claimed that his orders had come directly from William Hale.

Pike explained that Hale took pains never to say explicitly that Bryan had been involved in Anna's murder, but this was evident from what Hale was asking him to do. If Pike was telling the truth, it meant that Hale—a seeming paragon of law and order who had held himself up as Mollie Burkhart's most staunch protector—had been lying all these years about Anna's murder. Pike could not answer what White wanted to know most: Was Hale merely protecting Bryan, or was he part of a more intricate, nefarious design?

Pike, though, told agents one more thing that was startling. When he met with Hale and Bryan, Pike said, there was sometimes another person present: Ernest Burkhart. Pike added that Ernest was careful never to "discuss this case or talk it over with him in the presence of Mollie Burkhart."

The first time that Tom White saw a criminal hanged he was just a boy, and the executioner was his father. In 1888, his father, Robert Emmett White, was elected sheriff of Travis County, Texas, which included Austin, then a city of fewer than fifteen thousand people. A towering man with a dense mustache, Emmett, as Tom's father liked to be called, was poor, stern, hardworking, and pious. In 1870, at the age of eighteen, he migrated from Tennessee to the still-wild frontier of central Texas. Four years later, he married Tom's mother, Maggie. They lived in a log cabin, in the desolate hill country outside Austin, where they herded cattle and scratched the earth for whatever food it might yield. Tom, who was born in 1881, was the third of their five children; among them was Doc, the youngest, and Dudley, Tom's bruising older brother with whom he was particularly close. The nearest schoolhouse—which had one room and a single teacher for eight grades—was three miles away, and to get there, Tom and his siblings had to walk.

When Tom was six, his mother died, apparently from complications after childbirth. Her body was laid in a plot where Tom could see the grass growing over her. Emmett was left to raise Tom and his siblings, all of whom were under the age of ten. A nineteenth-

〝〝〝 *Tom (standing to the left) and his brothers, including Doc (on the donkey) and Dudley (far right)*

century book profiling distinguished Texans said of Emmett, "Mr. White belongs to that class of solid, substantial farmers of which Travis county can boast.... He is well known in the county, and the people have the greatest confidence in his energy and integrity of character." In 1888, a delegation of townsfolk beseeched Emmett to run for county sheriff, which he did, winning easily. And so Tom's father became the law.

As sheriff, Emmett was in charge of the county jail, in Austin, and he moved with his children into a house adjoining the building. The jail resembled a fortress, with barred windows and cold stone passageways and tiered cells. In Emmett's first year, the jail held nearly three hundred prisoners, including four murderers, sixty-five thieves, two arsonists, twenty-four burglars, two forgers, five rapists, and twenty-four inmates classified as lunatics. Tom later recalled, "I was raised practically right in the jail. I could look down from my bedroom window and see the jail corridor and the doors to some of the cells."

It was as if the Scripture were unfolding before his eyes: good and evil, redemption and damnation. One time, a melee broke out in the prison. As Sheriff White tried to quell the riot, his children ran to the nearby courthouse, calling for help. The *Austin Weekly Statesman* published a story about the incident under the headline BLOOD, BLOOD, BLOOD; THE COUNTY JAIL TURNED INTO A VERITABLE SLAUGHTER PEN. The reporter described the scene that young Tom had encountered: "The writer has seen many bloody and sickening sights in his experience in newspaper work, but none of them approached the disgusting sight that met his gaze when he entered the county jail yesterday afternoon about half past five o'clock. Turn which way he might nothing was to be seen but blood."

After the incident, in which five men were badly injured, Emmett White became a firm, even unyielding, sheriff. Still, he showed remarkable consideration toward the people in his custody and insisted on making arrests without brandishing his six-shooter. He did not philosophize about the law or his responsibilities, but Tom noticed that he always maintained the same manner, no matter whether the prisoners were black or white or Mexican. At the time, extrajudicial lynchings, particularly of blacks in the South, were one of the most egregious failures of the American legal system. Whenever Emmett heard that locals were planning to throw a "necktie party," he would rush out to try to stop it. "If a mob attempts to take the negro" from the sheriff, a reporter noted in one case, "there will be trouble." Emmett refused to put young, nonviolent prisoners in the jail alongside older, more dangerous convicts, and because there was no other place for them, he let them stay in his own house, living with his children. One girl remained with them for weeks on end. Tom never knew why she was in jail, and his father never discussed it.

Tom often puzzled over why criminals did what they did. Some of the prison's inmates seemed bad through and through, the devil born in them. Some seemed sick in the head, seeing things that other people couldn't see. Many of the prisoners, though, had been driven to a desperate act—often, something violent and despicable—and afterward they were penitent, seeking redemption. In some ways, these convicts were the most frightening to contemplate, for they demonstrated that badness could take hold of anyone. Tom attended a local Baptist church with his family, and the preacher said that everyone was a sinner—even Emmett, the upholder of justice. These were mysteries that Tom might never solve, though he seemed to spend most of his life trying.

Tom watched his father work. At all hours of the day, including on the Sabbath, Emmett would be summoned to hunt men. Criminology was still primitive: Emmett grabbed his gun, canvassed any witnesses to the crime, then mounted his horse and went in pursuit. He also kept a pack of bloodhounds, which he sometimes deployed in the chase.

Tom's father oversaw the county jail, in Austin.

One summer day in 1892, when Tom was eleven, his father hurried out with the bloodhounds: a family man had been gunned down while riding his horse. Tom's father noticed that, thirty paces from where the victim lay, there was a spot of trampled earth and a burned ammunition wad; it was the place where the killer had stood. White unleashed the hounds and they picked up the killer's trail, which curiously led right back to the dead man's house. As Sheriff White gathered evidence from witnesses, he learned that the victim's slayer was his own son.

A few weeks later, Tom's father was summoned again, this time in pursuit of a rapist. A headline in the *Statesman* read "RAVISHED IN BROAD DAY … Mrs. D. C. Evans Dragged from Her Buggy, Brutally Assaulted and Then Outraged—the Officers Hot on the Trail of the Brutal Wretch." Despite a grueling chase, the rapist eluded capture. In such cases, Tom's father withdrew into himself, as if tormented by some dreadful sickness. Once, before he apprehended a fugitive, a reporter observed, "Truth to tell, Sheriff White's every thought day and night" was of the man, so much so that "his capture soon became a part of Sheriff White's very existence."

Every time the sheriff headed out into the dark, the bloodhounds howling, Tom had to live with the terrible uncertainty that his father might never return—that, like Tom's mother, he might disappear from this world forever. Though it took enormous courage and virtue to risk your life in order to protect society, such selflessness also contained, at least from the vantage point of your loved ones, a hint of cruelty.

Once, a desperado put a gun to Emmett's head; somehow, he managed to wrestle the weapon free. Another time, at the jail, a prisoner pulled a knife and stabbed his father from behind. Tom could see the knife protruding from his father's back, blood gushing onto the floor. It was amazing how much blood was inside a man, inside his father. The prisoner tried to twist the knife, and his father seemed ready to give up the ghost, when suddenly he drove his finger into the prisoner's eye, causing the eye to pop out—Tom could see it dangling from the socket. His father subdued the prisoner. But Tom would relive that scene all his life. How could one forgive a sinner who tried to kill one's own father?

———

The first hanging that Tom witnessed was carried out in January 1894. A nineteen-year-old black man, Ed Nichols, had been convicted of raping a girl and sentenced to be "hung by the neck until he is dead." The duty of performing an execution, which hadn't occurred in the county for a decade, fell to the sheriff.

Tom's father hired a carpenter to construct the gallows near the southern wall of the prison, the only place where the ceiling was sufficiently high. The location was ten feet from Nichols's cell, and the condemned man—who maintained his innocence and still hoped for a reprieve from the governor—could hear the planks being sawed and nailed, sawed and nailed, the pace quickening. Tom's father was determined to make the killing mercifully swift, and once the apparatus was completed, he repeatedly tested it with sacks of sand.

The governor rejected Nichols's final appeal, saying, "Let the law take its course." Tom's father broke the news to Nichols, who was in his cell, deep in prayer. Nichols tried to stay calm, but his hands began to tremble. He said that he'd like to be clean-shaven and wear a fine black suit for his appointment with death, and Tom's father promised to honor his wishes.

On the day of the execution, Tom, who was twelve years old, stood on a tier inside the jail. No one shooed him away, not even his father, and he could see Nichols, who was dressed in his new suit, being led by Tom's father to the scaffolding, time measured in each step and breath. As Tom listened, a preacher read Nichols's final statement: "Sheriff White has been very accommodating to me indeed. I feel prepared to meet death. My soul is at peace with all mankind." Then the preacher offered his own holy words. "Ed Nichols is to swing into eternity," he said. "Sheriff Death is on his black steed, is but a short distance away, coming to arrest the soul of this man to meet the trial at the higher bar where God himself is supreme ruler, Jesus, his son the attorney, and the Holy Ghost the prosecutor."

When the preacher finished, Tom heard a familiar voice. It was his father, reading the death warrant. The noose was fitted around Nichols's neck, and a black hood placed over his head. Tom could no longer see Nichols's face, but he could see his father holding the lever for the trapdoor. At two minutes before four in the afternoon, his father sprang the trap. The body fell before jerking violently upward. Then a sound of astonishment and horror rippled through the crowd. Despite all the meticulous construction, Nichols was still moving, still trembling with life. "He kicked and jerked around a long time," Tom later recalled. "It seemed like he would never give up and die." Finally, his body stopped moving and was cut down from the rope.

Perhaps because he witnessed this—and other executions—or perhaps because he had seen the effect of the ordeal on his father, or perhaps because he feared that the system could doom an innocent man, Tom grew to oppose what was then sometimes called "judicial homicide." And he came to see the law as a struggle to subdue the violent passions not only in others but also in oneself.

In 1905, when Tom was twenty-four, he enlisted in the Texas Rangers. Created in the nineteenth century as a volunteer citizen militia to fight American Indians on the frontier and, later, Mexicans along the border, the Rangers had evolved into a kind of state police force. American Indians and Mexicans had long despised the Rangers for their brutal, shoot-first methods. But among white Texans they were widely mythologized. As Lyndon B. Johnson later put it, "Every school boy in Texas cuts his eye teeth on stories about the Texas Rangers. I wasn't any exception."

Tom's brother Dudley, equally entranced by the Ranger mystique, entered the force the same year as Tom, and Doc soon joined them. Later, Tom's brother Coley followed even more closely in their father's footsteps, becoming the sheriff of Travis County. Doc recalled the simple advice that his father gave him upon becoming a lawman: "Get all the evidence you can, son. Then put yourself in the criminal's place. Think it out. Plug up those holes, son."

Like Doc and Dudley, who were each placed in separate Ranger companies, Tom received a meager salary of $40 per month—"the same as a cowpuncher," as he put it. Tom joined his company at a campsite sixty-five miles west of Abilene. Another Ranger had once observed upon arriving in camp, "Here was a scene worthy of the pencil. Men in groups with long beards and moustaches, dressed in every variety of garment, with one exception, the slouched hat, the unmistakable uniform of a Texas Ranger, and a belt of pistols around their waists, were occupied drying their blankets, cleaning and fixing their guns, and some employed cooking at different fires, while others were grooming their horses. A rougher looking set we never saw."

Tom learned to be a lawman by following the example of the most skilled officers. If you observed carefully, and if you weren't too busy liquoring or whoring (which many of the Rangers were), you could learn how to track a horse through the brush—even if, as Tom once found, the thieves had deceptively turned the horseshoes backward. You picked up little tricks: overturning your boots each morning in case a scorpion or some other critter had crept inside; shaking out your blanket for rattlesnakes before lying down at night. You discovered how to avoid quicksand and how to locate streams in otherwise parched land. You understood that it was better to ride a black horse and dress in black like a personification of evil, so as not to be scoped by a gunman in the night.

Tom soon received the orders for one of his first missions: he was to accompany his captain and his sergeant in pursuit of cow rustlers in Kent County, north of Abilene. At one point, Tom and the sergeant paused at a store to get provisions. They tied up their

_{^^^^} *In back row, from left to right, are Tom's brothers Doc, Dudley, and Coley. In front are Tom's father, his grandfather, and then Tom.*

_{^^^^} *A group of Texas lawmen that includes Tom White (No. 12) and his three brothers, Doc (No. 6), Dudley (No. 7), and Coley (No. 13)*

horses and were heading inside when the sergeant asked Tom where his Winchester rifle was. Tom told him that it was in his scabbard, on his horse. The sergeant, a man of explosive temperament, yelled, "You don't never do that!... Go get your Winchester right now and bring it in here, and keep it right with you all the time."

Tom, chastened, retrieved his rifle, and it was not long before he understood the sergeant's urgency: they were being tracked by the rustlers. They had to dodge being shot several times before they finally arrested the gang.

Tom became increasingly adept at dealing with what he called "rascality": cow rustlers, horse thieves, scalawags, pimps, rumrunners, stagecoach robbers, desperadoes, and other human transgressors. When he was sent with another Ranger, Oscar Roundtree, to clean up the lawless town of Bowie, a pastor wrote to White's captain, saying that he had witnessed "the lawless element completely driven from our town by the two Rangers you sent here."

During his time as a Ranger, Tom investigated several murders. Tom's brother Doc recalled, "We had nothing—not even fingerprints. We had to use mostly witnesses, and they were sometimes hard to come by." Even more troublesome, some Rangers had no patience for the niceties of the law. One member of Tom's company would seek out the most ruthless bad man in town and then provoke a fight, so he could kill him. Tom, who believed that a lawman could usually "avoid killing if you didn't lose your head," later told a writer that he had heated discussions with this Ranger. It didn't seem right for any man to play judge, jury, and executioner.

═══

In 1908, while Tom was stationed in Weatherford, a town east of Abilene, he met a young woman named Bessie Patterson. She was petite, at least beside him, and she had short brown hair and sincere eyes. Tom, who'd spent much of his life in male company, was taken with her. Where he was a man of stillness, she was outspoken and a whirl of motion. She ordered him around in a way that few dared, but he didn't seem to mind; for once, it was not incumbent upon him to be in command of the world around him or the emotions inside him. His job, however, was ill-suited for marriage. Doc's captain once said, "An officer who hunts desperate criminals has no business having a wife and family."

Before long, Tom was tugged away from her. With N. P. Thomas, a Ranger who was one of his closest friends, he was sent to deal with a plague of rascality in Amarillo, in the Texas Panhandle. A Ranger reported that the city had some of the hardest crooks around and that the sheriff's office had provided no assistance in removing them; what's more, the Ranger noted, "the Sheriff has two sons who live at the whore house."

Thomas had already had several run-ins with the deputy sheriff, and one January morning in 1909 N. P. Thomas was sitting in the county prosecutor's office when the deputy leveled his gun and shot him in the face. Thomas fell forward, blood gushing from his mouth. When the medics arrived, he was still breathing, but they couldn't stop the bleeding and he died in agony.

Many of the men with whom Tom had served in the Rangers went prematurely to their deaths. Tom saw both inexperienced and veteran officers die. He saw irresponsible lawmen die and conscientious ones, too. Roundtree, who became a deputy sheriff, was shot in the head by a rich landowner. The Ranger with whom Tom argued about usurping the law joined a posse of vigilantes and was accidently shot and killed by one of his own men. Tom's sergeant was shot six times by an assailant, while a bystander was struck twice. As the sergeant lay on the ground, bleeding, he asked for a slip of paper and scribbled on it a message for Ranger headquarters: "I am shot all to pieces. Everything quiet." Somehow, he survived his wounds, but the innocent bystander died. Then there was the time that a new recruit in Tom's company was gunned down while trying to stop an assault. Tom collected the Ranger's body and transported it to the home of his parents, who couldn't fathom why their boy was in a box succoring maggots.

After N. P. Thomas's death, Tom felt a lawlessness within him. A friend of Tom's who wrote a short sketch of his life said, "Tom's emotional struggle was brief but violent. Should he... attempt to avenge [Thomas's] death?" Tom decided to leave the Rangers altogether and marry Bessie. The adjutant general wrote to Tom's captain, saying that Tom had "proved an excellent officer" and that he would "regret to see him quit the service." But his decision was final.

He and Bessie settled in San Antonio, where the first of their two sons was born. Tom became a railroad detective, and the steady wage made it possible to raise a family. Though he still chased bandits on horseback, the work was generally less dangerous; in many cases, it involved unmasking individuals who had filed false claims for reimbursements. Tom found these people cowards and, therefore, more contemptible than the desperadoes who risked their lives to hold up a train.

Tom was a dedicated family man, but like his father he was attracted to the darkness, and in 1917 he took the oath to become a special agent of the Bureau of Investigation. He swore, "I will support and defend the Constitution of the United States against all enemies.... SO HELP ME GOD."

===

In July 1918, not long after Tom joined the bureau, his brother Dudley went with another Ranger to arrest a pair of deserters in a remote, wooded area in East Texas known as the Big Thicket. It was during an obliterating drought, and amid the dust and heat Dudley and his partner searched a clapboard house where the two wanted men were believed to be hiding out. The suspects weren't there, so Dudley and his partner decided to wait on the porch. At three in the morning, the darkness was suddenly ablaze with gun-

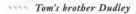
Tom's brother Dudley

fire. The deserters had ambushed them. Dudley's partner was shot twice, and as he lay bleeding on the porch, he could see Dudley standing and firing one of his six-shooters. Then Dudley was falling, as if someone had undercut his legs, his massive frame smashing against the porch. His partner later recalled that he "fell, and did not get up again." A bullet had struck Dudley near the heart.

Tom was overcome by the news; his brother—who was married and had three children under the age of eight—had seemed invulnerable to Tom. The two deserters were caught and prosecuted for murder, and Tom's father attended each day of the trial until both men were convicted.

After the shooting, Dudley's corpse was transported home. A Ranger report noted clinically, "One wagon sheet, one bed sheet, one pillow, used in shipping Ranger White's body." Tom and his family retrieved Dudley's possessions, including the soft-nosed, steel-jacketed bullet that had killed him. He was buried in a cemetery near the ranch where he was born. As the Bible said, "For dust you are and to dust you will return." An obelisk by his grave read,

> JOHN DUDLEY WHITE, SR
> HDQTRS CO TEXAS RANGERS
> KILLED IN LINE OF DUTY . . .
> JULY 12, 1918

Two weeks after the funeral, a cool rain finally began to fall, washing over the prairie. By then, Tom had returned to the Bureau of Investigation.

In September 1925, as White tried to determine what secrets William Hale and his nephews Ernest and Bryan were hiding, he wondered if one person had previously uncovered them: Bill Smith, Mollie Burkhart's brother-in-law. It was Smith who had first suspected that Lizzie was poisoned, and he who had investigated whether there was a larger conspiracy connected to the family's oil wealth. If Smith was killed because of what he had learned, that information might be the key to unlocking the inside world.

After the explosion destroyed the Smiths' house, agents asked the nurse who had been on duty when Bill was being treated in the hospital whether he had mentioned anything about the murders. She said that Bill had often muttered names in his feverish sleep, but she had been unable to make them out. Sometimes, when he woke up, he seemed worried that he might have said something in his sleep—something that he shouldn't have. Shortly before Bill died, the nurse recalled, he had met with his doctors, James and David Shoun, and with his lawyer. The doctors had asked the nurse to leave the room. It was clear that they didn't want her to overhear their conversation with Bill, and she suspected that he had given some sort of statement indicating who was responsible for blowing up his house.

White, already suspicious of the Shouns owing to the missing bullet in the Anna Brown case, began to question each person who had been in the room with Bill. Later, federal prosecutors also questioned these men. According to a transcript of these interrogations, David Shoun acknowledged that he and his brother had summoned the lawyer, believing that Bill might name his killers, but nothing came of it. "If Bill Smith had an idea who blowed him up, he never said," the doctor recalled.

One of the prosecutors pressed him about why it had been so important for the nurse to leave the room. Shoun explained that nurses "often leave when the doctors come in."

"If she says that you asked her to step out, she lies?"

"No, sir. If she says that, I did." Shoun said he would swear a dozen times that Bill never identified his killers. Pointing to his hat, he added, "Bill Smith gave me that hat, and he is my friend."

James Shoun, David's brother, was equally adamant, telling the prosecutor, "He never did say who blew him up."

"He must have talked about that."

"He never did say who blew him up."

"Did he talk about who blew him up?"

"He didn't talk about who blew him up."

When Bill Smith's lawyer was questioned, he, too, insisted that he had no idea who was responsible for blowing up the Smiths' house. "Gentlemen, it is a mystery to me," he said. But as he was being grilled, he revealed that in the hospital Bill Smith had said, "You know, I only had two enemies in the world," and that those enemies were William K. Hale, the King of the Osage Hills, and his nephew Ernest Burkhart.

The investigators asked James Shoun about this, and eventually he divulged the truth: "I would hate to say positively that he said ... that Bill Hale blew him up, but he did say Bill Hale was his only enemy."

"What did he say about Ernest Burkhart?" a prosecutor asked.

"He said they were the only two enemies he knew of."

The Shouns were close to Hale and the Burkharts, having been their families' physicians, and not long after the conversation at the hospital one of the Shoun brothers informed the nurse that Bryan Burkhart was ill. She was asked to visit Bryan at his house, and she agreed to do so. While she was there, Hale showed up. He conferred privately with Bryan, then approached the nurse. After some small talk, he asked her if Bill Smith had named his killers before he died. The nurse told him, "If he did I would not be telling it." Hale seemed to be trying to ascertain whether she knew anything and, perhaps, to be warning her not to divulge a word if she did.

———

As White and agents dug deeper into the hospital statement, they began to suspect that the doctors had orchestrated the private meeting with Bill Smith not for his testimony but, rather, for another, ulterior motive. During the meeting, James Shoun was named the administrator of the estate of Bill Smith's murdered wife, Rita, which allowed him to execute her will. Such a position was coveted by whites, for it paid unconscionably high fees and provided ample opportunities for graft.

After White's team uncovered this scheme, one of the prosecutors questioned David Shoun about it. "You understand in your study of medicine the requisite of a dying declaration," he said. "You weren't undertaking to get anything like that?"

"No," Shoun replied meekly.

It was now clear why the doctors had summoned not the sheriff or a prosecutor but Bill Smith's personal attorney. They had asked him to bring the paperwork for Bill to sign before he died.

Another prosecutor asked David Shoun if Bill was even lucid enough to make such a decision. "Did he know what he was signing?"

"I suppose he did; he was supposed to be rational."

"You are a doctor, was he rational?"

"He was rational."

"And he made arrangements for your brother to be appointed for his wife's estate?"

"Yes, sir." After further interrogation, he conceded, "A very wealthy estate."

The more White investigated the flow of oil money from Osage headrights, the more he found layer upon layer of corruption. Although some white guardians and administrators tried to act in the best interests of the tribe, countless others used the system to swindle the very people they were ostensibly protecting. Many guardians would purchase, for their wards, goods from their own stores or inventories at inflated prices. (One guardian bought a car for $250 and then resold it to his ward for $1,250.) Or guardians would direct all of their wards' business to certain stores and banks in return for kickbacks. Or guardians would claim to be buying homes and land for their wards while really buying these for themselves. Or guardians would outright steal. One government study estimated that before 1925 guardians had pilfered at least $8 million directly from the restricted accounts of their Osage wards. "The blackest chapter in the history of this State will be the Indian guardianship over these estates," an Osage leader said, adding, "There has been millions—not thousands—but millions of dollars of many of the Osages dissipated and spent by the guardians themselves."

This so-called Indian business, as White discovered, was an elaborate criminal operation, in which various sectors of society were complicit. The crooked guardians and administrators of Osage estates were typically among the most prominent white citizens: businessmen and ranchers and lawyers and politicians. So were the lawmen and prosecutors and judges who facilitated and concealed the swindling (and, sometimes, acted as guardians and administrators themselves). In 1924, the Indian Rights Association, which defended the interests of indigenous communities, conducted an investigation into what it described as "an orgy of graft and exploitation." The group documented how rich Indians in Oklahoma were being "shamelessly and openly robbed in a scientific and ruthless manner" and how guardianships were "the plums to be distributed to the faithful friends of the judges as a reward for their support at the polls." Judges were known to say to citizens, "You vote for me, and I will see that you get a good guardianship." A white woman married to an Osage man described to a reporter how the locals would plot: "A group of traders and lawyers sprung up who selected certain Indians as their prey. They owned all the officials.... These men had an understanding with each other. They cold-bloodedly said,

〜〜〜 *The Osage chief Bacon Rind protested that "everybody wants to get in here and get some of this money."*

'You take So-and-So, So-and-So and So-and-So and I'll take these.'
They selected Indians who had full headrights and large farms."

Some of the schemes were beyond depraved. The Indian Rights
Association detailed the case of a widow whose guardian had
absconded with most of her possessions. Then the guardian falsely
informed the woman, who had moved from Osage County, that she
had no more money to draw on, leaving her to raise her two young
children in poverty. "For her and her two small children, there was
not a bed nor a chair nor food in the house," the investigator said.
When the widow's baby got sick, the guardian still refused to turn
over any of her money, though she pleaded for it. "Without proper
food and medical care, the baby died," the investigator said.

The Osage were aware of such schemes but had no means to
stop them. After the widow lost her baby, evidence of the fraud was
brought before a county judge, only to be ignored. "There is no
hope of justice so long as these conditions are permitted to remain,"
the investigator concluded. "The human cry of this... woman is a
call to America." An Osage, speaking to a reporter about the guardians, stated, "Your money draws 'em and you're absolutely helpless.
They have all the law and all the machinery on their side. Tell
everybody, when you write your story, that they're scalping our
souls out here."

One day that September, the undercover operative who was pretending to be an insurance salesman stopped at a filling station in Fairfax and struck up a conversation with a woman working there. When the operative told her that he was looking to buy a house in the vicinity, she mentioned that William Hale "controlled everything" in these parts. She said that she'd purchased her own home from Hale, which was on the edge of his pasture. One night, she recalled, thousands of acres of Hale's land had been set on fire. Nothing was left behind but ashes. Most people didn't know who had started the blaze, but she did: Hale's workers, on his orders, had torched the land for the insurance money—$30,000 in all.

White tried to learn more about another suspicious matter: How had Hale become the beneficiary of Henry Roan's $25,000 life-insurance policy? After Roan turned up with a bullet in the back of his head, in 1923, Hale had the most obvious motive. Yet the sheriff had never investigated Hale, nor had other local lawmen—an oversight that no longer seemed incidental.

White tracked down the insurance salesman who had originally sold Roan the policy in 1921. Hale had always insisted that Roan, one of his closest friends, had made him the beneficiary because he had lent Roan a lot of money over the years. But the salesman told a different story.

As the salesman recalled it, Hale had independently pushed for the policy, saying, "Hells bells, that's just like spearing fish in a keg." Hale had promised to pay an extra premium on such a policy, and the salesman had responded, "Well, we might write him for $10,000."

"No, I want it for $25,000," Hale said.

The salesman had told Hale that because he wasn't Roan's relative, he could become his beneficiary only if he were his creditor. Hale had said, "Well, he owes me a lot of money, he owes me $10,000 or $12,000."

White found it hard to believe that this debt was real. If Roan had really owed Hale that amount of money, then all Hale would have had to do was present proof of the debt to Roan's wealthy estate, which would have reimbursed him. Hale had no need to get an insurance policy on his friend's life—a policy that wouldn't have a significant return unless Roan, who was then in his late thirties, suddenly died.

The salesman, who was close to Hale, admitted that he had no proof of the debt and that he had simply desired his commission. He was yet another person bound up in the "Indian business." Roan seemed to have been unaware of these machinations; he trusted that Hale, his supposedly closest friend, was helping him. But there remained one impediment to Hale's scheme. A doctor had to examine Roan—a heavy drinker who had once wrecked his car while intoxicated—and deem him a safe risk for the insurance company. Though one physician said that nobody would approve that "drunken Indian," Hale shopped for doctors until he found a man in Pawhuska willing to recommend Roan; one of the seemingly ubiquitous Shoun brothers, James, also recommended Roan.

White discovered that the insurance company had rejected the first application. A company representative later noted dryly of Hale's effort to secure a $25,000 policy, "I don't think it would seem regular." Undeterred, Hale approached a second insurance company. The application asked if Roan had previously been turned down by a competitor. The answer "no" was filled in. An insurance agent who reviewed the application later told authorities, "I knew the questions in it had been answered falsely."

This time, Hale had produced a creditor's note to prove that he was owed money by Roan. The debt that Hale had originally claimed—$10,000 or $12,000—had grown inexplicably to $25,000, the exact amount of the insurance policy. The creditor's note was purportedly signed by Roan and was dated "Jany, 1921"; this was important, because it indicated that the note predated efforts to obtain the insurance, giving legitimacy to Hale's claim.

Handwriting and document analysis were emerging tools in the field of criminal investigation. Although many people greeted the new forensic sciences with reverence, attributing to them a godlike power, they were often susceptible to human error. In 1894, the French criminologist Bertillon had helped to wrongfully convict Alfred Dreyfus of treason, having presented a wildly incorrect handwriting analysis. But when applied carefully and discreetly, document and handwriting analysis could be helpful. In the infamous Nathan Leopold and Richard Loeb murder case, in 1924, investigators had correctly detected similarities between Leopold's typed school notes and the typed ransom note.

Agents working on Roan's murder case later showed the creditor's note to an analyst at the Treasury Department, who was known as the "Examiner of Questioned Documents." He detected that the date initially typed on the document had said "June," and that someone had then carefully rubbed out the u and the e. "Photographs taken by means of slanting light show clearly the roughening and raising of the fibres of the paper about the date due to mechanical erasure," the examiner wrote. He determined that somebody had replaced the u with an a, and the e with a y so that the date read "Jany."

White suspected that Hale had ginned up the document while trying to obtain the insurance policy, and altered it after realizing that he had blundered on the date. Later, a federal official questioned the man who Hale claimed had typed up the note. He denied ever having seen the document. Asked if Hale was lying, he said, "Absolutely."

The second insurance company approved the policy after Hale took Roan to the Pawhuska doctor again for the required medical examination. The doctor recalled asking Hale, "Bill, what are you going to do, kill this Indian?"

Hale, laughing, said, "Hell, yes."

———

After Hale served as a pallbearer at Roan's funeral, White learned, local lawmen did more than ignore Hale as a suspect: they tried to build a case against Roy Bunch, the man who'd been having an affair with Roan's wife. White and his agents spoke to Bunch, who maintained his innocence and told a curious story about Hale. After Roan's murder, Hale had approached Bunch and said, "If I were you, I'd get out of town."

"Why should I run? I didn't do it."

"People think you did," Hale said.

He offered Bunch money to help him flee. Afterward, Bunch spoke to a friend, who persuaded him not to take off, because it would only make him look guilty. "If you run, they'll hang it on you for sure," his friend said.

White and his men thoroughly investigated Bunch and ruled him out as a suspect; as one agent noted, the "notorious relations between Bunch and Roan's wife were calculated to furnish a good screen" for the real murderers. And the person who seemed most intent on framing Bunch was the King of the Osage Hills. After Roan's murder, Hale had visited Roan's widow several times to try to get her to sign various papers regarding claims against Roan's estate. Once, Hale had left a bottle of whiskey for her as a gift. But she refused to taste the moonshine: she feared that it was poisoned.

Though White had gathered circumstantial evidence implicating Hale in the murder of Roan, there were still huge holes in the case. There was no proof—no fingerprints, no credible eyewitnesses—that Hale had shot Roan or that he had ordered one of his nephews or another henchman to do so. And while the suspicious life-insurance policy seemed to tie Hale to Roan's murder, it did not provide a motive for the other Osage killings.

Yet, as White studied the Roan case further, one detail stood out. Before Hale obtained the life-insurance policy on Roan, he had attempted to purchase Roan's headright—his share in the tribe's mineral trust, which was more precious than any cache of diamonds or gold. Hale knew that the law prevented anyone from buying or selling a headright, but he'd been confident that lobbying pressure from influential whites would soon eliminate this prohibition. Indeed, Hale once said, "I, like many other good men, believed it would be only a short time until Congress would pass a law permitting every educated Indian who had his certificate of competency to sell or convey his or her mineral rights to whom they wished." Yet the law had not been changed, and White suspected that this setback had prompted Hale to turn to the insurance murder plot.

There was one legal way, though, that someone could still obtain a headright: inheritance. As White examined probate records for many of the murder victims, it was evident that with each successive death more and more headrights were being directed into the hands of one person—Mollie Burkhart. And it just so happened that she was married to Hale's nephew Ernest, a man who, as an agent wrote in a report, "is absolutely controlled by Hale." Kelsie Morrison, the bootlegger and bureau informant, said to agents that both Ernest and Bryan Burkhart did exactly what their uncle told them to do. Morrison added that Hale was "capable of anything."

White studied the pattern of deaths in Mollie's family. Even the chronology no longer seemed haphazard but was part of a ruthless plan. Anna Brown, divorced and without children, had bequeathed nearly all her wealth to her mother, Lizzie. By killing Anna first, the mastermind made sure that her headright would not be divided between multiple heirs. Because Lizzie had willed most of her headright to her surviving daughters, Mollie and Rita, she became the next logical target. Then came Rita and her husband, Bill Smith. White realized that the unusual method of the final killing—a bombing—had a vicious logic. The wills of Rita and Bill stipulated that if they died simultaneously, much of Rita's headright would go to her surviving sister, Mollie. Here, the mastermind had made one miscalculation. Because Bill unexpectedly outlived Rita by a few days, he had inherited much of her wealth, and upon his death the money went to one of his relatives. Still, the bulk of the family's headrights had been funneled to Mollie Burkhart, whose wealth was controlled by Ernest. And Hale, White was convinced, had secretly forged an indirect channel to this fortune through his subservient nephew. As White later reported to Hoover, "MOLLIE appears to have been the first means to draw HALE, through the BURKHARTS, the assets of the entire family."

White couldn't determine whether Ernest's marriage to Mollie—four years before Anna's murder—had been conceived from the outset as part of the plot, or if Hale had prevailed upon his nephew to betray her after they married. In either case, the plan was so brazen, so sinister, that it was hard to fathom. It demanded that Ernest share a bed with Mollie, and raise children with her, all while plotting and scheming against her family. As Shakespeare wrote in *Julius Caesar:*

> *Where wilt thou find a cavern dark enough*
> *To mask thy monstrous visage? Seek none, conspiracy:*
> *Hide it in smiles and affability.*

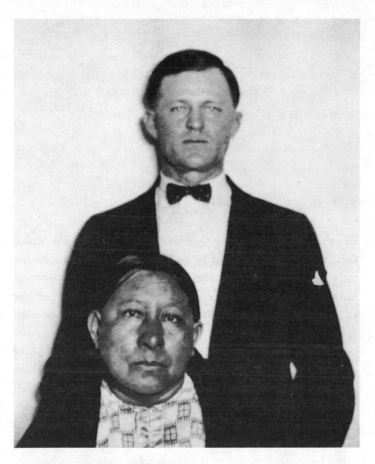

Ernest and Mollie Burkhart

White and his men felt a growing sense of progress. A Justice Department prosecutor sent Hoover a note, saying that in the few months since White had assumed command of the investigation, "many new angles of these cases were successfully developed" and a "new and enthusiastic spirit seemed to pervade the hearts of all of us."

Still, White faced the same problem with the investigation of Mollie Burkhart's murdered family that he did with his inquiry into Roan's death. There was no physical evidence or witnesses to prove that Hale had carried out or ordered any of the killings. And without an airtight case White knew that he'd never be able to bring down this man who hid behind layers of respectability—who called himself the Reverend—and who used a network of patronage to influence the sheriff's office, prosecutors, judges, and some of the highest state officials.

In a stark report, agents noted that Scott Mathis, the Big Hill Trading Company owner and a guardian of Anna Brown and Lizzie, was "a crook and evidently in the power of Hale"; that an associate of Mathis's served as a "spy for Bill Hale and the Big Hill Trading Company, and does all the framing for them in their crooked deals in skinning the Indians"; that the chief of police in Ponca City had "taken money from Bill Hale"; that the chief of police in Fairfax "will do nothing against Hale whatsoever"; that a local banker and guardian "will not talk against the Hale faction, for the reason that Hale has too much on him"; that the mayor of Fairfax, "an arch crook," was Hale's close friend; that a longtime county prosecutor was part of Hale's political machine and was "no good" and "crooked"; and that even a federal official with the Office of Indian Affairs was "in the power of Bill Hale and will do what Hale says."

White realized that his struggle to obtain justice was just beginning. As a bureau report would put it, Hale "dominated local politics and seemingly could not be punished." Hoover had earlier praised White, saying that because of his handling of the case "conditions have been peaceful and I have had no complaint or criticism whatsoever, and this has been a great relief to me." Yet Hoover— that "slender bundle of high-charged electric wire," as one reporter described him—was growing increasingly impatient.

Hoover wanted the new investigation to be a showcase for his bureau, which he had continued to restructure. To counter the sordid image created by Burns and the old school of venal detectives, Hoover adopted the approach of Progressive thinkers who advocated for ruthlessly efficient systems of management. These systems were modeled on the theories of Frederick Winslow Taylor, an industrial engineer, who argued that companies should be run "scientifically," with each worker's task minutely analyzed and quantified. Applying these methods to government, Progressives sought to end the tradition of crooked party bosses packing government agencies, including law enforcement, with patrons and hacks. Instead, a new class of technocratic civil servants would manage burgeoning bureaucracies, in the manner of Herbert Hoover— "the Great Engineer"—who had become a hero for administering humanitarian relief efforts so expeditiously during World War I.

As the historian Richard Gid Powers has noted, J. Edgar Hoover found in Progressivism an approach that reflected his own obsession with organization and social control. What's more, here was a way for Hoover, a deskbound functionary, to cast himself as a dashing figure—a crusader for the modern scientific age. The fact that he didn't fire a gun only burnished his image. Reporters noted that the "days of 'old sleuth' are over" and that Hoover had "scrapped the old 'gum shoe, dark lantern and false moustache' traditions of the Bureau of Investigation and substituted business methods of procedure." One article said, "He plays golf. Whoever could picture Old Sleuth doing that?"

Yet an ugliness often lurked beneath the reformist zeal of Progressivism. Many Progressives—who tended to be middle-class white Protestants—held deep prejudices against immigrants and blacks and were so convinced of their own virtuous authority that they disdained democratic procedures. This part of Progressivism mirrored Hoover's darkest impulses.

As Hoover radically streamlined the bureau, eliminating overlapping divisions and centralizing authority, White, like other special agents in charge, was given greater command over his men in the field, but he also became more accountable to Hoover for anything the agents did, good or bad. White had to constantly fill out Efficiency Rating sheets, grading agents, on a scale of 0 to 100, in such categories as "knowledge," "judgment," "personal appearance," "paper work," and "loyalty." The average score became an agent's overall grade. After White told Hoover that he had occasionally given an agent a 100 rating, Hoover responded sharply, writing, "I regret that I am unable to bring myself to believe that any agent in the jurisdiction of the Bureau is entitled to a perfect or 100% rating."

Hoover, who believed that his men should conquer their deficiencies the way he had conquered his childhood stutter, purged anyone who failed to meet his exacting standards. "I have caused the removal from the service of a considerable number of employ-ees," he informed White and other special agents. "Some have been lacking in educational ability and others have been lacking in moral stamina." Hoover often repeated the maxim "You either improve or deteriorate."

Though Hoover conceded that some might deem him a "fanatic," he reacted with fury to any violations of the rules. In the spring of 1925, when White was still based in Houston, Hoover expressed outrage to him that several agents in the San Francisco field office were drinking liquor. He immediately fired these agents and ordered White—who, unlike his brother Doc and many of the other Cowboys, wasn't much of a drinker—to inform all of his personnel that they would meet a similar fate if caught using intoxicants. He told White, "I believe that when a man becomes a part of the forces of this Bureau he must so conduct himself as to remove the slightest possibility of causing criticism or attack upon the Bureau."

The new policies, which were collected into a thick manual, the bible of Hoover's bureau, went beyond codes of conduct. They dictated how agents gathered and processed information. In the past, agents had filed reports by phone or telegram, or by brief-ing a superior in person. As a result, critical information, including entire case files, was often lost.

Before joining the Justice Department, Hoover had been a clerk at the Library of Congress—"I'm sure he would be the Chief Librarian if he'd stayed with us," a co-worker said—and Hoover had mastered how to classify reams of data using its Dewey decimal–like system. Hoover adopted a similar model, with its classifications and numbered subdivisions, to organize the bureau's Central Files and General Indices. (Hoover's "Personal File," which included infor-mation that could be used to blackmail politicians, would be stored separately, in his secretary's office.) Agents were now expected to standardize the way they filed their case reports, on single sheets

~~~~ *Tom White and Hoover*

of paper. This cut down not only on paperwork—another statistical measurement of efficiency—but also on the time it took for a prosecutor to assess whether a case should be pursued.

White himself could be a demanding superior. An agent who worked under him in Oklahoma recalled that each of his men was "supposed to know his job and do it." Another man who later worked under White said he could be "honest till it hurt." Yet White was more forgiving of frailty than Hoover was, and he often tried to shield his men from the boss man's anger. When Hoover became inflamed after one of White's agents failed to use the one-page format in a report on the Osage murder cases, White told Hoover, "I feel that I, myself, am altogether to blame for I looked over this report and gave it my approval."

Under Hoover, agents were now seen as interchangeable cogs, like employees in a large corporation. This was a major departure from traditional policing, where lawmen were typically products of their own communities. The change helped insulate agents from local corruption and created a truly national force, yet it also ignored regional difference and had the dehumanizing effect of constantly uprooting employees. Speaking only "with the betterment of the service in mind," White wrote to Hoover that he believed an agent who was familiar with a region and its people was more effective. He noted that one of his agents who had gone undercover as a Texas cattleman in the Osage case was ideally suited to working on the frontier—"but put him in Chicago, New York or Boston and he is almost worthless." Hoover was unmoved. As one of his yes-men wrote in a memo, "I do not agree with Mr. White at all on this matter. An Agent who is only acquainted with the characteristics of inhabitants of one section of the country had better get into some other line of work."

At a makeshift training school in New York, agents were indoctrinated in the new regulations and methods. (Hoover later turned the program into a full-fledged academy at Quantico, Virginia.) Agents were increasingly trained in what Hoover hailed as "scientific policing," such as fingerprint and ballistics techniques. And they were taught formal rules of evidence gathering, in order to avoid cases being dropped or stalled, as had happened with the first Osage investigation.

Some agents, especially older ones, despised Hoover and his edicts. One veteran agent advised new recruits, "The first thing you've got to do is unlearn everything they taught you at the Seat of Government. The second is get rid of those damn manuals." In 1929, an agent resigned with the complaint that Hoover's initiatives were "directed against the personnel rather than against the criminal."

White, too, sometimes chafed at Hoover's rules and whims. But he clearly relished being part of the bureau, being swept up in events greater than himself. He tried to neatly type up his reports and touted the virtues of scientific policing. Later, he would replace his cowboy hat with a fedora and, like Hoover, take up golf, putting the ball across the immaculate greens, where the new American men of money and power and leisure gathered. White would become almost indistinguishable from one of Hoover's college boys.

During the fall of 1925, White tried to reassure Hoover that he'd gather enough evidence to put away Hale and his accomplices. White sent Hoover a memo reporting that an undercover operative was on Hale's ranch that very moment, spying. White was feeling pressure not just from Hoover. In the short time that White had been on the case, he had seen the lights burning each night around the homes of the Osage, and seen that members of the community wouldn't let their children go into town alone, and seen more and more residents selling their homes and moving to distant states or even other countries like Mexico and Canada. (Later, one Osage called it a "diaspora.") The desperation of the Osage was unmistakable, as was their skepticism toward the investigation. What had the U.S. government done for them? Why did they, unlike other Americans, have to use their own money to fund a Justice Department investigation? Why had nobody been arrested? An Osage chief said, "I made peace with the white man and lay down my arms never to take them up again and now I and my fellow tribesmen must suffer."

White had come to understand that prejudiced and corrupt white citizens would not implicate one of their own in the killing of American Indians, and so he decided to change his strategy. He would try to find a source, instead, among the most disreputable, dangerous group of Oklahomans: the outlaws of the Osage Hills. Reports from agents and informants like Morrison suggested that several of these desperadoes had knowledge about the murders. These men might not be any less racist. But because some of them had recently been arrested, or convicted of crimes, White would at least hold some leverage over them. The name of one outlaw, in particular, kept coming up: Dick Gregg, a twenty-three-year-old stickup man who used to run with the Al Spencer Gang and who was now in a Kansas penitentiary serving a ten-year sentence for robbery.

Gregg had once told Agent Burger that he knew something about the murders, though he remained coy, insisting that he couldn't betray a confidence. In a report, Agent Burger noted in frustration, "Gregg is 100 percent criminal and will tell as little as he can." Comstock, the attorney and guardian, knew Gregg's father well and provided legal counsel for the family. Hoover still didn't trust Comstock, but it was Comstock who used his relationship with Gregg's father to help persuade the young outlaw to cooperate with the bureau.

Eventually, White met with Gregg himself. White liked to take mental notes about the criminals he encountered, in order to fix them in his memory—a skill honed from his time on the frontier when he could not rely on mug shots or fingerprints. Decades later, when White was asked to describe Gregg, he wrote with remarkable precision: "A very small man, I should say 5'6" and weighed 125 lbs, fair complexion, blue eyes and light brown hair. A good looking youngster." Gregg's pretty looks were deceiving, according to a prosecutor, who said that he was "a cold cruel calculating type of criminal" who "would not hesitate to commit murder." Still, in White's view, Gregg belonged to that category of outlaw who was not inherently bad and who might even have "gone places" with proper training.

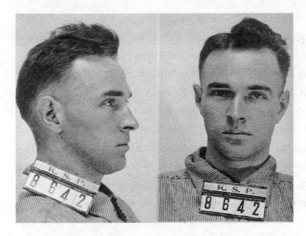

~~~~ *Dick Gregg had been a member of the Al Spencer Gang.*

Though Gregg was known for his nerve as a stickup man, he was reluctant to cross Hale. If word got out, Gregg said, "my life would not be worth a damn." But, hoping to shave time off his robbery sentence, he agreed to divulge to White and other agents what he knew. Sometime in the summer of 1922, he recalled, the outlaw Al Spencer told him that Hale wanted to meet with the gang, and so Spencer, Gregg, and several associates headed to one of Hale's pastures near Fairfax. Hale rode up fiercely on his horse, emerging from the tall prairie grasses. The group convened by the edge of a creek and shared some whiskey. Then Hale asked Spencer to step aside with him, and the two went off to talk. After they returned and the meeting broke up, Spencer relayed their conversation.

Hale told Spencer that he'd pay him and his gang at least $2,000 to bump off a couple—an old man and his blanket, meaning an Indian woman. Spencer asked Hale whom he wanted dead. "Bill Smith and his wife," he said. Spencer told Hale that he might be cold-blooded but he wouldn't kill a woman for silver. As he put it, "That's not my style." Hale said he hoped that Gregg, at least, would go through with the plan. But Gregg agreed with Spencer.

White thought that Gregg was being "on the level" and that his refusal to kill for hire showed him to be "an outlaw with some honor." But though Gregg's testimony offered the clearest indication yet that Hale had ordered the murders, it was of limited legal value. After all, the statement was coming from a crook seeking to shorten his sentence, and Spencer, the one person who could corroborate Gregg's testimony, had since been gunned down by a posse of lawmen. (The *Pawhuska Daily Capital* had reported: WITH $10,000 BONDS IN ONE HAND AND WINCHESTER CLUTCHED IN THE OTHER, FAMOUS BANDIT DIES IN HIS BOOTS WHILE HILLS WHICH GAVE HIM SHELTER IN LIFE ARE HIS SEPULCHER IN DEATH.)

During one of his interrogations, Gregg said that agents should find Curley Johnson, an outlaw who ran with the stickup man Blackie Thompson. "Johnson knows all about the Smith blow up and will squeal if made to do so," Gregg promised. But Johnson, it turned out, was also rotting underground. Less than a year earlier, he'd died suddenly—word was of poisoned alcohol.

White's desperate search for a witness soon led him to Henry Grammer, the rodeo star and gunslinging bootlegger who, every year or so, seemed to draw down on another man because of a dispute. (HENRY GRAMMER SHOOTS AGAIN, one headline put it.) Though Grammer and Hale generally moved in different circles, White established that they'd known each other for years, from the time when Hale had first appeared in Osage territory, at the turn of the century. In a rodeo contest in 1909, they'd com-

A photograph of Al Spencer, after he was shot dead on September 15, 1923.

Hale (fourth from left) and Grammer (third from left) competing in a roping contest in 1909

peted with the Osage Cowboys against the Cherokee Cowboys. CHEROKEES NO MATCH FOR THE OSAGE ROPERS, declared the *Muskogee Times-Democrat.* By 1925, Hale had shed his past, but there remained a faded photograph from the contest; it showed Hale and Grammer sitting proudly on their horses, holding up coiled ropes.

Just before the Smith house blew up, Hale had told friends that he was heading out of town to attend the Fat Stock Show in Fort Worth, Texas. White looked into Hale's alibi and was told that Grammer had gone with him. A witness had overheard Hale talking to Grammer before the murders, murmuring something about being ready for "that Indian deal."

Like the other potential witnesses against Hale, however, Grammer was dead. On June 14, 1923, three months after the

Smiths' house was demolished, Grammer had been killed when his Cadillac spun out of control and flipped over. The legendary quick-draw artist had bled out on an empty country road.

Finally, a yegg—a safecracker—gave White and his team the name of another witness to the bombing plot: Asa Kirby, the gold-toothed outlaw who had been an associate of Grammer's. The yegg said that Kirby was the "soup man"—the expert in explosives—who had designed the bomb. But it turned out that Kirby couldn't testify, either. A few weeks after Grammer's fatal car crash, he'd broken into a store in the middle of the night in an attempt to steal a stash of diamonds, only to find that the shopkeeper had been tipped off beforehand and was lying in wait with his 12-gauge shotgun. In an instant, Kirby was blasted into the world beyond. The person who had tipped off the shopkeeper about the robbery, White was hardly surprised to learn, was William K. Hale.

By foiling the heist, Hale had reinforced his reputation for upholding law and order. But another outlaw told White that Hale had actually set up the robbery—that he'd told Kirby about the diamonds and suggested the ideal time to break in. It was, evidently, a plot within a plot, and White suddenly became suspicious of the litany of dead witnesses. He inquired about Grammer's car accident and was told by people who knew him that they believed his Cadillac's steering wheel and brakes had been tampered with. Curley Johnson's widow, meanwhile, was sure that her husband had been murdered—intentionally poisoned by Hale and his henchmen. And when White learned about a potential witness in the Roan murder case, he discovered that this person had been bludgeoned to death. Anyone who could implicate Hale, it seemed, was being eliminated. The yegg said that Hale was "taking care of too many people," adding, "I might be taken care of myself."

Having failed to locate any living witnesses, White found himself stymied, and Hale seemed aware that agents were onto him. "Hale knows everything," the informant Morrison had told agents, and there were signs that Morrison might be playing his own

William Hale

duplicitous game. Morrison, agents learned, had told a friend that he had all the dope on the murders and had saved Hale's "damned neck till now."

Hale had begun spreading even more patronage to solidify his power. In a report, Agent Wren wrote that Hale was "making all the propaganda he can to favor himself by giving presents, suits of clothes, as well as going on notes"—providing loans—"for different people." Hale was even "giving ponies away to young boys."

One of the undercover operatives who was playing a Texas cattleman had slowly become close with Hale. They shared stories about the old days cowboying, and the operative accompanied Hale as he inspected his herds of cattle. The operative reported that Hale seemed to be mocking investigators. Hale boasted to him, "I'm too slick and keen to catch cold."

White would see Hale on the streets of Fairfax, with his bow tie on and his chin up—the incarnation of what White and his brothers, and their father before them, had spent their lives chasing. He carried himself, White thought, "like he owned the world."

Sometimes, as the strain on White intensified, as each promising lead dead-ended, he would take his rifle and disappear into the countryside. Spotting a duck or some other flying prey, he would take aim and fire until the air was laced with smoke and blood drained into the soil.

Out of the blue, White received a tip. In late October 1925, he was meeting with the governor of Oklahoma, discreetly discussing the case. Afterward, an aide to the governor told White, "We've been getting information from a prisoner at McAlester"—the state penitentiary—"who claims to know a great deal about the Osage murders. His name is Burt Lawson. Might be a good idea to talk to him."

Desperate for a new lead, White and Agent Frank Smith rushed over to McAlester. They didn't know much about Lawson, other than that he was from Osage County and that he had had several brushes with the law. In 1922, he had been charged with murdering a fisherman but was acquitted after claiming that the fisherman had first come at him with a knife. Less than three years later, Lawson was convicted of second-degree burglary and sentenced to seven years.

White liked to interview a subject in a place that was unfamiliar to the person in order to unsettle him, and so he had Lawson taken to a room off the warden's office. White studied the man who appeared before him: short, portly, and middle-aged, with ghostly white long hair. Lawson kept referring to White and Smith as the "hot Feds."

White said to him, "We understand from the governor's office you know something about the Osage murders."

"I do," Lawson said, adding, "I want to make a clean breast of it."

In a series of interviews, Lawson explained that in 1918 he began working as a ranch hand for Bill Smith, and that he grew to know Hale and his nephews Ernest and Bryan Burkhart. In a signed statement, Lawson said, "Some time around the early part of 1921 I discovered an intimacy between my wife and … Smith, which finally developed in breaking up my family and caused me to leave the employment of Smith." Ernest knew of Lawson's hatred of Smith, and more than a year later he visited him. Lawson recalled that Ernest "turned to me and said, 'Burt, I have got a proposition I want to make to you.' I remarked, 'What is it, Ernest?' Ernest said, 'I want you to blow up and kill Bill Smith and his wife.'"

When Lawson wouldn't agree to do it, Hale came to see him and promised him $5,000 in cash for the job. Hale told him that he could use nitroglycerin and that all he had to do was place a fuse under the Smiths' house. "Hale then pulled from his pocket," Lawson recalled, "a piece of white fuse about three feet and said, 'I will show you how to use it.' He then took his pocket knife and cut off a piece about six inches long … then took a match from his pocket and lighted the end."

Lawson still said no, but shortly after he was arrested for killing the fisherman, Hale—who, as a reserve deputy sheriff, could come in and out of the jail as he pleased—visited him again and said, "Burt, you will be needing some attorneys pretty soon and I know you haven't got any money to pay them with, and I want that job pulled."

Lawson said, "All right Bill, I'll pull it."

One night not long after, Lawson recalled, another deputy sheriff opened his cell and led him to Hale, who was in a car outside. Hale drove Lawson to a building in Fairfax, where Ernest was waiting. Hale told Ernest to get "the box," and Ernest brought out a wooden container. Inside was a jug filled with nitroglycerin; a long coiled fuse was attached to the spout. After carefully loading the box in the car, the three of them made their way to the Smiths' house. "I got out and took the box and fuse, and Hale and Ernest drove on away," Lawson recounted. "I then went in the back way and into Smith's cellar, and placed the box in the far corner of the cellar, then laid the fuse out like Hale told me....I then sat down in the dark and waited." Lawson continued, "I saw the lights turned on. I suppose they all undressed and went to bed for pretty soon the lights went out. I sat there for quite a while, I had no way to tell what time it was, but I would figure it was about three quarters of an hour, and after I thought they were all asleep, I lighted a short piece of fuse....As soon as the long end began to smoke, I beat it as fast I could." He could hear the house breaking apart. Hale and Ernest picked him up in a spot nearby and returned him to the jail, where the other deputy sheriff snuck him into his cell. Before Hale left, he'd warned Lawson, "If you ever cheep this to anybody we will kill you."

White and Agent Smith felt a rush of excitement. There were still questions. Lawson had not mentioned the involvement of Kirby, the soup man. But Kirby could have prepared the bomb for Hale without interacting with Lawson. White would need to tie up these loose ends, but at last a witness had emerged who could directly implicate Hale in the plot.

On October 24, 1925, three months after White took over the case, he sent Hoover a telegram, unable to conceal a sense of triumph: "Have confession from Burt Lawson that he placed and set off the explosive that blew up Bill Smith's home; that he was persuaded, prompted and assisted to do it by Ernest Burkhart and W. K. Hale."

Hoover was elated. Via telegram, he quickly sent White a message: "Congratulations."

======

As White and his men worked to corroborate the details in Lawson's confession, they felt a growing urgency to get Hale and his nephews off the streets. The attorney and guardian Comstock, who White no longer doubted was helping investigators by persuading witnesses to talk, had begun to receive threats to his life. He was now sleeping in his office, in downtown Pawhuska, with his .44-caliber English Bulldog by his side. "Once, when he went to open the window, he found sticks of dynamite behind the curtain," a relative recalled. He was able to dispose of them. But, the relative added, "Hale and his bunch were determined to kill him."

White was also very concerned about the fate of Mollie Burkhart. Although White had received reports that she was sick with diabetes, he was suspicious. Hale had successfully arranged, corpse by corpse, for Mollie to inherit the majority of her family members' wealth. Yet the plot seemed unfinished. Hale had access to Mollie's fortune through Ernest, but his nephew did not yet directly control it, and would do so only if Mollie died and bequeathed it to him. A servant in Mollie's house had told an agent that one night Ernest had muttered to her while drunk that he was afraid something would happen to Mollie. Even Ernest seemed terrified of the plan's inevitable denouement.

John Wren, the Ute agent, had recently spoken to Mollie's priest, who said that she had stopped coming to church, which was unlike her, and that he had heard she was being forcibly kept away by family members. The priest was sufficiently alarmed that he had broken the tenet of parishioner confidentiality. Soon after, the priest reported that he had received a secret message from Mollie: she was afraid that someone was trying to poison her. Given that poisoned whiskey had been one of the killers' preferred methods, the priest sent word back warning Mollie "not to drink any liquor of any kind under any circumstances."

But Mollie's diabetes seemed to have provided an even more

devious way to deliver the poison. Some of the town's doctors, including the Shoun brothers, had been giving her injections of what was supposed to be insulin, but instead of improving, Mollie seemed to be getting worse. Government officials working for the Office of Indian Affairs were also concerned that Mollie was slowly being poisoned. A Justice Department official had noted that her "illness is very suspicious, to say the least." It was urgent, the official went on, to "get this patient to some reputable hospital for diagnosis and treatment free from the interference of her husband."

By the end of December 1925, White felt that he could no longer wait. He had not finished confirming many details in Lawson's confession, and there remained certain contradictions. In addition to Lawson having made mention of Kirby, he had insisted that Hale was in Fairfax at the time of the explosion rather than in Fort Worth with Grammer, as some witnesses had claimed. Nevertheless, White rushed to obtain arrest warrants for Hale and Ernest Burkhart for the murders of Bill and Rita Smith and their servant Nettie Brookshire. The warrants were issued on January 4, 1926. Because agents could not make arrests, they fanned out with U.S. marshals and other lawmen, including Sheriff Freas, who, after being expelled from office, had been reelected to the position.

Several lawmen quickly located Ernest Burkhart at his favorite dive, a pool hall in Fairfax, and transported him to the jail in Guthrie, eighty miles southwest of Pawhuska. Hale, however, could not be found. Agent Wren learned that he had ordered a new suit of clothes and had said that he was planning to leave town at a moment's notice. Authorities feared that Hale had disappeared for good when he suddenly strolled into Sheriff Freas's office. He looked as if he were heading to a formal party: he wore a perfectly pressed suit, shoes shined to a gleam, a felt hat, and an overcoat with his diamond-studded Masonic lodge pin fastened to the lapel. "Understand I'm wanted," he said, explaining that he was there to turn himself in—no need to put the fellas out.

As he was taken to the jail in Guthrie, he was confronted by a

〵〵〵 *Hale in front of the Guthrie jail*

local reporter. Hale's deep-set eyes burned, and he moved, in the words of the reporter, "like a leashed animal."

The reporter asked him, "Have you a statement to make?"

"What are you?" Hale demanded, not used to being questioned.

"A newspaperman."

"I'll not try my case in the newspapers, but in the courts of this county."

Hoping Hale might at least talk about himself, the reporter asked, "How old are you?"

"I'm fifty-one years of age."

"How long have you been in Oklahoma?"

"Twenty-five years, more or less."

"You are pretty well known, aren't you?"

"I think so."

"Have large numbers of friends?"

"I hope so."

"Wouldn't they like to have a statement from you, even though you merely say 'I am innocent'?"

"I'll try my case in the courts, not in the newspapers. Cold tonight, isn't it?"

"Yes. How's the cattle business this season?"

"Been fair."

"It's a long trip from Pawhuska, isn't it?"

"Yes, but we've had a car with curtains up."

"Now about that statement?"

Hale declined again and was led away by authorities. If Hale had momentarily been uneasy, he was confident by the time White spoke to him—even cocky, evidently convinced that he remained untouchable. He insisted that White had made a mistake. It was as if White were the one in trouble, not him.

White suspected that Hale would never admit his sins, certainly not to a lawman and perhaps not even to the God whom he so often invoked. Ernest Burkhart offered the only chance for a confession. "You could look at him and size him up as the weak sister," White observed. A prosecutor working with White put it more bluntly, "We all picked Ernest Burkhart the one to break."

=====

Burkhart was brought into a room on the third floor of a federal building in Guthrie, which was being used as a makeshift interrogation room: the box. He was wearing the same clothes that he had when he was arrested, and White thought that he looked like a "small-town dandy, well dressed in a western way, expensive cowboy boots, loud shirt, flashy tie, and a high-priced, tailored suit." He moved about nervously and licked his lips.

White and Agent Frank Smith questioned him. "We want to talk to you about the murder of Bill Smith's family and Anna Brown," White said.

"Hell, I don't know a thing about it," Burkhart insisted.

White explained that they had talked to a man named Burt Lawson in the pen, who said differently—said that Burkhart knew a good deal about the murders. The mention of Lawson did not seem to faze Burkhart, who insisted that he'd never had any dealings with him.

"He says you were the contact man in setting up the Smith house explosion," White said.

"He's lying," Burkhart said emphatically. A doubt seized White, a doubt that perhaps had been lurking somewhere inside him but had been suppressed: What if Lawson was lying and had simply picked up information from other outlaws in prison who had heard rumors about the case? Perhaps Lawson was lying in the hopes that prosecutors would reduce his jail time, in exchange for his testimony. Or maybe the whole confession had been orchestrated by Hale—another one of his plots within a plot. White still didn't know quite what to believe. But if Lawson was lying about anything, getting a confession from Burkhart was even more crucial; otherwise, the case would collapse.

For hours, in the hot, claustrophobic box, White and Smith went over the circumstantial evidence that they'd gathered on each of the murders, trying to trip up Burkhart. White thought that he detected some element of remorse in him, as if he wanted to unburden himself, to protect his wife and children. Yet, whenever White or Smith mentioned Hale, he stiffened in his chair, more afraid of his uncle, it seemed, than he was of the law.

"My advice to you is to tell it all," White said, almost pleadingly.

"There's nothing to tell," Burkhart said.

After midnight, White and Smith gave up and returned Burkhart to his cell. By the next day, White's case encountered even more trouble. Hale announced that he could prove positively that he had been in Texas at the time of the explosion, for he had received a telegram there and signed for it. If this was true—and White was inclined to believe that it was—then Lawson had indeed been lying all along. In White's desperation to get Hale, he'd committed the ultimate sin of an evidence man and believed, despite apparent contradictions, what he wanted to believe. White knew that he had only hours before Hale's lawyers would produce the record of this telegram and spring Hale, along with Burkhart—only hours before word got out that the bureau had humiliated itself, news that would then reach Hoover. As one of Hoover's aides said of the director, "If he didn't like you, he destroyed you." Hale's lawyers promptly tipped off a reporter who ran a story about Hale's "perfect" alibi, noting, "He's not afraid."

Desperate, White turned to the man who had embarrassed Hoover and become a pariah in the eyes of investigators: Blackie Thompson, the part-Cherokee outlaw who, during the bureau's early investigation, had been released from prison as an informant, only to murder a police officer. Since being caught, he'd been locked up at the state penitentiary, a blight on the bureau best unseen.

Yet, from the bureau's early reports on the case, White suspected that Blackie might have key information about the murders, and without consulting Hoover, White had him transported to Guthrie. If anything went wrong, if Blackie escaped or hurt a soul, White's career would be over. And White made sure that Luther Bishop—a state lawman who had gunned down Al Spencer—was in charge of transferring Blackie. When Blackie arrived at the federal building, he was in chains and flanked by a small army. On a nearby rooftop, White had placed a rifleman, who kept Blackie in his scope through a window.

Blackie was still hostile, sullen, mean, but when White asked him about Hale and Burkhart's role in the murders of the Osage, his mood seemed to change. A man filled with venom and bigotry, he'd once complained that Hale and Ernest Burkhart were "too much Jew—they want everything for nothing."

Agents told Blackie that they couldn't cut a deal with him to reduce his sentence, and he spoke grudgingly at first about the murders, but gradually he divulged more and more. He said that

The outlaw Blackie Thompson

Burkhart and Hale had once approached him and his old buddy Curley Johnson to kill Bill and Rita Smith. As part of the payment, they had proposed that Blackie steal Burkhart's car, and one night, while Burkhart was at home in bed with Mollie, Blackie had taken it from their garage. Blackie had later been picked up by the law for car theft and never went through with any of the killings.

It wasn't clear if Blackie would ever agree to testify in court to these matters, but White hoped that he had enough information to save the case. He left Blackie surrounded by guards and rushed with Agent Smith to interrogate Burkhart again.

Back in the box, White told Burkhart, "We're not satisfied with the answers you gave us last night. We believe there's a good deal you didn't tell us."

"All I know is what's common talk," Burkhart said.

White and Agent Smith played their last card: they told Burkhart that they had another witness who would testify to his involvement in the scheme to kill Bill and Rita Smith. Burkhart, knowing that he had been bluffed once, said that he didn't believe them.

"Well, I can go get him if you don't think we have got him," Agent Smith said.

"Bring him in," Burkhart said.

White and Smith went and got Blackie and escorted him into

the room. While the gunman on the roof kept Blackie in his scope through the window, the outlaw sat across from Burkhart, who looked stunned.

Agent Smith turned to Blackie and said, "Blackie, have you told me . . . the truth concerning the propositions made by Ernest Burkhart to you?"

Blackie replied, "Yes, sir."

Agent Smith added, "To kill Bill Smith?"

"Yes, sir."

"Did you tell me the truth when you told me Ernest gave you an automobile as part payment of that job?"

"Yes, sir."

Blackie, evidently enjoying himself, looked squarely at Burkhart and said, "Ernest, I have told them everything."

Burkhart appeared defeated. After Blackie was taken away, White thought that Burkhart was ready to confess and turn on Hale, but each time Burkhart came close to doing so, he stopped himself. Around midnight, White left Burkhart in the custody of the other agents and returned to his hotel room. There were no more tricks to play; exhausted, despairing, he collapsed on his bed and fell asleep.

Not long after, White was jolted awake by the phone. Facing the prospect that something else had gone wrong—that Blackie Thompson had sprung loose—he picked up the receiver and heard the urgent voice of one of his agents. "Burkhart's ready to tell his story," he said. "But he won't give it to us. Says it's got to be you."

=====

When White entered the box, he found Burkhart slumped in his seat, tired and resigned. Burkhart told White that he hadn't killed all those people, but he knew who had. "I want to tell," he said.

White reminded Burkhart of his rights, and Burkhart signed a paper that said, "After being so warned, and with no promises having been made me of immunity from prosecution, and of my own free will and accord, I now make the following statement."

Burkhart began speaking about William Hale—about how he had worshipped him as a boy, how he had done all types of jobs for him, and how he had always followed orders. "I relied on Uncle Bill's judgment," he said. Hale was a schemer, Burkhart said, and though he hadn't been privy to all the mechanics of Hale's plots, his uncle had shared with him details of a murderous plan: to kill Rita and Bill Smith. Burkhart said that he had protested when Hale had informed him of his intention to blow up the whole house and everyone in it, including his own relatives. Hale told him, What do you care? Your wife will get the money.

Burkhart said that he went along with Hale's plan, as he always did. Hale had first approached the outlaws Blackie Thompson and Curley Johnson to do the bloodletting. (In a later statement, Burkhart recalled, "Hale had told me to see Curley Johnson, and to find out how tough he was, and if he wanted to make some money, and told me to tell Johnson the job was to bump a squaw-man"—referring to Bill Smith.) Then, when Johnson and Blackie couldn't do the job, Hale sought out Al Spencer. After Spencer refused, Hale spoke to the bootlegger and rodeo star Henry Grammer, who promised to provide a man for the job. "Just a few days before the blow-up happened, Grammer told Hale that Acie"—Asa Kirby— "would do it," Burkhart recalled. "That is what Hale told me."

Burkhart said that Lawson had nothing to do with the explosion, explaining, "You have got the wrong pig by the tail." (Later, Lawson admitted to White, "All that story I told was a lie. All I know about the Smith blow-up was just what I heard in jail. . . . I done wrong and lied.") In fact, Burkhart indicated that Hale had gone with Grammer to Fort Worth so they would have an alibi. Before leaving, Hale told Burkhart to deliver a message to John Ramsey, the cow thief and bootlegger who worked for Henry

Grammer. The message was for Ramsey to tell Kirby that it was time to carry out "the job." Burkhart delivered the message and was home with Mollie on the night of the explosion. "When it happened I was in bed with my wife," he recalled. "I saw a light on the north side. My wife went to the window and looked out." She said that she thought somebody's house was on fire. "As soon as she said that I knew what it was."

Burkhart also provided crucial details about how Hale had arranged the murder of Roan for the insurance money. "I know who killed Henry Roan," Burkhart said, and he identified Ramsey—the cow thief—as the triggerman.

The case had broken wide open. White placed a call to Agent Wren, who was out in the field. "There's a suspect up there named John Ramsey," White told him. "Take him into custody right away."

Ramsey was picked up and brought into the box. He wore overalls over his tall, thin frame; his black hair was greasy, and he walked with a slight, menacing limp. A reporter said he seemed "like a nervy and, perhaps, a dangerous man."

According to the accounts of White and other agents, he looked at the agents warily, insisting he didn't know a thing. Then White laid Burkhart's signed statement in front of Ramsey, who stared at the paper, as if trying to assess its authenticity. Just as White and Smith had presented Burkhart with Blackie, they now brought in Burkhart to confirm his statement to Ramsey. And Ramsey threw up his hands and said, "I guess it's on my neck now. Get your pencils."

According to his sworn statement and other testimony, sometime in early 1923 Grammer told Ramsey that Hale had "a little job he wanted done." When Ramsey asked what it was, Grammer said that Hale needed an Indian knocked off. Ramsey, who referred to the plot as "the state of the game," eventually agreed, and he lured Roan down into the canyon, promising him whiskey. "We sat on the running board of his car and drank," Ramsey recounted. "The

Indian then got in his car to leave, and I then shot him in the back of the head. I suppose I was within a foot or two of him when I shot him. I then went back to my car and drove to Fairfax."

White observed the way Ramsey kept saying "the Indian," rather than Roan's name. As if to justify his crime, Ramsey said that even now "white people in Oklahoma thought no more of killing an Indian than they did in 1724."

═══

White still had questions about the murder of Mollie's sister Anna Brown. Ernest Burkhart remained cagey about the role of his brother Bryan, evidently not wanting to implicate him. But he revealed the identity of the mysterious third man who had been seen with Anna shortly before her death. It was someone whom the agents knew, knew all too well: Kelsie Morrison, their undercover informant who had supposedly been working with the agents to *identify* the third man. Morrison had not just been a double agent who had funneled information back to Hale and his henchmen. It was Morrison, Ernest said, who had put the fatal bullet in Anna Brown's head.

═══

While the authorities went to round up Morrison, they also made sure that a doctor went to check on Mollie Burkhart. She seemed near death, and based on her symptoms, authorities were certain that someone had been secretly poisoning her and doing it slowly so as not to arouse suspicions. In a later report, an agent noted, "It is an established fact that when she was removed from the control of Burkhart and Hale, she immediately regained her health."

Burkhart never admitted having any knowledge that Mollie was being poisoned. Perhaps this was the one sin that he couldn't bear to admit. Or perhaps Hale had not trusted him to kill his own wife.

The Shoun brothers were brought in and interrogated over what, exactly, they had been treating Mollie with. One of the prosecutors who was working with White asked James Shoun, "Weren't you giving her insulin?"

"I may have been," he said.

The prosecutor grew impatient. "Wasn't she taken away from you and taken to the hospital at Pawhuska? Weren't you administering insulin to her?"

Shoun said that maybe he'd misspoken: "I don't want to get balled up and don't want to get in bad."

The prosecutor asked again if he'd administered injections to her. "Yes, I gave her some," he said.

"For what?"

"For sugar diabetes."

"And she got worse?"

"I don't know."

"And she got so bad she was taken away from you and taken to a hospital at Pawhuska, and she got better immediately under the care of another doctor?"

James Shoun and his brother denied any wrongdoing, and White could not prove who was responsible for the poisoning. When Mollie was feeling better, she was questioned by authorities. Mollie was not one who liked to be seen as a victim, but for once she admitted that she was scared and bewildered. At times, she relied upon an interpreter to help with her English—a language that now seemed to convey secrets beyond comprehension. An attorney assisting the prosecution explained to her, "We are all your friends and working for you." He informed her that her husband, Ernest, had confessed that he knew something about these murder cases and that Hale had apparently engineered them, including the bombing of her sister Rita's house.

"Bill Hale and your husband are kin-folks, are they not?" he added.

"Yes, sir," she replied.

At one point, the attorney asked her if Hale was at her house around the time of the explosion.

"No, he was not there. Just my husband and my children was all that was at home."

"No one came there that night?"

"No."

"Was your husband at home all evening?"

"Yes, all evening."

He asked her if Ernest had ever told her anything about Hale's plot. She said, "He never told me anything about it." All she wanted, she said, was for the men who did this to her family to be punished.

"It makes no difference who they are?" the attorney asked.

"No," she said adamantly. But she couldn't, *wouldn't,* believe that Ernest had been involved in such a plot. Later, a writer quoted her saying, "My husband is a good man, a kind man. He wouldn't have done anything like that. And he wouldn't hurt anyone else, and he wouldn't ever hurt me."

Now the attorney asked her, "You love your husband?"

After a moment, she said, "Yes."

———

Once armed with the statements of Ernest Burkhart and Ramsey, White and Agent Smith confronted Hale. White sat across from this gentlemanly-looking figure who, he was convinced, had killed nearly all the members of Mollie's family and who had killed witnesses and co-conspirators. And White had discovered one more disturbing development; according to several people close to Anna Brown, Hale had had an affair with Anna and was the father of her baby. If true, it meant that Hale had killed his own unborn child.

White tried to contain the violent passions inside him as Hale greeted him and Agent Smith with the same politeness that he had demonstrated while being arrested. Burkhart once described Hale as the best man you "ever saw until after you found him out and knowed him," adding, "You could meet and you'd fall in love with him. Women were the same way. But the longer you stayed around him, he'd get to you. He'd beat you some way."

White did not waste time. As he later recalled, he told Hale, "We have unquestioned signed statements implicating you as the principal in the Henry Roan and Smith family murders. We have the evidence to convict you."

Even after White detailed the overwhelming evidence against him, Hale seemed unperturbed, as if he still held the upper hand. Kelsie Morrison had earlier told agents that Hale was certain that "money will buy the protection or acquittal of any man for any crime in Osage County."

White could not anticipate the bitter, sensational legal battle that was about to ensue—one that would be debated in the U.S. Supreme Court and would nearly destroy his career. Still, hoping to tie up the case as neatly and quickly as possible, he made one last attempt to persuade Hale to confess. "We don't think you want to expose [your family] to a long trial and all its sordid testimony, the shame and embarrassment," White said.

Hale stared at White with gleeful zeal. "I'll fight it," he said.

The revelations of the arrests and the horror of the crimes held the nation in their grip. The press wrote about "an evidently well-organized band, diabolic in its ruthlessness, to destroy with bullet, poison, and bomb the heirs to the oil-rich lands of the Osage"; about crimes that were "more blood-curdling than those of the old frontier days"; and about the federal government's effort to bring to justice the alleged "King of the Killers."

White had been consumed with the cases involving Roan and Mollie Burkhart's family members, and he and his men had not yet been able to connect Hale to all of the twenty-four Osage murders or to the deaths of the attorney Vaughan and the oilman McBride. Yet White and his team were able to show how Hale benefited from at least two of these other killings. The first was the suspected poisoning of George Bigheart, the Osage Indian who, before dying, had passed on information to Vaughan. White learned from witnesses that Hale had been seen with Bigheart just before he was rushed to the hospital, and that after his death Hale made a claim upon his estate for $6,000, presenting a forged creditor's note. Ernest Burkhart disclosed that Hale, before filling out the note, had practiced making his handwriting look like Bigheart's. Hale was also implicated in the apparent poisoning of Joe Bates, an Osage Indian, in 1921. After Bates, who was married and had six children, suddenly died, Hale had produced a dubious deed to his land. Bates's widow later wrote a letter to the Office of Indian Affairs, saying, "Hale kept my husband drunk for over a year. Hale would come to the house and ask him to sell his inherited shares in land. Joe always refused no matter how drunk he was. I never believed that he sold that land, he always told me he would not even up to a few days before his death.... Well, Hale got the land."

Despite the brutality of the crimes, many whites did not mask their enthusiasm for the lurid story. OSAGE INDIAN KILLING CON-SPIRACY THRILLS, declared the *Reno Evening Gazette*. Under the headline OLD WILD WEST STILL LIVES IN LAND OF OSAGE MUR-DERS, a wire service sent out a nationwide bulletin that the story, "however depressing, is nevertheless blown through with a breath of the romantic, devil-may-care frontier west that we thought was gone. And it is an amazing story, too. So amazing that at first you wonder if it can possibly have happened in modern, twentieth-century America." A newsreel about the murders, titled "The Tragedy of the Osage Hills," was shown at cinemas. "The true history of the most baffling series of murders in the annals of crime," a handbill for the show said. "A Story of Love, Hatred and Man's Greed for Gold. Based on the real facts as divulged by the startling confession of Burkhart."

Amid the sensationalism, the Osage were focused on making sure that Hale and his conspirators did not find a way to wriggle free, as many feared they would. Bates's widow said, "We Indians cannot get our rights in these courts and I have no chance at all of saving this land for my children." On January 15, 1926, the Society of Oklahoma Indians issued a resolution that said,

> Members of the Osage Tribe of Indians have been foully
> murdered for their headrights...
> Whereas, the perpetrators of these alleged crimes deserve to

be vigorously prosecuted and, if convicted, punished to the
full extent of the law...
THEREFORE, BE IT RESOLVED by this Society that we
commend the federal and state officials for their efforts in trying to ferret out and prosecute the criminals guilty of these
atrocious crimes.

Yet White knew that America's judicial institutions, like its
policing agencies, were permeated with corruption. Many lawyers and judges were on the take. Witnesses were coerced, juries
tampered with. Even Clarence Darrow, the great defender of the
downtrodden, had been charged with trying to bribe prospective
jurors. A *Los Angeles Times* editor recalled Darrow once telling him,
"When you're up against a bunch of crooks you will have to play
their game. Why shouldn't I?" Hale held enormous influence over
Oklahoma's fragile legal institutions; as a reporter who visited the
region noted, "Townspeople, from low to high, speak of him with
bated breath. His influence and that of his associates is felt everywhere."

Because of Hale's power, a federal prosecutor warned that it was
"not only useless but positively dangerous" to try him in the state
legal system. But, as with many crimes against American Indians,
the question of which government entity had jurisdiction over the
Osage murders was confounding. If a murder occurred on Indian
territory, then the federal authorities could claim jurisdiction. The
Osage territory, however, had been allotted, and much of the surface land where the murders had occurred, including the slaying of
Anna Brown, was no longer under the tribe's control. These cases,
Justice Department officials concluded, could only be tried by the
state.

Yet, as officials scoured the various cases, they thought that
they'd found an exception. Henry Roan was killed on an Osage
allotment that hadn't been sold to whites; moreover, the Osage
property owner was under guardianship and considered a ward of

the federal government. Prosecutors working with White decided to move forward with this case first, and Hale and Ramsey were charged in federal court with Roan's murder. They faced the death penalty.

The assembled prosecution team was formidable. It included two high-ranking officials in the Justice Department, as well as a young, newly appointed U.S. attorney, Roy St. Lewis, and a local attorney named John Leahy, who was married to an Osage woman and who had been hired by the Tribal Council to assist in the various trials.

Hale was aided by his own array of lawyers—some of the "ablest legal talent of Oklahoma," as one newspaper put it. Among them was Sargent Prentiss Freeling, a former Oklahoma attorney general and a staunch advocate of states' rights. He had often traveled around the region giving a lecture titled "The Trial of Jesus Christ

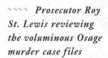

Prosecutor Roy St. Lewis reviewing the voluminous Osage murder case files

from a Lawyer's Standpoint," warning, "When a small-natured man indulges to the extent of his ability in villainy and goes as far as his contemptible nature will permit, he then employs some disreputable lawyer to assist him." To defend John Ramsey, Roan's alleged shooter, Hale hired an attorney named Jim Springer, who was known as a fixer. Under Springer's counsel, Ramsey quickly recanted his confession, insisting, "I never killed anyone." Ernest Burkhart told White that Hale had earlier assured Ramsey "not to worry, that he—Hale—was on the inside and had everything fixed from the road-overseer to the Governor."

Soon after the grand jury proceedings began, in early January, one of Hale's cronies—a pastor—was charged with committing perjury on the stand. At a later proceeding, another associate was arrested for trying to intoxicate witnesses. As the trial neared, crooked private eyes began trailing witnesses and even trying to make them disappear. The bureau put out a physical description for one private eye who agents feared might be hired as an assassin: "Long face ... gray suit and light Fedora hat ... several gold teeth ... has reputation as being very cunning and 'slippery.'"

Another gunman was hired to assassinate Kelsie Morrison's former wife, Katherine Cole, who was Osage and had agreed to testify for the prosecution. The gunman later recalled, "Kelsie said that he wanted to make some arrangement to get shed of Katherine, his wife, because she knew too much about the Anna Brown murder deal. Kelsie said that he would give me a note to Bill Hale and that Hale would fix the arrangements." Hale paid the gunman and told him to "get her out drunk and get rid of her." But at the last minute the gunman wouldn't go through with it, and after being picked up on a robbery charge, he told authorities about the plan. Still, the plots continued.

White, who had ordered his men to work in pairs for security, received a tip that a former member of the Al Spencer Gang had shown up in Pawhuska to kill federal agents. White told Agent Smith, "We'd better head this off," and armed with .45 automatics, they confronted the man at a house where he was staying. "We hear you've threatened to run us out of town," White said.

The outlaw assessed the lawmen and said, "I'm just a friend of Bill Hale's. Just happened in town, is all."

White subsequently informed Hoover, "Before this man could put into execution any of his 'dirty' work, he left . . . as he was given to understand that it would be healthier for him some other place."

White was extremely concerned about Ernest Burkhart. Hale later told one ally that Burkhart was the only witness he was afraid of. "Whatever you do, you get to Ernest," Hale told him. Otherwise, he said, "I'm a ruined man."

On January 20, 1926, Burkhart—whom the government had not yet charged, waiting to see the extent of his cooperation—told White that he was sure he was going to be "bumped off."

"I'll give you all the protection the government can afford," White promised him. "Whatever is necessary."

White arranged for Agent Wren and another member of his team to spirit Burkhart out of the state and guard him until the trial. The agents never registered Burkhart in hotels under his own name, and referred to him by the alias "E. J. Ernest." White later told Hoover, "We think that it is likely that they will endeavor to kill Burkhart. Of course, every precaution is being taken to prevent such a step, but there are many ways that this could be done, for friends of Ramsey and Hale could probably slip poison to him."

Mollie, meanwhile, still didn't believe that Ernest was "intentionally guilty." And when he did not return home for days, she became frantic. Her whole family had been decimated, and now it appeared as if she'd lost her husband, too. An attorney assisting the prosecution asked whether she'd feel better if agents brought her to see Ernest.

"That is all I wanted," she said.

Afterward, White and Mollie met. He promised her that Ernest would be back soon. Until then, White said, he would make sure that they could correspond.

After Mollie received a letter from Ernest saying that he was well and safe, she replied, "Dear husband, I received your letter this morning and was very glad to hear from you. We are all well and Elizabeth is going back to school." Mollie noted that she was no longer so sick. "I feel better now," she said. Clinging to the illusion of their marriage, she concluded, "Well Ernest I must close my short letter. Hoping to hear from you soon. Good by from your wife, Mollie Burkhart."

===

On March 1, 1926, White and the prosecution received a devastating setback. The judge, agreeing with a defense motion, ruled that even though Roan's murder had occurred on an individual Osage allotment, this was not the equivalent of tribal lands, and therefore the case could be adjudicated only in state court. Prosecutors appealed the decision to the U.S. Supreme Court, but with a ruling not expected for months, Hale and Ramsey would have to be released. "It appeared that Bill Hale's lawyers—just as his friends predicted—had clipped the government's tail feathers good," one writer observed.

Hale and Ramsey were celebrating in the courtroom, when they were approached by Sheriff Freas. He shook hands with Hale, then said, "Bill, I have a warrant for your arrest." White and prosecutors had worked with the Oklahoma attorney general to keep Hale and Ramsey behind bars by filing state charges against them for the bombing murders.

White and the prosecutors had no choice but to initiate the state case in Pawhuska, the Osage County seat and a Hale stronghold. "Very few, if any, believe that we can ever be able to get a jury in Osage County to try these parties," White told Hoover. "Trickeries and all methods of deceit will be resorted to."

At a preliminary hearing, on March 12, Osage men and women, many of them relatives of the victims, crammed into the courtroom to bear witness. Hale's wife, his eighteen-year-old daughter, and his many boisterous supporters clustered behind the defense table. Journalists jostled for space. "Seldom if ever has such a crowd gathered in a court room before," a reporter from the *Tulsa Tribune* wrote. "Here are well-groomed business men, contesting stand-ing room with roustabouts. There are society women sitting side by side with Indian squaws in gaudy blankets. Cowboys in broad brimmed hats and Osage chiefs in beaded garb drink in the tes-timony. Schoolgirls crane forward in their seats to hear it. All the cosmopolitan population of the world's richest spot—the Kingdom of the Osage—crowd to catch the drama of blood and gold." A local historian later ventured that the Osage murder trials received more media coverage than the previous year's Scopes "monkey trial," in Tennessee, regarding the legality of teaching evolution in a state-funded school.

Many people in the gallery gossiped about an Osage woman who was sitting on one of the benches, quiet and alone. It was Mollie Burkhart, cast out from the two worlds that she'd always straddled: whites, loyal to Hale, shunned her, while many Osage ostracized her for bringing the killers among them and for remain-ing loyal to Ernest. Reporters portrayed her as an "ignorant squaw." The press hounded her for a statement, but she refused to give one. Later, a reporter snapped her picture, her face defiantly composed, and a "new and exclusive picture of Mollie Burkhart" was transmit-ted around the world.

Hale and Ramsey were escorted into the courtroom. Though Ramsey appeared indifferent, Hale acknowledged his wife and daughter and supporters confidently. "Hale is a man of magnetic personality," the *Tribune* reporter wrote. "Friends crowd about him at every recess of court and men and women shout cheerful greet-ings." In jail, Hale had jotted down these lines from a poem as he remembered them:

> *Judge Not! The clouds of seeming guilt may dim thy brother's fame,*
> *For fate may throw suspicion's shade upon the brightest name.*

White sat down at the prosecution table. In an instant, one of Hale's lawyers said, "Your honor, I demand that T. B. White over there, head of the federal Bureau of Investigation in Oklahoma City, be searched for firearms and excluded from this courtroom."

Hale's supporters hooted and stamped their feet. White stood, opening his coat to show that he wasn't armed. "I will leave if the court orders it," he said. The judge said that this wouldn't be necessary, and White sat back down and the crowd quieted. The hearing proceeded uneventfully until that afternoon, when a man entered the courtroom who had not been seen in Osage County for weeks: Ernest Burkhart. Mollie watched her husband as he walked unsteadily down the long aisle to the stand. Hale glowered at his nephew, whom one of Hale's lawyers denounced as a "traitor to his own blood." Moments before, Burkhart had confided to a prosecutor that if he testified, "they'll kill me," and as Burkhart sat in the witness chair, it was evident that whatever strength he had mustered to reach this point was fading.

A lawyer for Hale rose and demanded to confer privately with Burkhart. "This man is my client!" he said. The judge asked Burkhart if this individual was really his attorney, and Burkhart, with one eye on Hale, said, "He's not my attorney...but I'm willing to talk to him."

White and the prosecutors watched incredulously as Burkhart stepped down from the stand and went with Hale's lawyers into the judge's chambers. Five minutes drifted by, then ten, then twenty; at last, the judge ordered the bailiff to retrieve them. Hale's lawyer Freeling emerged from the chamber and said, "Your Honor, I'd like to ask the court to allow Mr. Burkhart until tomorrow to confer with the defense." The judge agreed, and for a moment Hale personally buttonholed Burkhart in the courtroom, the plot unfolding this time right in front of White. Leahy, the prosecutor who had been hired by the Osage Tribal Council, considered all this to be the most "high-handed and unusual course of conduct I had

ever witnessed on the part of attorneys." As Burkhart left the courtroom, White strove to catch his attention, but Burkhart was swept
away by a mob of Hale's supporters.

═══

The next morning in court one of the prosecutors made the
announcement that White and everyone in the buzzing gallery
were expecting: Ernest Burkhart refused to testify for the state. In
a memo to Hoover, White explained that Burkhart's "nerve went
back on him and, after he was allowed to see Hale and once more
be placed under his domination, there was no hope of his testifying." Instead, Burkhart took the stand as a defense witness. One
of Hale's lawyers asked him if he'd ever spoken to Hale about the
murder of Roan or any other Osage Indian.

"I never did," Burkhart murmured.

When the lawyer asked if Hale had ever requested that he hire
someone to kill Roan, Burkhart said, "He never did."

Step-by-step, in a quiet monotone voice, Burkhart recanted.
Prosecutors tried to salvage their case by filing separate charges
against Burkhart, naming him as a co-conspirator in the bombing of the Smiths' house. Hoping to bolster their position against
Hale and Ramsey by gaining an early conviction against Burkhart,
prosecutors scheduled his trial first. But the two most important
pillars of evidence against Hale—the confessions of Burkhart and
Ramsey—had crumbled. White recalled that in the courtroom
"Hale and Ramsey gave us triumphant grins," adding, "The King
on top again."

When Burkhart's trial began, in late May, White found himself in the midst of an even greater crisis. Hale took the stand and
testified, under oath, that during his interrogation White and his
agents, including Smith, had brutally tried to coerce a confession
from him. Hale said that the men from the bureau had told him
that they had ways of making people talk. "I looked back," Hale

continued. "What caused me to look back was hearing a pistol cock behind me. Just as I looked back, Smith jumped across the room, grabbed me by the shoulder and shoved a big gun in my face."

Hale said that Smith had threatened to beat his brains out and that White had told him, "We will have to put you in the hot chair." Then, he said, the agents shoved him in a special chair, attached wires to his body, and put a black hood over his head and a device like a catcher's mask over his face. "They kept talking about putting the juice to me and electrocuting me and did shock me," Hale said.

Burkhart and Ramsey testified that they had received similar abuse, which was the only reason they had made their confessions. When Hale was on the stand, he gestured wildly, dramatizing how the electricity had allegedly jolted his body. One agent, he claimed, had sniffed the air and cried, "Don't you smell that human flesh burning?"

One morning in early June, Hoover was in Washington. He liked to eat a poached egg on toast for breakfast. A relative once observed that Hoover was "quite a tyrant about food" and that if the yolk seeped at all, he would send it back to the kitchen. Yet this morning it was not the food that disturbed him. He was stunned to pick up the *Washington Post* and find, above the fold, the following headline:

PRISONER CHARGES USE OF ELECTRICITY BY
JUSTICE AGENTS...
ATTEMPT TO FORCE HIM TO ADMIT MURDERS TOLD ON STAND. . . .
OFFICERS SNIFFED AT "FLESH BURNING," HE SAYS.

While Hoover had no particular devotion to the niceties of the law, he did not seem to believe that White was capable of such tactics. What worried Hoover was scandal or, to use his preferred term, "embarrassment." He sent White an urgent telegram demanding an explanation. Though White did not want to dignify the "ridiculous" allegations, he promptly responded, insisting that the charges were a "fabrication from start to finish as there was absolutely no third degree method used. I never used such tactics in my life."

White and his agents took the stand to refute the allegations. Still, William B. Pine—a U.S. senator from Oklahoma who was a wealthy oilman and had defended the guardianship system—began to lobby government officials for White and his men to be fired from the bureau.

At Ernest Burkhart's trial, tempers could no longer be contained. When a defense attorney alleged that the government had committed fraud, a prosecutor shouted, "I'll meet the man who says it out in the courtyard." The two men had to be separated.

With the government's case in trouble, prosecutors eventually called a witness who, they believed, could sway the jury in their favor: the bootlegger and former bureau informant Kelsie Morrison. White and his men had earlier confronted Morrison after learning of his deception. Morrison seemed to have only one guiding force: his own self-interest. When he thought that Hale was more powerful than the U.S. government, he'd served as a double agent for the King of the Osage; once he was caught and realized that the government controlled his fate, he flipped sides and admitted his role in the conspiracy.

Now, as rain fell and thunder clapped outside the courtroom, Morrison testified that Hale had plotted to eliminate all the members of Mollie's family. Hale had informed him that he wanted to get rid of "the whole damn bunch" so that "Ernest would get it all."

As for Anna Brown, Morrison said that Hale had recruited him to "bump that squaw off" and had given him the weapon—a .380 automatic. Bryan Burkhart had acted as his accomplice. After making sure that Anna was good and drunk, they drove out to Three Mile Creek. Morrison's wife at the time, Cole, was with them, and he told her to stay in the car. Then he and Bryan grabbed hold

Anna Brown

of Anna. She was too drunk to walk, Morrison recalled, and so they carried her down into the ravine.

Eventually, Bryan helped Anna sit up on a rock by the creek. "He raised her up," Morrison said. A defense attorney asked, "Pulled her up?"

"Yes, sir."

The courtroom was still. Mollie Burkhart looked on, listening.

The attorney continued, "Did you tell him in what position to hold her while you shot her in the head?"

"Yes, sir."

"You stood there and directed him how to hold this drunken helpless Indian woman down in the bottom of that canyon while you got ready to shoot a bullet into her brain?"

"Yes, sir."

"Then when he got her just in the position you wanted him to have her, then you shot a bullet from this .380 automatic?"

"Yes, sir."

"Did you move her after you shot her?"

"No, sir."

"What happened when you shot her?"

"Turned her loose and she fell back down."

"Just fell over?"

"Yes, sir."

"Did she make any outcry?"

"No, sir."

The attorney continued, "Did you stand there and watch her die?"

"No, sir."

"You had satisfied yourself that with that gun you shot that bullet into her brain you had killed her, didn't you?"

"Yes, sir."

Asked at one point what he had done after the shooting, he replied, "I went home and ate supper."

Morrison's former wife, Cole—who said she hadn't come forward right after the murder because Morrison had threatened to "stomp me to death"—corroborated his account. She said, "I stayed in the car alone about twenty-five or thirty minutes, until they returned. Anna Brown was not with them, and I never saw her alive again."

═══

On June 3, in the middle of the trial, Mollie was called away. Her younger daughter with Ernest, Anna, whom a relative had been raising since Mollie became seriously ill, had died. She was four years old. Little Anna, as she was called, had not been well of late, and doctors had attributed her death to illness, because there seemed to be no evidence of foul play. But for the Osage every death, every apparent act of God, was now in doubt.

Mollie attended the funeral. She had relinquished her daughter to another family so that she would be safe; now she watched as Little Anna, in her small plain box, disappeared into the grave. There were fewer and fewer Osage who knew the old prayers for the dead. Who would chant every morning at dawn for her?

After the burial, Mollie went straight to the courthouse—the cold stone building that seemed to hold the secrets to her grief and despair. She sat down in the gallery by herself, not saying a word, just listening.

═══

On June 7, several days after the death of his daughter, Ernest Burkhart was being escorted from the courtroom back to the county jail. When no one was looking, he slipped a note to the deputy sheriff. "Don't look at it now," he whispered.

Later, when the deputy unfolded the note, he discovered that it was addressed to John Leahy, the prosecutor. It said simply, "See me tonight in the county jail. Ernest Burkhart."

The deputy passed the note to Leahy, who found Burkhart in his cell pacing restlessly. He had deep circles around his eyes, as if he hadn't slept for days. "I'm through lying, judge," Burkhart said, the words rushing out of him. "I don't want to go on with this trial any longer."

"Being with the prosecution, I'm in no position to advise you," Leahy said. "Why don't you tell your lawyers?"

"I can't tell them," Burkhart said.

Leahy looked at Burkhart, not sure if the impending confession was yet another trick. But Burkhart looked sincere. The death of his daughter, the haunting face of his wife each day at the trial, the realization that the evidence against him was piling up—it was too much to withstand. "I'm absolutely helpless," Burkhart said. He beseeched Leahy to ask Flint Moss, an attorney whom Burkhart knew, to come see him.

Leahy agreed, and on June 9 Burkhart returned to the courtroom after having spoken to Moss. This time, Burkhart did not sit at the defense table with Hale's team of attorneys. He walked to the bench and whispered something to the judge. Then he stepped back, breathing loudly, and said, "I wish to discharge the defense attorneys. Mr. Moss will now represent me."

There were protests from the defense, but the judge agreed to the request. Moss stood beside Ernest and pronounced, "Mr. Burkhart wishes to withdraw his plea of not guilty and enter a plea of guilty."

Gasps filled the courtroom. "Is this your desire, Mr. Burkhart?" the judge asked.

"It is."

"Have state or federal officials offered you immunity or clemency if you changed your plea?"

"No."

He had decided to throw himself at the mercy of the court, having earlier told Moss, "I'm sick and tired of all this.... I want to admit exactly what I did."

Burkhart now read a statement admitting that he'd delivered a message from Hale to Ramsey, saying to let Kirby know it was time to blow up the Smith house. "I feel in my heart that I did it because I was requested to do it by Hale, who is my uncle," he said. "The truth of what I did I have told to many men, and as I see it the honest and honorable thing for me to do was to stop the trial and acknowledge the truth."

The judge said that before he accepted the plea, he needed to ask a question: Had federal agents forced Burkhart to sign a confession at gunpoint or under threat of electrocution? Burkhart said that other than keeping him up late, the men from the bureau had treated him just fine. (Later, Burkhart said that some of Hale's attorneys had prodded him to lie on the stand.)

The judge said, "Then your plea of guilty will be accepted."

The courtroom erupted. The *New York Times* reported on the front page, BURKHART ADMITS OKLAHOMA KILLING: CONFESSES HE HIRED MAN TO DYNAMITE SMITH HOME ... SAYS UNCLE HEADED PLOT.

White sent a message to Hoover. Burkhart, he reported, "was very much disturbed and, with tears in his eyes, told me that he had lied and that he was now going to tell the truth ... and would testify to any Court in the United States to that effect."

After Burkhart's admission, the campaign to fire White and his men ended. Oklahoma's attorney general said, "Too much credit cannot be given these gentlemen."

Yet only a fraction of the case had been completed. White and the authorities still had to convict the other henchmen, includ-

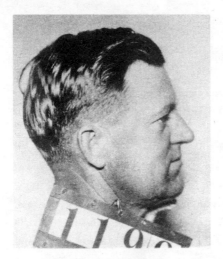

Ernest Burkhart's mug shot

ing Bryan Burkhart and Ramsey. And, most treacherous of all, they still had to bring down Hale. White, after witnessing the shenanigans in Ernest's trial, was less certain that Hale could be convicted, but he received at least one encouraging bit of news: the U.S. Supreme Court had ruled that the place where Roan had been murdered was indeed on Indian lands. "That put us back in federal district courts," White noted.

On June 21, 1926, Burkhart was sentenced to life imprisonment and hard labor. Even so, the people around him detected relief on his face. A prosecutor said that he was now someone "whose mind is at ease because he has relieved his tortured soul of a terrible secret and now seeks repentance and forgiveness." Before being led away in irons to the state penitentiary, Burkhart turned and smiled wanly at Mollie. But her expression remained impassive, perhaps even cold.

In the last week of July 1926, as the summer heat reached infernal temperatures, the trial of Hale and Ramsey for the murder of Henry Roan began at the redbrick courthouse in Guthrie. "The stage is set: the curtain rises slowly on the great tragedy of the Osage—the long-awaited federal trial of two old-time cowboys," the *Tulsa Tribune* reported. "The trial of Ernest Burkhart, although it ended in a melodramatic flourish with his confession to the Smith murder conspiracy implicating Hale, was merely a prologue to the life and death tragedy that goes on the boards today."

White stationed extra guards at the jail after attempts to break out the outlaws who were going to testify against Hale. Later, when Hale was being held on a separate tier from the cell housing Blackie Thompson, he passed him a note through a hole where a radiator pipe went through the ceiling. Blackie admitted to agents that Hale had asked him what he required to "not testify against him." Blackie added, "I wrote one note that I would not testify against him if he would get me out." Hale wrote back promising to arrange his escape in return for one more thing—that Blackie then kidnap Ernest Burkhart and make him disappear before he could testify.

"He wanted me to take Ernest Burkhart to Old Mexico," Blackie said, adding that Hale didn't "want Burkhart killed in this country where he would be found."

Given the abundance of evidence against Hale and Ramsey, White believed that the verdict would depend, in large part, on whether the witnesses and the jury became tainted. At Ernest Burkhart's trial, the first panel of prospective jurors had been dismissed after evidence surfaced that Hale had attempted to bribe them. Now, before selecting a jury, prosecutors probed prospective candidates to ascertain whether anyone had approached them. The judge then asked the twelve chosen jurors to swear that they would render a true verdict according to the law and the evidence—"so help you God!"

There was one question that the judge and the prosecutors and the defense never asked the jurors but that was central to the proceedings: Would a jury of twelve white men ever punish another

〰〰〰 *Hale (second from left) and Ramsey (third from left) with two U.S. marshals*

white man for killing an American Indian? One skeptical reporter noted, "The attitude of a pioneer cattleman toward the full-blood Indian...is fairly well recognized." A prominent member of the Osage tribe put the matter more bluntly: "It is a question in my mind whether this jury is considering a murder case or not. The question for them to decide is whether a white man killing an Osage is murder—or merely cruelty to animals."

On July 29, as testimony was set to begin, throngs of spectators arrived early in order to get a seat. The temperature outside was ninety degrees, and it was hard to breathe in the courtroom. John Leahy, the prosecutor, rose to give his opening statement. "Gentlemen of the jury," he said. "William K. Hale is charged with aiding and abetting to the killing of Henry Roan, while John Ramsey is charged with the killing." Leahy outlined the alleged facts of the insurance murder plot in a matter-of-fact voice. One observer noted that "the veteran of legal battles does not go in for fireworks or courtroom histrionics but he makes his points all the stronger for his quiet reserve." Looking on, Hale smiled ever so slightly, while Ramsey leaned back in his chair, fanning himself in the heat, a toothpick between his teeth.

On July 30, the prosecution called Ernest Burkhart to the stand. There was speculation that Burkhart would defect again and return to the fold of his uncle, but this time Burkhart answered the prosecution's questions forthrightly. Burkhart recalled that one time Hale and Henry Grammer had discussed how to eliminate Roan. The original plan was not for Ramsey to shoot Roan, Burkhart said. Instead, Hale intended to use one of his other primary methods—a batch of poisoned moonshine. Burkhart's testimony finally made public what the Osage had long known: members of the tribe had been systematically killed with intentionally contaminated alcohol. In the case of Roan, Burkhart said, Hale ultimately decided to have him shot, but Hale was furious when he later learned that Ramsey had not, as instructed, fired the bullet into the front of Roan's head and left the gun at the scene. "Hale said to me if John Ramsey had done it the way I told him to nobody would have known but that Roan had attempted suicide," Burkhart recalled.

On August 7, the prosecution rested, and the defense soon summoned Hale to the stand. Addressing the jurors as "gentlemen," he insisted, "I never devised a scheme to have Roan killed. I also never desired his death." Although Hale had made a compelling witness, White was confident the government had proven its case. In addition to Burkhart's testimony, White had testified to Ramsey's confession, and witnesses had described Hale's fraudulent acquisition of the insurance policy. The prosecutor Roy St. Lewis called Hale "the ruthless freebooter of death." Another prosecutor said, "The richest tribe of Indians on the globe has become the illegitimate prey of white men. The Indian is going. A great principle is involved in this case. People of the United States are following us through the press. The time has now come for you gentlemen to do your part."

On August 20, a Friday, the jury started its deliberations. Hours went by. The next day, the deadlock continued. The *Tulsa Tribune* said that though the government's case was strong, bets around Guthrie were "five to one for a hung jury." After five days of deliberations, the judge called the parties into the courtroom. He asked the jurors, "Is there any possibility of an agreement on a verdict?"

The foreman rose and said, "There is none."

The judge asked if the government had any remarks, and St. Lewis stood. His face was red, his voice trembling. "There are some good men on the jury and some that are not good," he said. He added that he had been informed that at least one, if not more, members of the panel had been bribed.

The judge considered this, then ordered that the jury be dismissed and the defendants held for further trial.

White was stunned. More than a year of his work, more than three years of the bureau's work, had reached an impasse. The jury was also hung when Bryan Burkhart was tried for the murder of

Hale leaving the courthouse

Anna Brown. It seemed impossible to find twelve white men who would convict one of their own for murdering American Indians. The Osage were outraged, and there were murmurings about taking justice into their own hands. White suddenly had to deploy agents to protect Hale, this man whom he so desperately wanted to bring to justice.

The government, meanwhile, began preparing to retry Hale and Ramsey for the murder of Roan. As part of this effort, White was asked by the Justice Department to investigate corruption during the first Hale trial. He soon uncovered that there had been a conspiracy to obstruct justice, including bribes and perjury. According to one witness, the defense attorney Jim Springer had offered him money to lie on the stand, and when he refused, Springer aimed what appeared to be a gun in his pocket at him and said, "I will kill you." In early October, a grand jury recommended filing charges against Springer and several witnesses for what it called flagrant attempts to obstruct justice. The grand jury issued a statement: "Such practices should not be endured, otherwise our courts will be a mockery, and justice defeated." Several witnesses were indicted and convicted, but prosecutors decided not to charge Springer, because he would demand delaying the second trial of Hale and Ramsey until his own case was resolved.

Before the retrial of Hale and Ramsey for the murder of Roan began, in late October, a Justice Department official advised St. Lewis, the prosecutor, that "this whole defense is a tissue of lies, and it is up to us to get at the facts." He added, "There will be no one to blame except ourselves if they succeed in fixing this jury." White's men were assigned to safeguard the jury.

The prosecution presented essentially the same case, though in more streamlined form. To the surprise of the courtroom, Mollie was briefly summoned to the stand by Hale's attorney Freeling.

"Will you state your name?" he asked her.

"Mollie Burkhart."

"Are you the present wife of Ernest Burkhart?"

"Yes, sir."

He then exposed the secret that she'd long kept from Ernest, asking, Was Henry Roan your husband at one time?

"Yes, sir," she said.

The prosecution protested that the question was immaterial, and the judge agreed. Indeed, there seemed to be no point to the line of questioning other than to inflict more suffering upon her. After she identified a photograph of Roan, she stepped down from the stand and returned to the gallery.

When Ernest Burkhart was on the stand, the prosecutor Leahy questioned him about his marriage to Mollie. "Your wife is an Osage Indian?" Leahy asked him.

"She is," Ernest replied.

At an earlier proceeding, he was asked what his profession was, and he said, "I don't work. I married an Osage."

One of Hale's lawyers now asked Ernest if he'd pleaded guilty to murdering his wife's sister by blowing up her house while she was inside.

"That is right," he said.

Hoping to place the blame for the killings on Ernest, Hale's lawyer recited the names of Mollie's murdered family members, one after the other. "Has your wife now any surviving relatives outside of the two children she has by you?"

"She has not."

There was a hush in the courtroom as Mollie looked on; her gaze could no longer be avoided. After only eight days of testimony, both parties rested. One of the prosecutors said in his closing statement, "The time now has come for you men to stand for law and order and decency, time to uncrown this King. You should say by your verdict as courageous men, decent men, that they shall hang by the neck until they are dead." The judge advised the jury members that they must set aside sympathies or prejudices for either side. He warned, "There never has been a country on this earth that has fallen except when that point was reached...where the citizens would say, 'We cannot get justice in our courts.'" On the evening of October 28, the jury began deliberating. By the next morning, word spread that the jurors had reached a decision, and the courtroom filled with the familiar participants.

The judge asked the foreman if indeed the jury had reached a verdict. "Yes, sir," he replied, and handed him a sheet of paper. The judge looked at it for a moment, then passed it on to the clerk. The courtroom was so quiet that the ticking of a clock on the wall could be heard. A reporter later observed, "Hale's face expressed a guarded eagerness; Ramsey's was a mask." Standing in front of the still room, the clerk read out that the jury found John Ramsey and William K. Hale guilty of first-degree murder.

Hale and Ramsey appeared shocked. The judge said to them, "A jury has found you guilty of the murder of an Osage Indian, Mr. Hale and Mr. Ramsey, and it becomes my duty to pass sentence. Under the law the jury may find you guilty and that carries the death penalty in a first-degree murder case. But this jury has qualified it with life imprisonment." The jurors were willing to punish the men for killing an American Indian, but they would not hang them for it. The judge told Hale and Ramsey, "Stand before the bench." Hale rose quickly, Ramsey hesitantly. The judge declared that he was sentencing them to the penitentiary for the "period of your natural lives." He then asked, "Have you anything to say, Mr. Hale?"

Hale stared straight ahead, vacantly. "No, sir," he said.

"And you, Mr. Ramsey?"

Ramsey simply shook his head.

Reporters rushed out of the courtroom to file their stories, proclaiming, as the *New York Times* put it, "KING OF OSAGE HILLS" GUILTY OF MURDER. The attorney Leahy would hail the outcome as "one of the greatest indications of law and justice that has been realized in the country." Mollie welcomed the verdict, but, as White knew, there were some things that no successful investigation, no system of justice, could restore.

A year later, when Anna Brown's murder was prosecuted, Mollie attended the trial. By then, Morrison had recanted his confession, shifting his allegiance yet again in the hope of securing compensation from Hale. Authorities had seized a note that he had sent to Hale in prison, in which he had promised to "burn" down the authorities "if I ever get the Chance." Prosecutors gave Bryan Burkhart immunity, believing that it was necessary to obtain Morrison's conviction. During the trial, Mollie listened again to the gruesome details of how Bryan, her brother-in-law, had gotten her sister drunk and then propped up her body while Morrison shot her in the back of the head—or, as Bryan put it, "watered" her.

Bryan recalled that a week after the shooting he had returned to the scene of the crime with Mollie and her family to identify Anna's rotting corpse. The memory had lingered with Mollie, but only now could she fully comprehend the scene: Bryan was standing near her, staring down at his victim while feigning grief.

"Did you go out to see this body?" an attorney asked Bryan.

"That is what we all went for," he said.

The shocked attorney asked him, "You knew Anna Brown's dead body was out there, didn't you?"

"Yes, sir."

Morrison had been among the onlookers. Ernest had been there, too, comforting Mollie, even though he had known that Anna's two killers were standing only a few feet away from them. Similarly, Ernest had known from the moment Rita and Bill Smith's house exploded who was responsible; he had known the truth when, later that evening, he had crept into bed with Mollie, and he had known the whole time she had been desperately searching for the killers. By the time Morrison was convicted of Anna's murder, Mollie could no longer look at Ernest. She soon divorced him, and whenever her husband's name was mentioned, she recoiled in horror.

═══

For Hoover, the Osage murder investigation became a showcase for the modern bureau. As he had hoped, the case demonstrated to many around the country the need for a national, more professional, scientifically skilled force. The *St. Louis Post-Dispatch* wrote of the murders, "Sheriffs investigated and did nothing. State's Attorneys investigated and did nothing. The Attorney General investigated and did nothing. It was only when the Government sent Department of Justice agents into the Osage country that law became a thing of majesty."

Hoover was careful not to disclose the bureau's earlier bungling. He did not reveal that Blackie Thompson had escaped under the bureau's watch and killed a policeman, or that because of so many false starts in the probe other murders had occurred. Instead, Hoover created a pristine origin story, a founding mythology in which the bureau, under his direction, had emerged from lawlessness and overcome the last wild American frontier. Recognizing that the new modes of public relations could expand his bureaucratic power and instill a cult of personality, Hoover asked White to send him information that he could share with the press: "There is, of course, as you can appreciate, a difference between legal aspects and human interest aspects and what the representatives of the press would have an interest in would be the human interest aspect, so I would like to have you emphasize this angle."

Hoover fed the story to sympathetic reporters—so-called friends of the bureau. One article about the case, which was syndicated by William Randolph Hearst's company, blared,

NEVER TOLD BEFORE! —

How the Government with the Most Gigantic Fingerprint System on Earth Fights Crime with Unheard-of Science Refinements; Revealing How Clever Sleuths Ended a Reign of Murder and Terror in the Lonely Hills of the Osage Indian Country, and Then Rounded Up the Nation's Most Desperate Gang

In 1932, the bureau began working with the radio program *The Lucky Strike Hour* to dramatize its cases. One of the first episodes was based on the murders of the Osage. At Hoover's request, Agent Burger had even written up fictional scenes, which were shared with the program's producers. In one of these scenes, Ramsey shows Ernest Burkhart the gun he plans to use to kill Roan, saying, "Look at her, ain't she a dandy?" The broadcasted radio program concluded, "So another story ends and the moral is identical with that set forth in all the others of this series.... [The criminal] was no match for the Federal Agent of Washington in a battle of wits."

Though Hoover privately commended White and his men for capturing Hale and his gang and gave the agents a slight pay increase—"a small way at least to recognize their efficiency and application to duty"—he never mentioned them by name as he promoted the case. They did not quite fit the profile of college-educated recruits that became part of Hoover's mythology. Plus, Hoover never wanted his men to overshadow him.

The Osage Tribal Council was the only governing body to

publicly single out and praise White and his team, including the undercover operatives. In a resolution, which cited each of them by name, the council said, "We express our sincere gratitude for the splendid work done in the matter of investigating and bringing to justice the parties charged." The Osage, meanwhile, had taken their own steps to protect themselves against future plots, persuading Congress to pass a new law. It barred anyone who was not at least half Osage from inheriting headrights from a member of the tribe.

======

Soon after Hale and Ramsey were convicted, White faced a momentous decision. The U.S. assistant attorney general, who oversaw the federal prison system, had asked White if he would take over as warden of Leavenworth prison, in Kansas. The oldest federal penitentiary, it was then considered one of the country's most dreaded places to be incarcerated. There had been allegations of corruption at the prison, and the assistant attorney general had told Hoover that White was ideal for the job: "I hate to give up the chances of getting a warden that I think will be as good as Mr. White."

Hoover did not want White to leave the bureau. He told the assistant attorney general that it would be a tremendous loss. Still, Hoover said, "I feel that I would be unfair to [White] if I should oppose his promotion. I have, as you know, the highest regard for him, personally and officially."

After some torment, White decided to leave the bureau. The job offered him greater pay and meant that he would no longer need to uproot his wife and young boys. It also offered him a chance to preside over a prison, just as his father had, although on a far larger scale.

On November 17, 1926, when White was still settling into the new job, two new inmates were convoyed up the prison's horseshoe driveway by U.S. marshals. The inmates took in their grim destination: Leavenworth was a 366,000-square-foot fortress, which, as a prisoner once described, rose out of the surrounding cornfields like a "giant mausoleum adrift in a great sea of nothingness." As the two inmates approached the entryway in shackles, White walked toward them. Their faces were pale from a lack of sunlight, but White recognized them: Hale and Ramsey.

"Why, hello, Tom," Hale said to White.

"Hello, Bill," White answered.

Ramsey said to White, "Howdy."

White shook hands with both inmates, who were then led away to their cells.

It was like wandering through the catacombs of memory. As White walked along the cell block tiers, he could see figures from his past, their eyes peering out from behind bars, their bodies gleaming with sweat. He saw Hale and Ramsey. He encountered members of the old Al Spencer Gang and the former head of the Veterans Bureau, who had committed bribery during the scandalous Harding administration. And White came upon the two deserters who had killed his older brother, Dudley, though White never mentioned the connection, not wanting to cause them any distress.

White lived with his family on the prison grounds. His wife was initially unable to sleep, wondering, "How do you raise two young boys in this kind of environment?" The challenges of managing the prison—which was designed to hold twelve hundred inmates but instead had three times that number—were overwhelming. In the summer, the temperatures inside rose as high as 115 degrees, which is why prisoners would later call Leavenworth the Hot House. One August day in 1929, when it was so nightmarishly hot that the milk in the prison's kitchen soured, a riot erupted in the mess hall. Red Rudensky, an infamous safecracker, recalled that there was "ugly, dangerous, killing hate" and that White rushed in to quell the unrest: "Warden White showed his courage, and came within a few feet of me, although cleavers and broken, jagged bottles were inches from him."

White tried to improve conditions in the prison. A custodian who later worked under him recalled, "The Warden was strict with the inmates but would never stand for any mistreatment or heckling of them." White once sent Rudensky a note that said, "It takes a good deal of nerve to change a course that you have been on for years and years—more so, maybe than I realize, but if it is in you, now is the time to show it." Because of White's support, Rudensky recalled, "I had a ray of hope."

Though White encouraged efforts at rehabilitation, he had few illusions about many of the men contained in the Hot House. In 1929, Carl Panzram—a repeat killer who'd confessed to slaying twenty-one people and insisted, "I have no conscience"—beat a member of the prison staff to death. He was sentenced to be hanged inside the penitentiary, and White, though opposed to capital punishment, was given the grim task of overseeing the execution, much as his father had done in Texas. On September 5, 1930, as the sun rose over the prison dome, White went to take Panzram from his cell to the newly built gallows. White made sure that his two boys weren't present when the noose was looped around the neck of Panzram, who shouted at his executioners to hurry up: "I could hang a dozen men while you're fooling around." At 6:03 a.m., the trap opened and Panzram swung to his death. It was the first time that White had helped to end a human life.

═══

After arriving at Leavenworth, William Hale was assigned to duty on the tuberculosis ward. Later, he toiled on the prison farm, where he tended pigs and other animals the way he had during his early days on the frontier. A prison report said, "He does high grade work caring for stock, and is able to do such operations as opening of abscesses and castrating of animals."

In November 1926, when a reporter wrote to White fishing for gossip about Hale, White refused to provide any, insisting that Hale would be "treated as other prisoners are treated." White went out of his way so that Hale's wife and daughter never felt slighted by prison officials. Hale's wife once wrote a letter to White, saying, "Would I be imposing to ask your permission to see my husband next Monday? It will be almost three weeks since my last visit and of course I realize your regulations allow us only one visit each month but . . . if you could please grant me this I would surely appreciate it." White wrote back that she would be welcome at the prison.

Over the years, Hale never admitted ordering any of the murders: not the killing of Roan, for which he was convicted, or the countless other murders that the evidence showed he had orchestrated but that he wasn't prosecuted for after he had received a life sentence. Despite his refusal to admit responsibility, he had given, during trial testimony, a rather cold statement about a different attempt that he'd made to swindle a headright—a statement that seemed to reveal his ethos: "It was a business proposition with me."

Whereas White had once turned to preachers to illuminate this thing of darkness, he now also searched for a scientific explanation. In prison, Hale was given a neurological and psychological examination. The evaluator found that Hale showed no obvious "evidence of repression nor of frank psychosis" but nevertheless had "extremely vicious components in his make-up." Cloaking his savagery under the banner of civilization, Hale portrayed himself as an American pioneer who had helped forge a nation out of the raw wilderness. The evaluator observed, "His poor judgment is further evidenced by his continued denial of his obvious guilt. His affect is not suitable. . . . He has put behind him any feeling of shame or repentance he may have had." White read the evaluator's psychological study of Hale, but there was some evil that seemed beyond the scope of science. Though Hale conformed to prison regulations, he continued to scheme to secure his release. He allegedly arranged for an appeals court to be bribed, and when these efforts

›››› *Mollie Burkhart*

failed to win him freedom, he boasted, as the evaluator noted, of "his probable release through influence of friends."

Yet for the first time in ages life in Osage County went on without his overwhelming presence. Mollie Burkhart began again to socialize and attend church. She eventually fell in love with a man named John Cobb, who was part white and part Creek. According to relatives, their love was genuine, and in 1928 they were married.

There was another dramatic change in Mollie's life. She and the Osage had fought to end the corrupt system of guardianships, and on April 21, 1931, a court ruled that Mollie was no longer a ward of the state: "IT IS FURTHER ORDERED, ADJUDGED AND DECREED BY THE COURT, that the said Mollie Burkhart, Osage Allottee No. 285, . . . is hereby restored to competency, and the order heretofore made adjudging her to be an incompetent person is hereby vacated." At forty-four, Mollie could finally spend her money as she pleased, and was recognized as a full-fledged American citizen.

———

On December 11, 1931, White was in his warden's office when he heard a noise. He stood and went to the door and found himself staring into the barrel of a gun. Seven of the most dangerous convicts—including two Al Spencer Gang members and a bandit who was nicknamed Boxcar, because of his giant size—were attempting to escape. The group was armed with a Winchester rifle, a sawed-off shotgun, and six sticks of dynamite, which had been smuggled into the prison. The convicts took White and eight members of his staff hostage and used them as shields as they pushed forward. Once outside the front gate, the prisoners released the other hostages and headed out to the main road with White— their insurance policy, as they called him. The inmates commandeered an approaching vehicle, forced White inside, and sped away.

White's captors reminded him that there'd be nothing left of him to bury if anything went wrong. Everything was going wrong. The car slipped off the muddy road and got stuck, forcing the prisoners to flee on foot. Soldiers from Fort Leavenworth joined the manhunt. Planes were flying overhead. The inmates ran into a farmhouse and seized an eighteen-year-old girl and her younger brother. White pleaded with the prisoners, saying, "I know you're going to kill me. But don't kill these two—they aren't in it at all."

Boxcar and another inmate went to look for a second car, taking White with them. At one point, White could see that the girl had broken free and was running. The gang seemed ready to start killing, and White grabbed the barrel of the gun being held by one of his captors, who yelled at Boxcar, "Shoot him! He's got my gun." As Boxcar leveled his shotgun at White's chest, only inches away, White lifted his left forearm to shield himself. Then he heard the blast and felt the bullet boring through his arm, through flesh and blood and bone, the buckshot fragmenting, some pieces going through his arm and into his chest. Yet White was standing. It was like a miracle; he had been shot to pieces, and yet he was still breathing in the cold December air, and then he felt the butt of the rifle smashing into his face and he crumbled, all 225 pounds of him, and fell into a ditch, bleeding out and left to die.

———

Nearly a decade later, in December 1939, the acclaimed newspaper reporter Ernie Pyle stopped at La Tuna prison, near El Paso, Texas. He asked to meet the warden and was led in to see Tom White, who was then nearly sixty years old. "White asked me to stay for lunch," Pyle later wrote. "So I did, and we sat and talked, and finally he told me the story, as I was hoping all the time he would. The story about his left arm."

White described how, after being shot by Boxcar, he was found in the ditch and rushed to the hospital. For several days, it was uncertain whether he would live, and doctors contemplated amputating his arm. But he survived, somehow, and he even kept his arm, though it still had bullet fragments lodged inside and dangled uselessly. White didn't mention one detail to Pyle: the girl who had been taken hostage credited White with protecting her and her brother. "I am sure they intended to kill all of us, and only Warden White's bravery saved us," she said.

None of the convicts managed to get away. They believed that if you touched a prison official, especially a warden, it was better, as one of them remarked, never to "come back because if you do you are going to have a hard, hard time." And so when the authorities caught up with Boxcar and the other escapees, Boxcar shot his two companions, then put a bullet in his own forehead. The other inmates prepared to kill themselves by detonating the dynamite, but before they could light the fuse, they were apprehended. One of them said, "The funny part is that when we got back to the institution they never laid a hand on us. Warden White was a hell of a man. He left strict orders, 'No hands on these people, leave them alone. Treat them just like the rest of the prisoners.'" He added, "Otherwise we'd have got our heads broken in."

White learned that Rudensky had been recruited to assist with the escape but had refused. "He had begun to develop a sense of responsibility," White told another writer. "He realized that I had been fair with him and was sincerely trying to help him establish himself as a member of 'legitimate' society." In 1944, Rudensky was released on parole and had a successful career as an author and a businessman.

When White had sufficiently recovered, he took over as warden of La Tuna, a job that was less strenuous. Pyle wrote of the shooting, "The experience affected Warden White, as it would anyone. It didn't make him afraid, but it made him jumpy, and kind of haunted." Pyle continued, "I don't see how, after an experience like that, you could look upon any convict with anything but hatred. But Warden White isn't that way. He is thoroughly professional about his job. He is a serious, pleasant man, and he has trained himself to control his emotions."

If J. Edgar Hoover used the Osage murder probe as a showcase for the bureau, a series of sensational crimes in the 1930s stoked public fears and enabled Hoover to turn the organization into the powerful force recognized today. These crimes included the kidnapping of Charles Lindbergh's baby and the Kansas City Massacre, where several lawmen were killed in a shootout while transporting the Al Spencer Gang member Frank "Jelly" Nash. White's old colleague, Agent Frank Smith, was among the convoy but survived. (The journalist Robert Unger later documented how Smith and another agent who originally claimed that they hadn't been able to identify the shooters, suddenly vividly recalled them after pressure from Hoover to resolve the cases.) In the wake of these incidents, Congress passed a series of New Deal reforms that gave the federal government its first comprehensive criminal code and the bureau a sweeping mission. Agents were now empowered to make arrests and carry firearms, and the department was soon renamed the Federal Bureau of Investigation. "The days of the small Bureau were over," Hoover's biographer Curt Gentry observed. "Gone, too, were the days when special agents were merely investigators." White's brother Doc was involved in many of the bureau's biggest cases during this period—from hunting public enemies like John Dillinger to killing Ma Barker and her son Fred. Tom White's son had also joined the bureau, making three generations of White lawmen.

Hoover ensured that the identity of the bureau was indistinguishable from his own. And while presidents came and went, this bureaucrat, now thick around the waist and with jowls like a bulldog, remained. "I looked up and there was J. Edgar Hoover on his balcony, high and distant and quiet, watching with his misty kingdom behind him, going on from President to President and decade to decade," a reporter for *Life* magazine wrote. The many details of Hoover's abuses of power would not be made public until after his death, in 1972, and despite White's perceptiveness he was blind to the boss man's megalomania, his politicization of the bureau, and his paranoid plots against an ever-growing list of perceived enemies, among them American Indian activists.

Over the years, White wrote periodically to Hoover. Once, White invited him to a relative's ranch: "We do not have to rough it on his ranch, for he has every convenience except air cooling and you don't need that." But Hoover politely declined. He was too busy now and had to be prodded to take note of his former star agent. When White, at the age of seventy, stepped down as warden of La Tuna in 1951, Hoover sent him a card only after another agent reminded him how much White would "appreciate a personal note from the director on his retirement."

J. Edgar Hoover

In the late 1950s, White learned that Hollywood was about to shoot a movie, *The FBI Story*, starring James Stewart as a crime-busting agent, that would feature a segment on the murders of the Osage. White sent Hoover a letter, asking if the filmmakers might want to talk to him about the case. "I would be glad to afford the information as I know it from start to finish," White said. Hoover replied that he would "certainly bear you in mind," but he never followed up. Hoover made a cameo appearance in the 1959 movie, which further enshrined him in the popular imagination.

But, even though the movie was popular, the Osage case was fading from memory, eclipsed by more recent celebrated cases. Soon, most Americans had forgotten it. In the late 1950s, White contemplated writing a story to document the case. He wanted to record the crimes against the Osage and wanted to make sure that the agents who had worked with him were not erased from history. They had all since died in obscurity and often in poverty. When one of the undercover operatives was dying, his wife wrote that she wished he had a retirement fund, and an agent who knew him advised Hoover that the family was "confronted with a very gloomy situation."

Several years after the Osage murder investigation, Wren, the Ute agent, was forced out of the bureau again, this time for good. As he left, he cursed and threw items from his desk. His treatment, he later wrote to Hoover, had been "unjust, unfair and unwarranted." Wren's anger eventually dissipated, and before he died, in 1939, he sent Hoover a letter that said, "Often when I read of you and your men I swell up with much pleasure and pride, then I begin to think again of the long time ago. I am very proud of you and still call you my old chief." He continued, "Many of my old friends have gone to the happy hunting grounds. Many of the tall beautiful trees have been destroyed, many have been cut down by the white man. The wild turkey, the deer, the wild horses, and the wild cattle have gone, and do not live anymore among the beautiful hills."

Along with documenting the roles of other agents, White no doubt hoped to secure himself a small place in history, though he'd never say so himself. He wrote a few stilted pages, which read, in part,

> After the Director Mr. J. Edgar Hoover briefed me on the importance of the case, he instructed me to return to Houston, arrange my affairs there, and go as soon as possible to take charge of the Oklahoma City office. He told me I was to select my investigators necessary in this case from men I knew best fitted in this line of work.... We realized the importance of men working under cover more than ever when we arrived on the ground and found the frightened state of mind the Indians were living under.

White recognized that he wasn't much of a writer, and by 1958 he had teamed up with Fred Grove, an author of Western novels who was part Osage and who, as a boy, had been staying in Fairfax at the time of the Smith explosion, an event that haunted him. As Grove worked on the book, White asked him, in a letter, if the narrative could be told in the third person. "I would like to keep the big 'I' out of it all I can, because I don't want it conveyed that I am the whole story," White explained. "If it had not been for the good agents I had on the job we could never have made it. Then too our boss man J. Edgar Hoover, the directing head of the F.B.I., is to be reckoned with."

In a letter to Hoover, White asked if the bureau would release to him some of the old case files to help him prepare the book. He also inquired whether Hoover would write a brief introduction. "I hope this will not be asking too much of you," White said. "I feel that this would be invaluable to us all who were then and are now vitally interested in our great organization, the Federal Bureau of Investigation. You and I are about the only ones of the originals left now." In an internal memo, Clyde Tolson, the associate direc-

〈〈〈〈 *Tom White*

tor of the bureau, who had become Hoover's longtime companion, spawning rumors that they were romantically involved, said, "We should furnish only limited, routine material, if any."

White's body was beginning to fail him. He had arthritis. He tripped walking (walking!) and injured himself. In September 1959, White's wife told Grove, "Sickness of any kind is really very terrible to him and puts him out considerably. We still hope he will improve so that he can go to Dallas the last of October to attend the National Convention of Ex-FBI Agents." Even in his ailing state White assisted Grove with the book, as if he were consumed by an unsolved case, until the manuscript was completed. In a letter to Grove, White wrote, "I am hoping that all the good luck in the world will come our way from a good publisher," adding that he would be keeping his fingers crossed. But publishers found the account less than captivating. And though Grove would eventually release a fictionalized version called *The Years of Fear*, the original historical account was never published. "I am sincerely sorry this letter couldn't bring better news," an editor said.

===

On February 11, 1969, Doc, who was staying on the ranch where he and Tom had grown up, died at the age of eighty-four. In a letter, White shared the news with Hoover, noting that he and his four siblings had been "born on this land." He added wistfully, "And now I am the only one left."

In October 1971, White collapsed from an apparent stroke. He was ninety and had no more miraculous escapes. On December 21, in the early morning hours, he stopped breathing. A friend said, "He died as he had lived, quietly and with a calm dignity." An agent urged Hoover to send condolences to White's widow, emphasizing that there was nothing in White's files to "militate against such action." And so Hoover sent a bouquet of flowers, which was laid upon the casket as it disappeared into the ground.

For a moment, before he receded from history, too, White was eulogized as a good man who had solved the murders of the Osage. Years later, the bureau would release several of its files on the Osage investigation in order to preserve the case in the nation's memory. But there was something essential that wasn't included in these and other historical records, something that White himself had missed. There was another layer to the case—a deeper, darker, even more terrifying conspiracy, which the bureau had never exposed.

THE
REPORTER

We have a few old mouth-to-mouth tales; we ex-
hume from old trunks and boxes and drawers letters
without salutation or signature, in which men and
women who once lived and breathed are now merely
initials or nicknames out of some now incompre-
hensible affection which sound to us like Sanskrit or
Chocktaw; we see dimly people, the people in whose
living blood and seed we ourselves lay dormant and
waiting, in this shadowy attenuation of time possess-
ing now heroic proportions, performing their acts of
simple passion and simple violence, impervious to
time and inexplicable.

—William Faulkner, *Absalom, Absalom!*

So much is gone now. Gone are the big petroleum companies and the forests of derricks as the vast oil fields have been increasingly depleted. Gone is the Million Dollar Elm. Gone are the railroads, including where Al Spencer and his gang pulled off the last train robbery in Oklahoma, in 1923. Gone, too, are the outlaws, many of whom died as spectacularly as they lived. And gone are virtually all the boomtowns that smoldered from morning until night. Little remains of them but shuttered buildings colonized by bats and rodents and pigeons and spiders, while in the case of Whizbang there is nothing save stone ruins submerged in a sea of grass. Several years ago, a longtime resident of one of the boomtowns lamented, "Stores gone, post office gone, train gone, school gone, oil gone, boys and girls gone—only thing not gone is graveyard and it git bigger."

Pawhuska is filled with its share of abandoned buildings, but it is one of the few towns that remain. It has a population of thirty-six hundred. It has schools, a courthouse (the same one where Ernest Burkhart was tried), and several restaurants, including a McDonald's. And Pawhuska is still the capital of the vibrant Osage Nation,

〝〝〝 *A now shuttered bar in Ralston, the town where Bryan Burkhart took Anna Brown to drink the night she was killed*

which, in 2006, ratified a new constitution. The nation maintains its own elected government and has twenty thousand members. The majority are scattered in other parts of the state or the country, but around four thousand reside in Osage County, above the underground reservation. The Osage historian Louis F. Burns observed that after "only shreds and tatters remained" of his people, they had risen "from the ashes of their past."

One summer day in 2012, after traveling from New York, where I live and work as a reporter, I visited Pawhuska for the first time, hoping to find information on the Osage murder cases, which, by then, were nearly a century old. Like most Americans, when I was in school, I never read about the murders in any books; it was as if these crimes had been excised from history. So when I stumbled upon a reference to the murders, I began to look into them. Since then, I had been consumed with trying to resolve lingering questions, to fill in the gaps in the FBI's investigation.

In Pawhuska, I stopped at the Osage Nation Museum, where I had arranged to meet with its longtime director, Kathryn Red Corn. A woman in her seventies, with a broad face and short graying hair, she had a gentle, scholarly manner that masked an inner intensity. She showed me an exhibit of photographs of many of the 2,229 allotted members of the tribe, including several of her relatives, who had each received a headright in 1906. In one of the display cases, I spotted a photograph of Mollie Burkhart sitting happily with her sisters. Another photograph showed their mother, Lizzie, and everywhere I turned while touring the exhibit I recognized another victim of the Reign of Terror. Here, a young, striking George Bigheart in a cowboy hat. There, Henry Roan with his long braids. Over there, a dashing Charles Whitehorn wearing a suit and bow tie.

The most dramatic photograph in the museum spanned an entire side of the room. Taken at a ceremony in 1924, it was a panoramic view of members of the tribe alongside prominent local white businessmen and leaders. As I scanned the picture, I noticed that a section was missing, as if someone had taken a scissors to it. I asked Red Corn what happened to that part of the photograph. "It's too painful to show," she said.

When I asked why, she pointed to the blank space and said, "The devil was standing right there."

She disappeared for a moment, then returned with a small, slightly blurred print of the missing panel: it showed William K. Hale, staring coldly at the camera. The Osage had removed his image, not to forget the murders, as most Americans had, but because they cannot forget.

A few years ago, Red Corn told me, she was at a party in Bartlesville and a man approached her. "He said that he had Anna Brown's skull," she recalled. It was evidently the part of Brown's skull that the undertaker had kept, in 1921, and given to bureau

The missing panel of the photograph that shows Hale (far left), dressed in a suit and cap and wearing glasses. The entire panoramic photograph—which includes Hale on the very far left—is shown on the title page at the beginning of the book.

agents for analysis. Outraged, Red Corn told the man, "That needs to be buried here." She called the Osage chief, and Anna's skull was retrieved and, at a quiet ceremony, interred with her other remains.

Red Corn gave me the names of several Osage who, she thought, might have information about the murders, and she promised to later share with me a related story about her grandfather. "It's hard for us to talk about what happened during the Reign of Terror," she explained. "So many Osage lost a mother or a father or a sister or a brother or a cousin. That pain never goes away."

———

Over several weekends each June, the Osage hold their ceremonial dances, *I'n-Lon-Schka*. These dances—which take place, at different times, in Hominy, Pawhuska, and Gray Horse, three areas where the Osage first settled when they came to the reservation, in the 1870s—help preserve fading traditions and bind the community together. The Osage come from all over to attend the dances, which provide a chance to see old family and friends and cook out and reminisce. The historian Burns once wrote, "To believe that the Osages survived intact from their ordeal is a delusion of the mind. What has been possible to salvage has been saved and is dearer to our hearts because it survived. What is gone is treasured because it was what we once were. We gather our past and present into the depths of our being and face tomorrow. We are still Osage. We live and we reach old age for our forefathers."

During a subsequent visit to the region, I headed to Gray Horse to see the dances and meet one of the people Red Corn had suggested I find —someone who had been profoundly affected by the murders. Almost nothing remained of the original Gray Horse settlement but some rotted beams and bricks buried in the wild grasses, which the wind ruffled in ghostly rhythms.

To accommodate the dances, the Osage had erected, amid the encroaching wilderness, a pavilion, with a mushroom-shaped metal roof and a circular earth floor surrounded by concentric rows of wooden benches. When I arrived on a Saturday afternoon, the pavilion was crowded with people. Gathered in the center, around a sacred drum used to commune with Wah'Kon-Tah, were several male musicians and singers. Ringed around them were the "lady singers," as they are called, and in a circle farther out were dozens of male dancers, young and old, wearing leggings, brightly colored ribbon shirts, and bands of bells below their knees; each of these dancers had on a headdress—typically made of an eagle feather, porcupine quills, and a deer tail—which stood up like a Mohawk.

At the sound of the drumming and singing, these dancers stepped in a counterclockwise circle to commemorate the rotation of the earth, their feet pounding the soft earth, their bells jangling. As the drumming and choral singing intensified, they crouched slightly and stepped more quickly, moving together with precision.

One man nodded his head while another flapped his arms like an eagle. Others gestured as if they were scouting or hunting.

There was a time when women were not allowed to dance at these events, but they now joined in as well. Wearing blouses and broadcloth skirts and handwoven belts, they formed a slower-moving, dignified circle around the male dancers, keeping their torsos and heads straight as they bobbed up and down with each step.

Many Osage looked on from the benches, fanning themselves in the heat; a few stole glances at cell phones, but most watched reverently. Each bench bore the name of an Osage family, and as I walked around to the southern side of the pavilion, I found the one I was looking for: "Burkhart."

Before long, an Osage woman walked toward me. In her early fifties, she wore a powder-blue dress and stylish glasses, and her long black glossy hair was pulled back in a ponytail. Her expressive face seemed vaguely recognizable. "Hi, I'm Margie Burkhart," she said, extending her hand. Margie is the granddaughter of Mollie Burkhart. She serves on a board that directs health-care services for the Osage, and she had driven from her home in Tahlequah, seventy miles southeast of Tulsa, to the dances with her husband, Andrew Lowe, a Creek Seminole.

The three of us sat on the wooden bench and, while watching the dancers, spoke about Margie's family. Her father, now deceased, was James "Cowboy" Burkhart—the son of Mollie and Ernest Burkhart. Cowboy and his sister, Elizabeth, also now dead, had witnessed the Reign of Terror from inside their father's house of secrets. Margie said of Ernest, "He took away everything from my dad—his aunts, his cousins, his trust." Though Cowboy was haunted by the knowledge of what Ernest had done, he adored Mollie. "He always spoke fondly of her," Margie recalled. "When he was little, he'd get these real bad earaches, and he said she'd blow in his ears to make the pain go away."

Margie Burkhart, the granddaughter of Mollie and Ernest

After Mollie divorced Ernest, she lived with her new husband, John Cobb, on the reservation. Margie was told that it had been a good marriage, a period of happiness for her grandmother. On June 16, 1937, Mollie died. The death, which wasn't considered suspicious, received little notice in the press. The *Fairfax Chief* published a short obituary: "Mrs. Mollie Cobb, 50 years of age... passed away at 11 o'clock Wednesday night at her home. She had been ill for some time. She was a full-blood Osage."

Later that year, Ernest Burkhart was paroled. The Osage Tribal Council issued a resolution, protesting that "anyone convicted of such vicious and barbarous crimes should not be freed to return to the scene of these crimes." The *Kansas City Times,* in an editorial, said, "The parole of Ernest Burkhart from the Oklahoma state penitentiary recalls what was possibly the most remarkable murder case in the history of the Southwest—the wholesale slaying of Osage Indians for their oil headrights.... The freeing of a principal in so cold-blooded a plot, after serving little more than a decade of a life sentence, seems to reveal one of the besetting weaknesses of the parole system."

Margie said that after Ernest got out, he robbed an Osage home and was sent back to prison. In 1947, while Ernest was still in jail, Hale was released, having served twenty years at Leavenworth. Parole board officials maintained that their ruling was based on the grounds of Hale's advanced age—he was seventy-two—and his record as a good prisoner. An Osage leader said that Hale "should have been hanged for his crimes," and members of the tribe were convinced that the board's decision was the last vestige of Hale's political influence. He was forbidden to set foot again in Oklahoma, but according to relatives he once visited them and said, "If that damn Ernest had kept his mouth shut we'd be rich today."

Margie told me that she never met Hale, who died in 1962, in an Arizona nursing home. But she saw Ernest after he got out of prison again, in 1959. Barred from returning to Oklahoma, he had initially gone to work on a sheep farm in New Mexico, earning $75 a month. A reporter noted at the time, "It will be a far cry from the days of affluence as the husband of an oil-rich Osage Indian woman." In 1966, hoping to return to Oklahoma, Ernest applied for a pardon. The records no longer exist, but his appeal, which went before a five-member review board in Oklahoma, was based at least partly on his cooperation with the bureau's investigation of the murders. (White had always credited Burkhart's confession as salvaging his case.) Despite intense protests from the Osage, the board ruled, three to two, in favor of a pardon, which the governor then granted. HEADRIGHTS KILLER WINS PARDON VOTE, the *Oklahoman* declared, adding, OSAGES TERRORIZED.

Stooped and with thinning hair, Ernest went back to Osage County, where at first he stayed with his brother Bryan. "When I met Ernest, I had just become a teenager," Margie recalled. "I was very surprised he looked so grandfatherly. He was very slight with graying hair; his eyes looked so kind. He wasn't rough even after all those years in prison. And I couldn't fathom that this man had done all that…" Her voice trailed off amid the insistent beating of the drum. After a while, she continued, "It was so hard on my dad. He and Liz were ostracized by the tribe, and that hurt so much. They needed family and support, and they didn't have any."

The experience made her father angry—angry at the world. Andrew, Margie's husband, pointed out that Elizabeth was also deeply affected. "She was kind of paranoid," he said.

Margie nodded and said, "Aunt Liz couldn't stay in one place and was always changing her address and phone number."

Elizabeth showed little interest in seeing Ernest, who eventually moved in to a mice-infested trailer just outside Osage County, but Cowboy occasionally visited. "I think a part of him longed for a father," Margie said. "But he knew what his father had done. He called him Old Dynamite." When Ernest died, in 1986, he was cremated, and his ashes were given to Cowboy in a box. Ernest had left instructions with Cowboy to spread them around the Osage Hills. "Those ashes were in the house for days, just sitting there," Margie

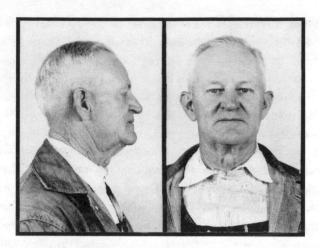

~~~~ *Ernest Burkhart*

~~~~ *Cowboy and Elizabeth with their father, Ernest,*
whose face was torn out of the photograph years later

recalled. "Finally, one night my dad got real mad and took the box and just chucked it over a bridge."

━━━

During a break in the dancing, as the sun began its descent in the sky, Margie offered to show me around Gray Horse. The three of us got in her car, and she began driving down a narrow, dusty road. Not far from the pavilion, almost concealed amid the black-jacks, was one of the few houses standing in Gray Horse. "That's where I grew up," Margie said. To my surprise, it was a small, spare, wooden house, more like a cabin than a mansion. The Great Depression had wiped out many Osage fortunes that had already been diminished by guardians and thieves. Margie said that Mollie's was no exception. The price of a barrel of oil, which reached more than $3 during the boom years, plummeted to 65 cents in 1931, and an annual headright payment fell to less than $800. The following year, the *Literary Digest* published an article headlined OSAGE OIL WEALTH FADING. It reported, "These Indians became accustomed to lives of glorious ease. But now... their income from oil is rapidly disappearing, and that was practically all they had." Compounding the situation was the gradual depletion of the oil fields. In 1929, even before the stock market crash, a national news-paper story reported, "In five years, if the oil map continues to shift, the tribe may have to go back to work."

Over the next few decades, most of the boomtowns, including Gray Horse, began to die off. "When I was little, I could hear the oil wells pumping," Margie recalled. "Then one day they stopped." Today more than ten thousand wells remain scattered across the reservation, but they are generally what oilmen call "stripper" wells, each one generating less than fifteen barrels a day. When an auction for Osage oil leases was held in Tulsa in 2012, three leases sold for less than $15,000 in total. Margie, who inherited a little more than half of a headright from her father, still receives a quarterly check for her share in the mineral trust. The amount varies depending on the prices of oil but in recent years has usually amounted to a few thousand dollars. "It certainly helps, but it's not enough to live on," she said.

The Osage have found new sources of revenue, including from seven casinos that have been built on their territory. (They were formerly called the Million Dollar Elm Casinos.) They generate tens of millions of dollars for the Osage, helping to fund their government, educational programs, and health-care benefits. The Osage were also able to retrieve at least a portion of the oil funds mismanaged over decades by the U.S. government. In 2011, after an eleven-year legal battle, the government agreed to settle a lawsuit brought by the Osage for $380 million.

As we drove through Gray Horse, we came upon a clearing in the woods, where there was an old cemetery. We got out of the car, and Margie paused in front of a tombstone bearing Mollie Burkhart's name. The epitaph said, "She was a kind and affectionate wife and a fond mother and a friend to all." Nearby were the plots for Mollie's murdered sisters and her murdered brother-in-law, Bill Smith, and her murdered mother, Lizzie, and her murdered first husband, Henry Roan. Margie looked around at the tombs and asked, "What kind of person could do this?"

Margie had earlier laid flowers around the graves, and she bent down and straightened one. "I always try to decorate the stones," she said.

We resumed driving and cut along a dirt road through the prairie. Lush tall grasses spread as far as the eye could see, a rolling green expanse that was disturbed only by a few small, rusted oil pumps and by cattle grazing here and there. Earlier, when I drove to Gray Horse, I'd been startled by the sight of bison roaming through the prairie with their bowed heads and massive woolly bodies supported seemingly impossibly on narrow legs. In the nineteenth century, bison were extinguished from the prairie, but in recent years they have been reintroduced by conservationists. The media mogul Ted Turner had been raising bison on a forty-

The graves of Mollie and her murdered family members

thousand-acre ranch between Fairfax and Pawhuska—a ranch that in 2016 was bought by the Osage Nation.

As Margie and her husband and I continued across the prairie, the sun floated above the rim of the earth—a perfect orange sphere that soon became half a sun, then a quarter, before dying off with a burst of dazzling light. Margie said, "I like it when the sky gets pink like this."

We seemed to be driving aimlessly, riding up and down over the undulating land, like a ship adrift in the waves. Suddenly, at a peak, Margie jolted the car to a stop. In the distance was a ravine and, at the bottom, a meandering creek. "Over there, that's where they shot Anna," Margie said. "My dad took me horseback riding and showed me the spot. I was young and we only had our horses. It was kind of scary."

In 2009, an Osage named Elise Paschen published a poem called "Wi'-gi-e," which means "prayer" in Osage. Narrated from

Mollie Burkhart's point of view, the poem is about the murder of
Anna Brown:

> *Because she died where the ravine falls into water.*
> *Because they dragged her down to the creek.*
> *In death, she wore her blue broadcloth skirt.*
> *Though frost blanketed the grass she cooled her feet in the spring.*
> *Because I turned the log with my foot.*
> *Her slippers floated downstream into the dam.*
> *Because, after the thaw, the hunters discovered her body.*

The poem ends with these lines:

> *During Xtha-cka Zhi-ga Tze-the, the Killer of the Flowers Moon.*
> *I will wade across the river of the blackfish, the otter, the beaver.*
> *I will climb the bank where the willow never dies.*

By the time Margie drove on, the prairie was shrouded in the
dark of night. Only the beams from the headlights illuminated the
dusty road. Margie said that her parents first told her what Ernest
and Hale had done when she was a child. "I used to worry whenever I did something naughty, 'What if I'm the bad seed?'" Margie
recalled. She said that occasionally *The FBI Story* would air on local
television, and she and her family would watch it and cry.

As she spoke, I realized that the Reign of Terror had ravaged—
still ravaged—generations. A great-grandson of Henry Roan's once
spoke of the legacy of the murders: "I think somewhere it is in the
back of our minds. We may not realize it, but it is there, especially if
it was a family member that was killed. You just have it in the back
of your head that you don't trust anybody."

We emerged from the prairie and headed into downtown Fairfax. Although still officially a town, it seemed on the verge of obliv-
ion. Year by year, its population had shrunk; now it was fewer than
fourteen hundred. The main street was lined with the western-

style buildings that had been constructed during the boom, but they were abandoned. We paused by the largest storefront, its window darkened with grime and cobwebs. "That was the Big Hill Trading Company," Margie said. "When I was growing up, it was still in business. It was huge and had these great wooden banisters and old wood floors. Everything smelled of wood." I looked down the street, trying to envision what Mollie Burkhart and Tom White had seen—the Pierce-Arrow motorcars and the cafés and the oilmen and the aristocratic Osage, the wild furies that had once burned there. Now, even on a Saturday night, it was a "ghost town," as Margie put it.

She drove on again and turned off the main street into a small residential area. A few of the old mansions remained, but they were deserted and decaying; some were completely imprisoned in vines. At one point, Margie slowed down, as if searching for something.

"What are you looking for?" her husband asked.

"The place where the house was blown up."

"Isn't it back the other way?" he said.

"No, it's—ah, here it is," she said, pulling over by the lot, where another house had since been built.

Margie then mentioned something that I had not seen in any of the FBI records. Her father had told her that on the night of the explosion he and his sister and Mollie had been planning to spend the night at the Smiths' house. But Cowboy had a bad earache, and they had stayed home. "That's why they escaped," Margie said. "It was just fate." It took a moment for the implication to sink in. "My dad had to live knowing that his father had tried to kill him," Margie said.

For a while, we sat in the car in the darkness, trying to comprehend what could not be comprehended even after all these years. Finally, Margie shifted into forward and said, "Well, why don't we go back to the dances?"

History is a merciless judge. It lays bare our tragic blunders and foolish missteps and exposes our most intimate secrets, wielding the power of hindsight like an arrogant detective who seems to know the end of the mystery from the outset. As I combed through the historical records, I could see what Mollie could not see about her husband. (An Osage had told me, "Who would believe that anyone would marry you and kill your family for your money?") I could see White unable to recognize Lawson's bogus confession or Hoover's sinister motives. And as I dug deeper into the Osage murder cases—into the murk of autopsies and witness testimony and probate records—I began to see certain holes in the bureau's investigation.

The authorities insisted that once Hale and his conspirators were given life sentences, they'd found the guilty parties. And after White had taken the job at Leavenworth, the cases were closed, closed with great triumph, even though the bureau had not yet connected Hale to all twenty-four murders. Was he really responsible for every one of them? Who, for example, had abducted the oilman McBride in Washington, D.C., or thrown W. W. Vaughan off the speeding train?

Hale relied on others to do his bloodletting, but there was no evidence that Hale's usual coterie of henchmen—including Bryan Burkhart, Asa Kirby, John Ramsey, and Kelsie Morrison—had trailed McBride to the nation's capital or were with Vaughan on the train. Whoever had murdered these men had seemed to get away scot-free.

I could not find any new leads on the McBride case, but one day when I was doing research in Oklahoma City, I called Martha Vaughan, a granddaughter of W. W. Vaughan's. She was a social worker who lived in Sallisaw, Oklahoma, which is 160 miles from the state capital. She was eager to talk about her grandfather and offered to drive to see me. "Let's meet at the Skirvin Hotel," she said. "It'll give you a glimpse of some of the riches that oil brought to Oklahoma."

When I arrived at the hotel, I understood what she meant. Built in 1910 by the oilman W. B. Skirvin, it was once billed as the finest hotel in the Southwest, with a ballroom that seated five hundred people and chandeliers imported from Austria and pillars topped with busts of Bacchus, the Greek god of wine. Hale's attorney Sargent Prentiss Freeling died—apparently of a cerebral hemorrhage—in one of the hotel rooms while playing solitaire. In 1988, amid a devastating oil downturn, the hotel closed and remained shuttered for years. But nearly two decades later, after undergoing a $55 million renovation, it reopened as part of the Hilton chain.

I waited for Martha in the lobby, which still has the original arched wooden entryway and the faces of Bacchus peering down from the ceiling. When Martha arrived, she was accompanied by her cousin Melville Vaughan, a biology professor at the University of Central Oklahoma. "He knows a lot about Grandpa Vaughan," Martha said.

Melville was carrying two thick binders, and as we sat at the bar, he laid them before me. They were filled with research that over decades the family had obsessively collected about W. W.

Vaughan's murder. The binders included faded newspaper clip-pings (PAWHUSKA MAN'S NUDE BODY FOUND), Vaughan's death certificate, and an informant's statement to the FBI that Vaughan, shortly before being killed, had mentioned having collected "suf-ficient evidence to put Bill Hale in the electric chair."

Martha and Melville said that Vaughan's widow, Rosa, was left with ten children to raise and no income. They had to move from their two-story house into a storage garage. "They didn't have money to eat," Martha said. "The Osage banded together and basi-cally helped feed the family." Some of Vaughan's children, includ-ing Martha's father, went to live with Osage families, where they grew up speaking Osage and learning the traditional dances. "My father felt safe among the Osage," Martha said.

She explained that though many members of her family believed that Hale had wanted Vaughan silenced, they suspected that there was more to the murder. They wondered who the assassin was and how the killing was carried out: Was Vaughan murdered before he was thrown off the train, or did the impact kill him? Someone with influence had made sure that the inquest was a sham—the cause of death was listed as "unknown."

For a while, we discussed elements of the case. Melville explained that Vaughan was big and strong, which meant that the assassin had to have been physically powerful or helped by accom-plices. Vaughan, I recalled, had told his wife that he had stashed evidence on the murders—as well as money for the family—in a secret hiding place. I asked Melville and Martha how the killer could have determined where this hiding place was. Martha said that there were only two possibilities: the killer either forced the information out of Vaughan before throwing him off the train, or the killer was someone whom Vaughan trusted enough to confide such information.

Melville said that after Hale had gone to jail, a relative tried to continue investigating the case, but he received an anonymous threat that if he and the family pressed the matter any further they'd all end up like W. W. Vaughan. After that, the family stopped digging. Martha said, "I remember talking to my oldest uncle; my sister and I were visiting with him before he died. We said, 'Who did this to Grandpa Vaughan?' He mentioned the warning to the family and said not to go there. He was still frightened."

I asked if Rosa, or anyone else in the family, had ever mentioned any potential suspects besides Hale.

No, Martha said. But there was a man who'd embezzled money from Grandpa Vaughan's estate after he died and whom Rosa then sued in civil court. I asked what the man's name was, and Martha said, "Something Burt."

"Yes, H. G. Burt," Melville said. "He was president of a bank."

I wrote down the name in my notebook, and when I looked up, I could see the eagerness in their eyes. I suddenly feared that I'd stirred false hope. "It's been a long time," I said. "But I'll see what I can find out."

=====

The southwest branch of the U.S. National Archives is in a warehouse, in Fort Worth, Texas, that is bigger than most airport hangars. Inside, stacked in fifteen-foot-high rows, in humidity-controlled conditions, are more than a hundred thousand cubic feet of records. They include transcripts from the U.S. District Courts of Oklahoma (1907–1969), logs on the deadly Galveston hurricane of 1900, materials on the assassination of John F. Kennedy, documents on slavery and Reconstruction, and reports from many of the Bureau of Indian Affairs field offices. The archive reflects the human need to document every deed and directive, to place a veil of administrative tidiness over the disorder of famines and plagues and natural disasters and crimes and wars. Within these voluminous files, I hoped to find a clue regarding the murder of W. W. Vaughan.

I had already reviewed court records about the lawsuit that Rosa Vaughan had filed against H. G. Burt. At first glance, the dispute, which began in 1923, seemed mundane. Vaughan and Burt, who was the president of a bank in Pawhuska, were considered close friends, and Vaughan had long acted as one of Burt's attorneys. According to Rosa, Burt owed her deceased husband $10,000, which she was seeking to recover.

Yet the devilry is in the details, and as I delved deeper, I discovered that the money in dispute was connected to another victim of the Reign of Terror, George Bigheart. Vaughan had also been Bigheart's attorney. And before Bigheart disclosed critical information about the murders to Vaughan—and before he died of suspected poisoning at the hospital in Oklahoma City—he had sought a "certificate of competency" from authorities. With this document, he would no longer be designated a ward of the government, and he could spend his headright payments as he pleased. Vaughan had successfully helped him file his application, and for this and other legal services Bigheart had planned to pay him as much as $10,000—a sum that is comparable today to nearly $140,000. Burt, however, had somehow collected the money. Days later, both Bigheart and Vaughan were dead.

Rosa Vaughan's suit against Burt, who was represented by one of the same law firms that had represented Hale in the murder trials, was initially dismissed in state court. Martha had told me the family was sure that the jury had been rigged, and on appeal the Oklahoma Supreme Court eventually reversed the decision and ordered Burt to turn over to Rosa Vaughan $5,000, plus interest. "What kind of person tries to steal from a penniless widow with ten children?" Martha had said to me.

As I reviewed various records at the National Archives as well as information from other sources, I began to piece together a clearer portrait of Burt. Born in Missouri in 1874, he was the son of a farmer. Census records indicate that by 1910 he had moved to Pawhuska, apparently one of the legions of acquisitive, dreaming, desperate settlers. He opened a trading store and later became president of a bank. A 1926 photograph shows him dressed in the same style as Hale, with a sharp suit and a hat—an itinerant farmer's son transformed into a respectable businessman.

Much of his wealth, though, flowed from the deeply corrupt "Indian business"—the swindling of millionaire Osage. A court record noted that Burt had run a loan business targeting the Osage. During a 1915 hearing before a joint commission of Congress that was investigating American Indian affairs, a tribal attorney said that Burt would borrow money from other whites and then relend it to the Osage at astronomical interest rates. "Mr. Burt is one of the men whom I say and believe is on the inside of affairs at Pawhuska," the attorney testified. "He told me that he was only paying 6 per cent for this money, and he could make a great deal more out of it by loaning it back to the Indians." He continued, "He is getting the money for 6 per cent and probably will be able to get—I would be afraid to guess how much—but somewhere from 10 to 50 per cent."

Burt employed bizarre accounting methods in order to conceal his fleecing of the Osage. At a probate hearing after the death of George Bigheart, an attorney expressed bafflement at why loans ostensibly from Burt's bank to the Osage were issued from Burt's personal checkbook. Burt insisted that he'd "never made any deals I have to cover up."

"I did not mean anything personal Mr. Burt, but that is just a little unusual."

"It is the way we have always handled it."

At the archive in Fort Worth, I pulled records from the U.S. Attorney's Office for the Western District of Oklahoma that dealt with the murders of the Osage. They contained something that I'd never seen anywhere before: the secret testimony of the grand jury that in 1926 investigated the murders of the Osage. Among the witnesses who testified were many of the principal figures in the case, such as Ernest Burkhart and Dick Gregg. There was no mention of Burt's testifying. However, the life-insurance agent who had issued a policy to Henry Roan, which had named Hale as the beneficiary, testified that Burt had also recommended another American Indian to target with an insurance-policy scheme.

I later found, amid the thousands of pages of records on the murders archived by the Bureau of Investigation, two other references to Burt. The first was an agent's report from a conversation with a trusted informant, who had indicated that Burt and Hale were "very intimate" associates. What's more, the informant said that Burt and Hale had "split on the boodle"—the sum of money—obtained from Bigheart. It wasn't clear from the report what, exactly, the amount was, but the bureau had noted that after Bigheart's death Hale successfully made a claim upon his estate for $6,000, by presenting a bogus creditor's note. Perhaps "the boodle" also included the $10,000 that Burt had tried to make off with.

Still, unlike the invaluable headrights involved in the slaying of Mollie's family members—or the $25,000 life-insurance policy in Roan's death—none of these sums, especially if divided, represented a significant incentive for murder. This may explain why the Justice Department never prosecuted Hale for Bigheart's killing or pursued Burt further. Yet it was evident that White and his men were deeply suspicious of Burt. In a second report that I found in the bureau files, agents described Burt as a "murderer."

For days, I returned to the archive trying to find a financial motive for the killing of Bigheart. I looked through probate records to see who would have benefited from his death. In an e-mail, Martha had written to me, "As Ol' Pappy always said, 'Follow the money.'" There was no evidence that Hale or Burt or any other white man had inherited Bigheart's fortune, which was passed down to Bigheart's wife and his young daughter. Bigheart's daughter, however, had a guardian, and this man would have had control of the money. I flipped through the records until I saw the name of her guardian: H. G. Burt.

I felt my heart quickening as I reviewed the facts. I knew that Burt had been a close associate of Hale's who had been enmeshed in the systematic exploitation of the Osage. I knew that Burt had gained access to Bigheart's fortune by becoming the guardian of his daughter. I knew, from government records, that Burt had also been the guardian of several other Osage, including one who had died. I knew that Burt had been with Bigheart around the time he succumbed to apparent poisoning—a local lawman had noted that Burt and Hale had both visited with Bigheart shortly before he died. And I knew that the bureau considered Burt a killer.

Other pieces of evidence also implicated Burt in a crime. Court records showed, for instance, that Burt had stolen money that Bigheart had intended for Vaughan, even though Burt purported to be Vaughan's close friend. Perhaps Vaughan, blind to his friend's machinations, had mentioned the investigation that he had been pursuing and confided the location of the hideout containing his money and evidence. And when Vaughan had gone to see Bigheart on his deathbed, perhaps Bigheart had incriminated not only Hale but also Burt in the murder plots.

The theory of Burt's involvement in the murder of Bigheart and Vaughan, though, was still based on circumstantial evidence. I didn't even know who was with Vaughan when he was thrown from the train. Then, while searching through old newspapers, I found an article in the *Pawhuska Daily Capital* about Vaughan's funeral. Partway through the story, it mentioned that Burt had boarded the train with Vaughan in Oklahoma City and was on the journey when Vaughan disappeared from his berth. According to another story in the newspaper, it was Burt who reported Vaughan's disappearance.

Before I left the National Archives in Fort Worth, I came across a folder that contained an interview with a bureau informant who had been close to Hale and who had provided critical evidence against him in the other murder cases. The informant was asked if he had any information regarding the murder of Vaughan.

"Yes," he replied. "I think Herb Burt pulled that."

═══

I was conscious of the unfairness of accusing a man of hideous crimes when he could not answer questions or defend himself. And when I called Martha Vaughan to tell her about my findings, I underscored the limitations of what we could know for sure. I then went through the research I had gathered. I also mentioned that at a library in New Mexico I had come across notes from an unpublished interview with the Fairfax town marshal, who had investigated the murders of the Osage. He indicated that Burt had been involved in Vaughan's killing and that a mayor of one of the boomtowns—a local tough—had helped Burt throw Vaughan off the train. The town marshal also indicated that during the bureau's investigation into the Osage murders, in 1925, Burt was so scared that he considered fleeing. Indeed, Burt abruptly moved to Kansas that same year. When I finished going through all the details, Martha fell silent, then sobbed softly.

"I'm sorry," I said.

"No, it's a relief. This has been with my family for so long."

While researching the murders, I often felt that I was chasing history even as it was slipping away, and not long after we spoke, I learned that Martha had died from heart failure. She was only sixty-five. A heartbroken Melville told me, "We lost another link to the past."

One night in May 2013, the Constantine Theater, in Pawhuska, was scheduled to show a video recording of a performance of the Osage ballet *Wahzhazhe*. The Osage have long been linked to the world of classical dance, having produced two of the greatest ballerinas, the sisters Maria and Marjorie Tallchief. Maria, considered America's first major prima ballerina, was born in Fairfax in 1925. In her autobiography, she recalled the oil riches and observed that her Osage father seemed to own the town: "He had property everywhere. The local movie theater on Main Street, and the pool hall opposite, belonged to him. Our ten-room, terra-cotta-brick house stood high on a hill overlooking the reservation." She also recalled that a house nearby had been "firebombed and everyone inside killed, murdered for their headrights."

Wahzhazhe chronicled the sweeping history of the Osage, including the period of the Reign of Terror. *Wahzhazhe* means "Osage." I was eager to see the ballet, even if it was only a recording of one of the performances, and after buying a ticket, I headed into the Pawhuska theater where Mollie and Ernest Burkhart had once sat in the velvety chairs and where the oil barons had gathered for auctions during bad weather. In the early 1980s, the theater had

The courthouse where Ernest Burkhart was tried still looms over Pawhuska.

been on the verge of demolition, but a group of local citizens volunteered to restore it, clearing away spiderwebs and vermin, polishing the brass plates on the front door, and removing layers of gunk on the lobby floor to reveal a mosaic in the shape of a star.

The auditorium was crowded, and I found my seat as the lights dimmed and the film began. An opening statement read, "In early missionary journals Osages were often described as being 'the happiest people in the world.' ... They had a sense of freedom because they didn't own anything and nothing owned them. But the Osage Nation was in the way of the economic drive of the European world ... and life as they once knew it would never be the same." The statement continued, "Today our hearts are divided between two worlds. We are strong and courageous, learning to walk in these two worlds, hanging on to the threads of our culture and tra-

ditions as we live in a predominantly non-Indian society. Our history, our culture, our heart, and our home will always be stretching
our legs across the plains, singing songs in the morning light, and
placing our feet down with the ever beating heart of the drum. We
walk in two worlds."

The ballet powerfully evoked these two colliding worlds. It
showed the Osage from the time they roamed the plains to their
first encounter with European explorers and missionaries, and to
the black-gold rush. At one point, the dancers appeared dressed as
flappers, twirling wildly to jazzy music. Suddenly, they were inter-
rupted by the sounds of an explosion. The music and the dancing became mournful as a succession of funereal dances conveyed
the murderous Reign of Terror. One of the mourners, representing
Hale, wore a mask to hide his face of evil.

A subsequent scene depicted the Osage's contributions to U.S. military efforts: Clarence Leonard Tinker, a member of the tribe, was the first Native American to reach the rank of major general and died when his plane was lost during World War II. To my surprise, a familiar figure appeared on-screen. It was Margie Burkhart, who had a brief, non-dancing role in the ballet, as the mother of one of the departing soldiers. She moved gracefully across the stage, wearing a shawl around her shoulders, echoing the way Mollie used to wear her Indian blanket.

At the conclusion of the show, many people in the audience lingered. I didn't see Margie in attendance, but she later told me that when she first saw the ballet's depiction of the Reign of Terror, "it hit me in the stomach." She added, "I didn't think it would affect me like that, but it did. There was so much emotion." Now, in the audience, I encountered the museum director Kathryn Red Corn. She asked me how my research was going. When I mentioned the likely involvement of H. G. Burt—someone who had never been publicly linked to the killings—she showed little surprise and told me to come see her at the museum the following morning.

When I arrived, I found her sitting at her desk in her office, surrounded by artifacts. "Look at this," she said, handing me a copy of a brittle old letter. It was written in neat script and was dated November 27, 1931. "Look at the signature on the bottom," Red Corn said. The name was "W. K. Hale."

She explained that Hale had sent the letter from prison to a member of the tribe and that not long ago a descendant had donated it to the museum. As I read through the letter, I was struck by the buoyant tone. Hale wrote, "I am in perfect health. I weigh 185 lbs. I haven't got a grey hair." When he got out of jail, he said, he hoped to return to the reservation: "I had rather live at Gray Horse than any place on earth." And he insisted, "I will always be the Osages true Friend."

Red Corn shook her head. "Can you believe it?" she said.

I assumed that she had invited me to the museum in order to

show me the letter, but I soon discovered that she had another reason. "I thought this might be a good time to tell you that story I mentioned before, about my grandfather," she said. She explained that after her grandfather divorced her grandmother, he wed a white woman, and in 1931 he began to suspect that he was being poisoned—by his second wife. When relatives visited her grandfather's home, Red Corn recalled, he was scared. He would tell them, "Don't eat or drink anything in this house." Not long after, Red Corn's grandfather dropped dead; he was forty-six years old. "Up until then he'd been in good health," Red Corn said. "There was nothing wrong with him. His wife made off with a lot of the money." The family was convinced that he had been poisoned, but there was never an investigation: "Back then, everyone covered these things up. The undertakers. The doctors. The police."

Red Corn did not know more than these fragmentary details relayed to her by relatives, and she hoped that I could investigate her grandfather's death. After a long pause, she said, "There were a lot more murders during the Reign of Terror than people know about. A *lot* more."

=====

During my years researching the murders of the Osage, I had turned my small office in New York into a grim repository. The floor and shelves were stacked with thousands of pages of FBI documents, autopsy reports, wills and last testaments, crime scene photographs, trial transcripts, analyses of forged documents, fingerprints, studies on ballistics and explosives, bank records, eyewitness statements, confessions, intercepted jailhouse notes, grand jury testimony, logs from private investigators, and mug shots. Whenever I obtained a new document, such as a copy of the Hale letter that Red Corn had shown me, I would label it and place it amid the stacks (my pitiful version of a Hoover filing system). Despite the darkness of the material, each new discovery gave me some hope that I might be able to fill in gaps in the historical chronicles—

˙˙˙˙ *Crime scene photograph of Blackie Thompson, who was gunned down in 1934 after he escaped from prison*

those spaces where there seemed to exist no recorded witnesses or voices, only the silence of the grave.

The case of Red Corn's grandfather was one of those voids. Because there had been no investigation into the death, and because all the principal figures were deceased, I couldn't find any trail of evidence to follow. Virtually all traces of the grandfather's life and death—of passions and turmoil and possible brutal violence—had seemingly been washed away.

The conversation with Red Corn, though, prompted me to probe more deeply into perhaps the most puzzling of the Osage murder cases—that of Charles Whitehorn. The murder, which bore all the markings of a Hale-orchestrated hit, took place in May 1921—the same time period as the slaying of Anna Brown, in what was considered the beginning of the four-year Reign of Terror. Yet no evidence had ever surfaced implicating Hale or his henchmen in Whitehorn's murder.

Though the case had never been solved, it had originally been a prime focus of investigators, and when I returned to New York, I gathered evidentiary material related to the crime. In one of the tottering piles in my office, I found the logs from the private detectives hired by Whitehorn's estate after his death. Their reports read as though they'd been torn from a dime-store novel, with lines such as "This dope is coming to me from a reliable source."

As I read through the reports, I jotted down key details:

Whitehorn last seen alive in Pawhuska on May 14, 1921. Witness spotted him around 8:00 p.m. outside Constantine Theater.

Body discovered two weeks later—on a hill about a mile from downtown Pawhuska.

According to undertaker, "The position of the body indicated that he had fallen in that position and had not been carried there."

Weapon: a .32 revolver. Shot—twice—between the eyes. A professional hit?

The reports noted that the attorney Vaughan had been eager to help the private eyes. "Vaughan who is well acquainted with the Indians stated that his real interest in the case was to...have the guilty party prosecuted," a private detective wrote. Neither the private detectives nor Vaughan had any inkling that Vaughan would eventually become a target—that within two years he, too, would be murdered—and I found myself pleading with them to see what they could not see.

Comstock—the attorney and guardian who, despite Hoover's initial suspicions, had proven to be trustworthy—had also tried to assist the private detectives investigating the murders. "Mr. Comstock had received some information," a private detective wrote, noting that Comstock had reported that on May 14 an unidentified man had been seen lurking on the hill where Whitehorn's body was subsequently found.

Because the Whitehorn case was officially unresolved, I expected the trails of evidence to disappear into a morass. In fact, the reports were bracing in their clarity. Based on leads from informants and from circumstantial evidence, the private detectives began to develop a crystalline theory of the crime. After Whitehorn's death, his part-white, part-Cheyenne widow, Hattie, had married an unscrupulous white man named LeRoy Smitherman. The private eyes learned that the marriage had been orchestrated by Minnie Savage—a "shrewd, immoral, capable woman," as one investigator put it, who ran a boardinghouse in Pawhuska. The private eyes suspected that she and Smitherman, as well as other conspirators, had arranged Whitehorn's killing in order to steal his headright and fortune. Over time, many of the investigators came to believe that Hattie Whitehorn, who had quickly spent some of her husband's fortune after his death, was also complicit. An informant told a private eye that there was no doubt Hattie Whitehorn was a "prime mover in killing Charley Whitehorn."

An undercover private eye was placed in Savage's boardinghouse. "He could hear what was said over the telephone," another detective wrote in his report, adding that the undercover "man will make good I think but will need some coaching." Meanwhile, Minnie Savage's sister became a rich source of information for investigators. She divulged that she had seen what was likely the murder weapon: "Minnie was making up the bed and the gun was under the pillow and Minnie picked it up.... It was a rather large gun, dark color." Despite all this, the private detectives somehow failed to secure enough evidence to prosecute any of the suspects, or perhaps the private eyes were bought off.

When the first federal agents from the Bureau of Investigation began to probe the case, in 1923, they also concluded that

Savage, Smitherman, and Hattie Whitehorn were responsible for the murder. "From the evidence thus far gathered," an agent wrote, it appeared that "Hattie Whitehorn caused him to be murdered in order that she might get hold of his estate." Hattie denied any involvement in the crime but told one agent, "I am as smart as you are. I have been warned about you." She added, "You are just getting into my confidence, and if I tell you you will send me to the electric chair."

By that point, there had been several disturbing twists in the case. Hattie's new husband, Smitherman, had fled the country for Mexico, taking with him her car and a chunk of her money. Then a man named J. J. Faulkner—whom an agent called an "unprincipled, hypocritical crook"—insinuated himself into Hattie's life, evidently blackmailing her with information that she'd shared with him about her role in the murder. (One of Hattie's sisters was heard yelling at Faulkner that he was an SOB and should stop extorting Hattie; Faulkner snapped back that he knew all about Hattie and the murder, and they'd better be careful about how they spoke to him.) In a report, Agent Burger and a colleague stated, "We are strongly of the belief that Faulkner has succeeded in obtaining some sort of confession from Hattie, and is using it to make her do as he sees fit, by threatening her with prosecution and exposing her, and that his object is to gain control of her... property at her death, and get money from her while she lives."

Before long, Hattie became incurably sick. Agents noted that she seemed "liable to die at any time." Remarkably, none of the agents expressed suspicions over the nature of her illness, even though so many victims during the Reign of Terror had been poisoned. Faulkner had a wife, and she told agents that he was "refusing to allow Hattie to be sent to a hospital... in order to keep her under his influence." According to Hattie's sisters, Faulkner had begun to steal money from her while she was "under the influence of a narcotic."

The sisters eventually managed to admit Hattie to a hospital.

Agents, believing that she was about to die, tried to persuade her to give a confession. In a report, agents wrote that she had admitted to Comstock that "she does know the facts and has never told what she knows" and that "they"—presumably Minnie Savage and other conspirators—had sent Hattie away at the time Whitehorn was murdered. But Hattie never disclosed anything further. Not surprisingly, she recovered from her mysterious illness after being dislodged from Faulkner's grip.

By the time Tom White showed up to begin his investigation, in 1925, the bureau had all but dropped the Whitehorn case. Agent Burger wrote dismissively that it was an "isolated murder," unconnected to the systematic killings. The case did not fit into the bureau's dramatic theory of the murders: that a lone mastermind was responsible for all the killings, and that when Hale and his henchmen were captured, the case of the Osage murders was solved. Yet, in hindsight, the fact that Hale appeared to have played no role in the Whitehorn plot was the very reason the killing was so important. Like the suspicious death of Red Corn's grandfather, the plot against Whitehorn—and the failed plot against his widow— exposed the secret history of the Reign of Terror: the evil of Hale was not an anomaly.

You must go out there and see what is happening," Kathryn Red Corn told me when I visited the Osage Nation again, in June 2015. And so following her directions, I drove through Pawhuska and headed west across the prairie, through the tall grasses, until I saw what she'd vividly described to me: scores of metallic towers invading the sky. Each one stood 420 feet tall, the equivalent of a thirty-story skyscraper, and had three whirring blades. A single blade was as long as the wings of an airliner. The towers were part of a windmill farm, which spanned more than eight thousand acres and was expected to eventually supply electricity to some forty-five thousand homes in Oklahoma.

More than a hundred years after oil was discovered in Osage territory, a new revolutionary source of energy was transforming the region. But this time the Osage viewed it as a threat to their underground reservation. "Did you see them?" Red Corn said of the turbines, when I returned. "This company came in here and put them up without our permission." The federal government, representing the Osage Nation, had filed a lawsuit against Enel, the Italian energy conglomerate that owned the wind farm. Citing the terms of the 1906 Allotment Act, the suit alleged that because the company had excavated limestone and other minerals while building the foundations for the turbines, it needed the Osage's approval to continue operations. Otherwise, Enel was violating the Osage's sovereignty over their underground reservation. The company insisted that it wasn't in the mining business, and thus did not need a lease from the Osage. "We don't disturb the mineral estate," a representative of the project told the press.

On July 10, 2015, at dawn, a chief and two dozen members of the Osage Nation gathered beneath the windmills for a prayer to Wah'Kon-Tah. As the first sunlight burned through the thin, blue mist and radiated off the blades, a prayer leader said that the Osage were a "humble people, asking for your help."

Not long after, a court sided with Enel, saying that though the government's interpretation of the Allotment Act would no doubt benefit the Osage, the "defendants have not marketed or sold minerals or otherwise engaged in mineral development. As a result,

The new windmill farm built above the Osage's underground reservation

they are not required to obtain a lease." Plans were already under
way for a second wind farm in the county.

New government environmental regulations for oil drilling
were having an even more profound effect on the Osage's underground reservation. The regulations, issued in 2014, were costly to
satisfy, and as a consequence oilmen had virtually stopped drilling
new wells, given that they produced only marginal returns. An oil
producer told a reporter, "For the first time in a hundred years,
there's no drilling in Osage County."

═══

I continued researching the murders, but there were fewer
archives to examine, fewer documents to find. Then one day at
the public library in Pawhuska I noticed, tucked amid volumes of
Osage history, a spiral-bound manuscript titled "The Murder of
Mary DeNoya-Bellieu-Lewis." It appeared to have been assembled
by hand, its pages printed on a computer. According to an intro-
ductory note, dated January 1998, the manuscript was compiled by
Anna Marie Jefferson, the great-great-grandniece of Mary Lewis.
"My great-grandmother . . . first told me the story about Mary," Jefferson wrote. "I first heard about this around 1975." Jefferson began
to gather, from relatives and newspaper clippings and other records,
bits of information about the murder—an endeavor that spanned
two decades. She must have left a copy of the manuscript with the
library, determined that the story not fall into the chasm of history.

I sat down and began to read. Mary Lewis, who was born in
1861, was an allotted member of the tribe. "With this money she
was able to enjoy a prosperous life," Jefferson wrote. Lewis had two
marriages that ended in divorce, and in 1918, in her mid-fifties, she
was raising a ten-year-old adopted child. That summer, Lewis took
her daughter on a trip to Liberty, Texas, a small city about forty
miles from Houston, on the banks of the Trinity River. Lewis was
accompanied by two white men: Thomas Middleton, who was a
friend, and a companion of his. With Lewis's money, they bought

a houseboat and stayed on the river. Then, on August 18, Lewis vanished. After authorities failed to investigate—"They never would have done anything," one of Lewis's relatives said—her family hired a private detective. He discovered that after Lewis's disappearance Middleton had pretended to be her adopted son in order to cash several of her checks. In January 1919, after the police detained Middleton and his companion, the private detective interrogated them. He told Middleton that he would "one hundred times rather find the old lady alive than dead," adding, "If you can give any information to locate her, that will help you."

Middleton insisted that he didn't know where she had gone. "I am not a bit afraid," he said.

He and his friend didn't divulge anything. But two witnesses revealed that on the day Lewis disappeared, they had seen, a few miles from her houseboat, a car heading toward a snake-infested swamp. On January 18, 1919, investigators, with their pant legs rolled up, began to comb the thicket of vegetation. A reporter said that one of the lawmen had "scarcely stepped in the water of the bayou when his feet struggled for freedom. When he reached to the bottom to disengage them he brought up a thick growth of woman's hair." Leg bones were dredged up next. Then came a human trunk and a skull, which looked as if it had been beaten with a heavy metal object. GREWSOME FIND ENDS QUEST FOR MARY LEWIS, a headline in a local newspaper said.

Middleton's companion confessed to beating Lewis over the head with a hammer. The plot was conceived by Middleton: after Lewis was killed, the plan was to use a female associate to impersonate her so that the friends could collect the headright payments. (This strategy was not unique—bogus heirs were a common problem. After Bill Smith died in the house explosion, the government initially feared that a relative claiming to be his heir was an impostor.) In 1919, Middleton was convicted of murder and condemned to die. "There was a point in Mary's family that they were relieved the ordeal was over," Jefferson wrote. "However, the feeling of satisfaction would be followed by disbelief and anger." Middleton's sentence was commuted to life. Then, after he had served only six and a half years, he was pardoned by the governor of Texas; Middletown had a girlfriend, and Lewis's family believed that she had bribed authorities. "The murderer had gotten only a slap on the hand," Jefferson wrote.

After I finished reading the manuscript documenting Lewis's murder, I kept returning to one detail: she had been killed for her headright in 1918. According to most historical accounts, the Osage Reign of Terror spanned from the spring of 1921, when Hale had Anna Brown murdered, to January 1926, when Hale was arrested. So Lewis's murder meant that the killings over headrights had begun at least three years earlier than was widely assumed, and if Red Corn's grandfather was poisoned in 1931, then the killings also continued long after Hale's arrest. These cases underscored that the murders of the Osage for their headrights were not the result of a single conspiracy orchestrated by Hale. He might have led the bloodiest and longest killing spree. But there were countless other killings—killings that were not included in official estimates and that, unlike the cases of Lewis or Mollie Burkhart's family members, were never investigated or even classified as homicides.

I returned to the archives in Fort Worth and resumed searching through the endless musty boxes and files. The archivist wheeled the newest batch of boxes on a cart into the small reading room, before rolling out the previous load. I had lost the illusion that I would find some Rosetta stone that would unlock the secrets of the past. Most of the records were dry and clinical—expenses, census reports, oil leases.

In one of the boxes was a tattered, fabric-covered logbook from the Office of Indian Affairs cataloging the names of guardians during the Reign of Terror. Written out by hand, the logbook included the name of each guardian and, underneath, a list of his Osage wards. If a ward passed away while under guardianship, a single word was usually scrawled by his or her name: "Dead."

I searched for the name of H. G. Burt, the suspect in W. W. Vaughan's killing. The log showed that he was the guardian of George Bigheart's daughter as well as of four other Osage. Beside the name of one of these wards was the word "dead." I then looked up Scott Mathis, the owner of the Big Hill Trading Company. According to the log, he had been the guardian of nine Osage, including Anna Brown and her mother, Lizzie. As I went down the list, I noticed that a third Osage Indian had died under Mathis's guardianship, and so had a fourth, and a fifth, and a sixth. Altogether, of his nine listed wards, seven had died. And at least two of these deaths were known to be murders.

I began to scour the log for other Osage guardians around this time. One had eleven Osage wards, eight of whom had died. Another guardian had thirteen wards, more than half of whom had been listed as deceased. And one guardian had five wards, all of whom died. And so it went, on and on. The numbers were staggering and clearly defied a natural death rate. Because most of these cases had never been investigated, it was impossible to determine precisely how many of the deaths were suspicious, let alone who might be responsible for any foul play.

Nevertheless, there were strong hints of widespread murder. In the FBI records, I found a mention of Anna Sanford, one of the names I had seen in the logbook with the word "dead" written next to it. Though her case was never classified as a homicide, agents had clearly suspected poisoning.

Another Osage ward, Hlu-ah-to-me, had officially died of tuberculosis. But amid the files was a telegram from an informant to the U.S. attorney alleging that Hlu-ah-to-me's guardian had deliberately denied her treatment and refused to send her to a hospital in the Southwest for care. Her guardian "knew that was the lone place she could live, and if she stayed in Gray Horse she must die," the informant noted, adding that after her death the guardian made himself the administrator of her valuable estate.

In yet another case, the 1926 death of an Osage named Eves Tall Chief, the cause was attributed to alcohol. But witnesses testified at the time that he never drank and had been poisoned. "Members of the family of the dead man were frightened," an article from 1926 said.

Even when an Osage ward was mentioned as being alive in the log, it did not mean that he or she had not been targeted. The Osage ward Mary Elkins was considered the wealthiest member of the tribe because she had inherited more than seven headrights. On May 3, 1923, when Elkins was twenty-one, she married a second-rate white boxer. According to a report from an official at the Office of Indian Affairs, her new husband proceeded to lock her in their house, whip her, and give her "drugs, opiates, and liquor in an attempt to hasten her death so that he could claim her huge inheritance." In her case, the government official interceded, and she survived. An investigation uncovered evidence that the boxer had not acted alone but had been part of a conspiracy orchestrated by a band of local citizens. Though the government official pushed for their prosecution, no one was ever charged, and the identities of the citizens were never revealed.

Then there was the case of Sybil Bolton, an Osage from Pawhuska who was under the guardianship of her white stepfather. On November 7, 1925, Bolton—whom a local reporter described as "one of the most beautiful girls ever reared in the city"—was found with a fatal bullet in her chest. Her death, at twenty-one, was reported by her stepfather to be a suicide, and the case was quickly closed without even an autopsy. In 1992, Bolton's grandson Dennis McAuliffe Jr., an editor at the *Washington Post,* had investigated her death after discovering numerous contradictions and lies in the official account. As he detailed in a memoir, *The Deaths of Sybil Bolton,* published in 1994, much of her headright money was stolen, and the evidence suggested that she had been assassinated outdoors, on her lawn, with her sixteen-month-old baby—McAuliffe's mother—beside her. According to the log, her guardian had four other Osage wards. They had also died.

Though the bureau estimated that there were twenty-four Osage murders, the real number was undoubtedly higher. The bureau closed its investigation after catching Hale and his henchmen. But at least some at the bureau knew that there were many more homicides that had been systematically covered up, evading their efforts of detection. An agent described, in a report, just one of the ways the killers did this: "In connection with the mysterious deaths of a large number of Indians, the perpetrators of the crime would get an Indian intoxicated, have a doctor examine him and pronounce him intoxicated, following which a morphine hypodermic would be injected into the Indian, and after the doctor's departure the [killers] would inject an enormous amount of morphine under the armpit of the drunken Indian, which would result in his death. The doctor's certificate would subsequently read 'death from alcoholic poison.'" Other observers in Osage County noted that suspicious deaths were routinely, and falsely, attributed to "consumption," "wasting illness," or "causes unknown." Scholars and investigators who have since looked into the murders believe that the Osage death toll was in the scores, if not the hundreds. To get a better sense of the decimation, McAuliffe looked at the *Authentic Osage Indian Roll Book,* which cites the deaths of many of the original allotted members of the tribe. He writes, "Over the sixteen-year period from 1907 to 1923, 605 Osages died, averaging about 38 per year, an annual death rate of about 19 per 1,000. The national death rate now is about 8.5 per 1,000; in the 1920s, when counting methods were not so precise and the statistics were segregated into white and black racial categories, it averaged almost 12 per 1,000 for whites. By all rights, their higher standard of living should have brought the Osages a *lower* death rate than America's whites. Yet Osages were dying at more than one-and-a-half times the national rate—and those numbers do not include Osages born after 1907 and not listed on the roll."

Louis F. Burns, the eminent historian of the Osage, observed, "I don't know of a single Osage family which didn't lose at least one family member because of the head rights." And at least one bureau agent who had left the case prior to White's arrival had realized that there was a culture of killing. According to a transcript of an interview with an informant, the agent said, "There are so many of these murder cases. There are hundreds and hundreds."

Even cases known to the bureau had hidden dimensions. During one of my last visits to the reservation, in June 2015, I went to the Osage Nation Court, where, in many criminal cases, the Osage now mete out their own justice. An Osage lawyer had told me that the Reign of Terror was "not the end of our history," adding, "Our families were victims of this conspiracy, but we're not victims."

In one of the courtrooms, I met Marvin Stepson. An Osage man in his seventies with expressive gray eyebrows and a deliberate manner, he served as the chief trial court judge. He was the grandson of William Stepson, the steer-roping champion who had died, of suspected poisoning, in 1922. Authorities never prosecuted anyone for Stepson's murder, but they came to believe that Kelsie Morrison—the man who had killed Anna Brown—was responsible. By 1922, Morrison had divorced his Osage wife, and after Stepson's death he married Stepson's widow, Tillie, making himself the guardian of her two children. One of Morrison's associates told the bureau that Morrison had admitted to him that he had killed Stepson so that he could marry Tillie and get control of her invaluable estate.

Stepson's death was usually included in the official tally of murders during the Reign of Terror. But as I sat with Marvin on one of the wooden courtroom benches, he revealed that the targeting of his family did not end with his grandfather. After marrying Morrison, Tillie grew suspicious of him, especially after Morrison was overheard talking about the effects of the poison strychnine. Tillie confided to her lawyer that she wanted to prevent Morrison from inheriting her estate and to rescind his guardianship of her children. But in July 1923, before she had enacted these changes, she, too, died of suspected poisoning. Morrison stole much of her fortune. According to letters that Morrison wrote, he planned to sell a portion of the estate he had swindled to none other than H. G. Burt, the banker who appeared to be involved in the killing of Vaughan. Tillie's death was never investigated, though Morrison admitted to an associate that he had killed her and asked him why

he didn't get an Indian squaw and do the same. Marvin Stepson, who had spent years researching what had happened to his grandparents, told me, "Kelsie murdered them both, and left my father an orphan."

And that was not the end of the plot. After William Stepson and Tillie died, Marvin's father, who was three years old at the time, became the next target, along with his nine-year-old half sister. In 1926, Morrison, while serving time in prison for killing Anna Brown, sent a note to Hale, which was intercepted by guards. The note, filled with grammatical errors, said, "Bill, you know Tillies kids are going to have 2 or 3 hundred thousand dollars in a few years, and I have those kids adopted. How can I get possession or control of that money when I get out. You know I belive I can take these kids out of the State and they cant do a dam thing… they Could not get me for Kidnapping." It was feared that Morrison planned to kill both children. An Osage scholar once observed, "Walking through an Osage cemetery and seeing the gravestones that show the inordinate numbers of young people who died in the period is chilling."

Marvin Stepson had the judicious air of someone who had

spent his whole career serving the law. But he told me that when he first learned what Morrison had done to his family, he feared what he might be capable of doing. "If Morrison walked in this room right now, *I'd...*" he said, his voice trailing off.

———

In cases where perpetrators of crimes against humanity elude justice in their time, history can often provide at least some final accounting, forensically documenting the murders and exposing the transgressors. Yet so many of the murders of the Osage were so well concealed that such an outcome is no longer possible. In most cases, the families of the victims have no sense of resolution. Many descendants carry out their own private investigations, which have no end. They live with doubts, suspecting dead relatives or old family friends or guardians—some of whom might be guilty and some of whom might be innocent.

When McAuliffe tried to find the killer of his grandmother, he initially suspected his grandfather Harry, who was white. By then, Harry had died, but his second wife was still alive and told McAuliffe, "You should be ashamed of yourself, Denny, digging up things about the Boltons. I can't understand why you'd want to do such a thing." And she kept repeating, "Harry didn't do it. He had nothing to do with it."

Later, McAuliffe realized that she was probably right. He came to believe, instead, that Sybil's stepfather was responsible. But there is no way to know with certainty. "I did not prove who killed my grandmother," McAuliffe wrote. "My failure was not just because of me, though. It was because they ripped out too many pages of our history.... There were just too many lies, too many documents destroyed, too little done at the time to document how my grandmother died." He added, "A murdered Indian's survivors don't have the right to the satisfaction of justice for past crimes, or of even knowing who killed their children, their mothers or fathers, brothers or sisters, their grandparents. They can only guess—like I was forced to."

═══

Before I left Osage County to return home, I stopped to see Mary Jo Webb, a retired teacher who had spent decades investigating the suspicious death of her grandfather during the Reign of Terror. Webb, who was in her eighties, lived in a single-story wooden house in Fairfax, not far from where the Smiths' home had exploded. A frail woman with a quavering voice, she invited me in and we sat in her living room. I had called earlier to arrange the visit, and in expectation of my arrival she had brought out several boxes of documents—including guardian expense reports, probate records, and court testimony—that she'd gathered about the case of her grandfather Paul Peace. "He was one of those victims who didn't show up in the FBI files and whose killers didn't go to prison," Webb said.

Mary Jo Webb

The open prairie north of Pawhuska

In December 1926, Peace suspected that his wife, who was white, was poisoning him. As the documents confirmed, he went to see the attorney Comstock, whom Webb described as one of the few decent white attorneys at the time. Peace wanted to get a divorce and change his will to disinherit his wife. A witness later testified that Peace had claimed his wife was feeding him "some kind of poison, that she was killing him."

When I asked Webb how her grandfather might have been poisoned, she said, "There were these doctors. They were brothers. My mother said that everyone knew that's where people would get the dope to poison the Osage."

"What was their name?" I asked.

"The Shouns."

I remembered the Shouns. They were the doctors who had claimed that the bullet that had killed Anna Brown had disappeared. The doctors who had initially concealed that Bill Smith had given a last statement incriminating Hale and who had arranged it so that one of them became the administrator of Rita Smith's invaluable estate. The doctors whom investigators suspected of giving Mollie Burkhart poison instead of insulin. Many of the cases seemed bound by a web of silent conspirators. Mathis, the Big Hill Trading Company owner and the guardian of Anna Brown and her mother, was a member of the inquest into Brown's murder that failed to turn up the bullet. He also managed, on behalf of Mollie's family, the team of private eyes that conspicuously never cracked any of the cases. A witness had told the bureau that after Henry Roan's murder, Hale was eager to get the corpse away from one undertaker and delivered to the funeral home at the Big Hill Trading Company. The murder plots depended upon doctors who falsified death certificates and upon undertakers who quickly and quietly buried bodies. The guardian whom McAuliffe suspected of killing his grandmother was a prominent attorney working for the tribe who never interfered with the criminal networks operating under his nose. Nor did bankers, including the apparent murderer Burt, who were profiting from the criminal "Indian business." Nor did the venal mayor of Fairfax—an ally of Hale's who also served as a guardian. Nor did countless lawmen and prosecutors and judges who had a hand in the blood money. In 1926, the Osage leader Bacon Rind remarked, "There are men amongst the whites, honest men, but they are mighty scarce." Garrick Bailey, a leading anthropologist on Osage culture, said to me, "If Hale had told what he knew, a high percentage of the county's leading citizens would have been in prison." Indeed, virtually every element of society was complicit in the murderous system. Which is why just about any member of this society might have been responsible for the murder of McBride, in Washington: he threatened to bring down not only Hale but a vast criminal operation that was reaping millions and millions of dollars.

On February 23, 1927, weeks after Paul Peace vowed to disinherit and divorce the wife he suspected of poisoning him, he was injured in a hit-and-run and left to bleed out on the road. Webb told me that the familiar forces had conspired to paper over his death. "Maybe you could look into it," she said. I nodded, though I knew that in my own way I was as lost in the mist as Tom White or Mollie Burkhart had been.

Webb walked me outside, onto the front porch. It was dusk, and the fringes of the sky had darkened. The town and the street were empty, and beyond them the prairie, too. "This land is saturated with blood," Webb said. For a moment, she fell silent, and we could hear the leaves of the blackjacks rattling restlessly in the wind. Then she repeated what God told Cain after he killed Abel: "The blood cries out from the ground."

ACKNOWLEDGMENTS

I am grateful to all the people who contributed to this project, and none more so than the Osage who entrusted me with their stories and encouraged me to dig deeper. Over the years, many Osage shared with me not only their insights but also their friendship. I want to especially thank Margie Burkhart, Kathryn Red Corn, Charles Red Corn, Raymond Red Corn, Joe Conner, Dolores Goodeagle, Dennis McAuliffe, Elise Paschen, Marvin Stepson, Mary Jo Webb, and the late Jozi Tall Chief.

My research odyssey led me to many other generous individuals. The late Martha Vaughan and her cousin Melville shed light on their grandfather W. W. Vaughan. Tom White's relatives—including James M. White, Jean White, John Sheehan White, and Tom White III—were invaluable sources. So was Tom White III's spouse, Styrous, who dug up and developed archival photographs. Alexandra Sands relayed details about her grandfather James Alexander Street, who was one of the undercover operatives. Frank Parker Sr. sent me photographs and papers concerning his father, Eugene Parker—another undercover agent. Homer Fincannon and his brother, Bill, shared a wealth of information about their great-grandfather A. W. Comstock.

A number of scholars and experts patiently answered my never-ending questions. Garrick Bailey, an anthropologist who specializes in Osage culture, went beyond any reasonable bounds of duty and read the entire manuscript before publication. He is not accountable for anything I wrote, but the book is infinitely better because of him.

The FBI historian John F. Fox was a tremendous and invaluable resource. So was Dee Cordry, a former special agent with the Oklahoma State Bureau of Investigation who has spent years researching and writing about western lawmen. Garrett Hartness, Roger Hall Lloyd, and Arthur Shoemaker all shared some of their immense knowledge about the history of Osage County. David A. Ward, a professor emeritus of sociology at the University of Minnesota, provided me with a transcript of his interview with one of the prisoners who took Tom White hostage.

Louise Red Corn, the publisher of the *Bigheart Times* and an indefatigable reporter, found photographs for me and along with her husband, Raymond, was a kind host whenever I visited Osage County. Joe Conner and his wife, Carol, opened their house to me and turned it into a central place to conduct interviews. Guy Nixon spoke to me about his Osage ancestors. And Archie L. Mason, a member of the Osage Nation Congress, sent me a copy of the astonishing panoramic photograph of William Hale and the Osage.

There is no greater gift to an author than the Dorothy and Lewis B. Cullman Center for Scholars and Writers at the New York Public Library. The Cullman fellowship allowed me essential time for research and the opportunity to plumb the library's miraculous archives. Everyone at the center—Jean Strouse, Marie d'Origny, and Paul Delaverdac, as well as the fellows—made for a year that was productive and fun.

The fellowship also guided me to an unexpected source. One day, Kevin Winkler, then the director of library sites and services, informed me that he knew about the Osage murders. It turned out that he was a grandson of Horace Burkhart, who was a brother of Ernest and Bryan Burkhart. Horace was considered the good brother, because he was not involved in any of the crimes. Winkler helped me to get in touch with his mother, Jean Crouch, and two of his aunts, Martha Key and Rubyane Surritte. They knew Ernest, and Key, who has sadly since died, had known Mollie as well. The three women spoke candidly about the family's history and shared with me a video recording of Ernest that was taken shortly before he died, in which he talked about Mollie and his past.

Several research institutions were critical to this project, and I am indebted to them and their staffs. Particularly, I want to thank David S. Ferriero, the archivist of the United States, as well as Greg Bognich, Jake Ersland, Christina Jones, Amy Reytar, Rodney Ross, Barbara Rust, and others at the National Archives; everyone at the Osage Nation Museum, including Lou Brock, Paula Farid, and the former director Kathryn Red Corn; Debbie Neece at the Bartlesville Area History Museum; Mallory Covington, Jennifer Day, Rachel Mosman, and Debra Osborne Spindle at the Oklahoma Historical Society; Sara Keckeisen at the Kansas Historical Society; Rebecca Kohl at the Montana Historical Society; Jennifer Chavez at New Mexico State University Library; Joyce Lyons, Shirley Roberts, and Mary K. Warren at the Osage County Historical Society Museum; Carol Taylor at the Hunt County Historical Commission; Carol Guilliams at the Oklahoma State Archives; Amanda Crowley at the Texas Ranger Hall of Fame and Museum; Kera Newby at the National Cowboy and Western Heritage Museum; and Kristina Southwell and Jacquelyn D. Reese at the University of Oklahoma's Western History Collections.

Several talented researchers assisted me in locating documents in distant corners of the country: Rachel Craig, Ralph Elder, Jessica Loudis, and Amanda Waldroupe. I can never thank enough Susan Lee, an extraordinarily gifted journalist who was indispensable to this project, helping me to ferret out records and devoting hours to fact-checking.

Aaron Tomlinson took exquisite photographs of Osage County and was a wonderful traveling companion. Warren Cohen, Elon Green, and David Greenberg are great journalists and even greater friends who provided wisdom and support throughout the process. And my friend Stephen Metcalf, who is one of the smartest writers, never tired of helping me to think through elements of the book.

At *The New Yorker*, I'm blessed to be able to draw on the advice of so many people brighter than I am, including Henry Finder, Dorothy Wickenden, Leo Carey, Virginia Cannon, Ann Goldstein, and Mary

Norris. Eric Lach was a relentless fact-checker and provided keen editorial suggestions. I asked far too much of Burkhard Bilger, Tad Friend, Raffi Khatchadourian, Larissa MacFarquhar, Nick Paumgarten, and Elizabeth Pearson-Griffiths. They pored over portions of the manuscript, and in some cases all of it, and helped me to see it more clearly. Daniel Zalewski has taught me more about writing than anyone, and he spread his magical dust over the manuscript. And David Remnick has been a champion since the day I arrived at *The New Yorker*, enabling me to pursue my passions and develop as a writer.

To call Kathy Robbins and David Halpern, at the Robbins Office, and Matthew Snyder, at CAA, the best agents would not do them justice. They are so much more than that: they are allies, confidants, and friends.

As an author, I have found the perfect home at Doubleday. This book would not have been possible without my brilliant editor and publisher, Bill Thomas. He is the one who first encouraged me to pursue this subject, who guided me through the highs and lows, and who has edited and published this book with grace and wisdom. Nor would this book have been possible without the unfailing support of Sonny Mehta, the chairman of the Knopf Doubleday Publishing Group. Nor would it have been possible without the remarkable team at Doubleday, including Todd Doughty, Suzanne Herz, John Fontana, Maria Carella, Lorraine Hyland, Maria Massey, Rose Courteau, and Margo Shickmanter.

My family has been the greatest blessing of all. John and Nina Darnton, my in-laws, read the manuscript not once, but twice, and gave me the courage to keep going. My sister, Alison, and my brother, Edward, have been an unbreakable ballast. So have my mother, Phyllis, who offered the kinds of perfect touches to the manuscript that only she can, and my father, Victor, who has always encouraged me; my only wish is that he were well enough to read this book now that it is done.

Finally, there are those for whom my gratitude goes deeper than words can express: my children, Zachary and Ella, who have filled my house with the madness of pets and the beauty of music and the joyfulness of life, and my wife, Kyra, who has been my best reader, my greatest friend, and my eternal love.

This book is based extensively on primary and unpublished materials. They include thousands of pages of FBI files, secret grand jury testimony, court transcripts, informants' statements, logs from private eyes, pardon and parole records, private correspondence, an unpublished manuscript co-authored by one of the detectives, diary entries, Osage Tribal Council records, oral histories, field reports from the Bureau of Indian Affairs, congressional records, Justice Department memos and telegrams, crime scene photographs, wills and last testaments, guardian reports, and the murderers' confessions. These materials were drawn from archives around the country. Some records were obtained through the Freedom of Information Act, while FBI documents that had been redacted by the government were provided to me, uncensored, by a former law-enforcement officer. Moreover, several private papers came directly from descendants, among them the relatives of the victims of the Reign of Terror; further information was often gleaned from my interviews with these family members.

I also benefited from a number of contemporaneous newspaper dispatches and other published accounts. In reconstructing the history of the Osage, I would have been lost without the seminal works of two Osage writers: the historian Louis F. Burns and the prose poet John Joseph Mathews. In addition, I was greatly aided by the research of Terry Wilson, a former professor of Native American studies at the University of California, Berkeley, and Garrick Bailey, a leading anthropologist of the Osage.

The writers Dennis McAuliffe, Lawrence Hogan, Dee Cordry, and the late Fred Grove had conducted their own research into the Osage murders, and their work was enormously helpful. So was Verdon R. Adams's short biography *Tom White: The Life of a Lawman*. Finally, in detailing the history of J. Edgar Hoover and the formation of the FBI, I drew on several excellent books, particularly Curt Gentry's *J. Edgar Hoover*, Sanford Ungar's *FBI*, Richard Gid Powers's *Secrecy and Power*, and Bryan Burrough's *Public Enemies*.

In the bibliography, I have delineated these and other important sources. If I was especially indebted to one, I tried to cite it in the notes as well. Anything that appears in the text between quotation marks comes from a court transcript, diary, letter, or some other account. These sources are cited in the notes, except in cases where it is clear that a person is speaking directly to me.

ARCHIVAL AND UNPUBLISHED SOURCES

Comstock Family Papers, private collection of Homer Fincannon
FBI   Federal Bureau of Investigation declassified files on the Osage
      Indian Murders
FBI/FOIA Federal Bureau of Investigation records obtained under the
      Freedom of Information Act
HSP   Historical Society of Pennsylvania
KHS   Kansas Historical Society
LOC   Library of Congress
NARA-CP National Archives and Records Administration, College Park,
      Md.
      Record Group 48, Records of the Office of the Secretary of the
      Interior
      Record Group 60, Records of the Department of Justice
      Record Group 65, Records of the Federal Bureau of Investigation
      Record Group 129, Records of the Bureau of Prisons
      Record Group 204, Records of the Office of the Pardon Attorney
NARA-DC National Archives and Records Administration, Washington,
      D.C.
      Records of the Center for Legislative Archives
NARA-FW National Archives and Records Administration, Fort Worth, Tex.
      Record Group 21, Records of District Court of the United States,
      U.S. District Court for the Western District
      Record Group 75, Records of the Bureau of Indian Affairs, Osage
      Indian Agency

Record Group 118, Records of U.S. Attorneys, Western Judicial District of Oklahoma

NMSUL   New Mexico State University Library
          Fred Grove Papers, Rio Grande Historical Collections
OHS   Oklahoma Historical Society
ONM   Osage Nation Museum
OSARM   Oklahoma State Archives and Records Management
PPL   Pawhuska Public Library
SDSUL   San Diego State University Library
TSLAC   Texas State Library and Archives Commission
UOWHC   University of Oklahoma Western History Collections
Vaughan Family Papers, private collection of Martha and Melville Vaughan

NOTES

1: THE VANISHING

5   In April, millions: For more information on the Osage's notion of the flower-killing moon, see Mathews's *Talking to the Moon*.

5   "gods had left": Ibid., 61.

5   On May 24: My description of Anna Brown's disappearance and the last day she visited Mollie Burkhart's house is drawn primarily from the testimony of witnesses who were present. Many of them spoke several times to different detectives, including FBI agents and private eyes. These witnesses also often testified at a number of court proceedings. For more information, see records at NARA-CP and NARA-FW.

6   "peculiar wasting illness": Quoted in Franks, *Osage Oil Boom*, 117.

6   "Lo and behold": Sherman Rogers, "Red Men in Gas Buggies," *Outlook*, Aug. 22, 1923.

6   "plutocratic Osage": Estelle Aubrey Brown, "Our Plutocratic Osage Indians," *Travel*, Oct. 1922.

6   "red millionaires": William G. Shepherd, "Lo, the Rich Indian!," *Harper's Monthly*, Nov. 1920.

7   "*une très jolie*": Brown, "Our Plutocratic Osage Indians."

7   "circle of expensive": Elmer T. Peterson, "Miracle of Oil," *Independent* (N.Y.), April 26, 1924.

7   "outrivals the ability": Quoted in Harmon, *Rich Indians*, 140.

7   "That lament": Ibid., 179.

8   "even whites": Brown, "Our Plutocratic Osage Indians."

8   "He was not the kind": *Oklahoma City Times*, Oct. 26, 1959.

12   Ernest's brothers, Bryan: His birth name was Byron, but he went by Bryan.
        To avoid any confusion, I have simply used Bryan throughout the text.

12   "All the forces": Statement by H. S. Traylor, U.S. House Subcommittee on
        Indian Affairs, *Indians of the United States: Investigation of the Field Service*, 202.

12   "very loose morals": Report by Tom Weiss and John Burger, Jan. 10, 1924,
        FBI.

13   "She was drinking": Grand jury testimony of Martha Doughty, NARA-FW.

14   "Do you know": Grand jury testimony of Anna Sitterly, NARA-FW.

14   "I thought the rain": Ibid.

14   Fueling the unease: Information concerning Whitehorn's disappearance
        is drawn largely from local newspapers and from private detectives and
        FBI reports at the National Archives.

14   Genial and witty: It should be noted that one newspaper account says that
        Whitehorn's wife was part Cherokee. However, the FBI files refer to her
        as part Cheyenne.

14   "popular among": *Pawhuska Daily Capital*, May 30, 1921.

15   "Oh Papa": Quotations from the hunters come from their grand jury tes-
        timony, NARA-FW.

16   "The body was": Report by Weiss and Burger, Jan. 10, 1924, FBI.

16   "It was as black": Grand jury testimony of F. S. Turton, NARA-FW.

16   "That is sure": Grand jury testimony of Andy Smith, NARA-FW.

2: AN ACT OF GOD OR MAN?

17   A coroner's inquest: My descriptions of the inquest were drawn primar-
        ily from eyewitness testimony, including that of the Shoun brothers. For
        more information, see records at NARA-CP and NARA-FW.

17   "not faintly": Quoted in A. L. Sainer, *Law Is Justice: Notable Opinions of Mr.
        Justice Cardozo* (New York: Ad Press, 1938), 209.

18   "A medical man": Quoted in Wagner, *Science of Sherlock Holmes*, 8.

19   "She's been shot": Grand jury testimony of Andy Smith, NARA-FW.

19   "An officer was": Quoted in Cordry, *Alive If Possible—Dead If Necessary*, 238.

20   "terror to evil": Thoburn, *Standard History of Oklahoma*, 1833.

20   "I had the assurance": Grand jury testimony of Roy Sherrill, NARA-FW.

20   "religion, law enforcement": *Shawnee News*, May 11, 1911.

20   "The brains": Grand jury testimony of David Shoun, NARA-FW.

21   "keep up the old": Quoted in Wilson, "Osage Indian Women During a
        Century of Change," 188.

22   Mollie relied: My description of the funeral is drawn primarily from
        statements by witnesses, including the undertaker, and from my inter-
        views with descendants.

22   "devotion to his": A. F. Moss to M. E. Trapp, Nov. 18, 1926, OSARM.

23   "It was getting": Statement by A. T. Woodward, U.S. House Committee
        on Indian Affairs, *Modifying Osage Fund Restrictions*, 103.

23   The funeral: The Osage used to leave their dead aboveground, in cairns. When an Osage chief was buried underground, in the late nineteenth century, his wife said, "I said it will be alright if we paint face of my husband; if we wrap blanket around my husband. He wanted to be buried in white man's grave. I said it will be all right. I said we will paint face of my husband and he will not be lost in heaven of Indian."

24   "It filled my little": From introduction to Mathews, *Osages*.

3: KING OF THE OSAGE HILLS

25   "TWO SEPARATE MURDER": *Pawhuska Daily Capital*, May 28, 1921.

25   "set adrift": Louis F. Burns, *History of the Osage People*, 442.

26   "Some day": *Modesto News-Herald*, Nov. 18, 1928.

26   So Mollie turned: My portrait of William Hale is drawn from a number of sources, including court records, Osage oral histories, FBI files, contemporaneous newspaper accounts, Hale's correspondence, and my interviews with descendants.

26   "fight for life": Sargent Prentiss Freeling in opening statement, *U.S. v. John Ramsey and William K. Hale*, Oct. 1926, NARA-FW.

27   "He is the most": Article by Merwin Eberle, "'King of Osage' Has Had Long Colorful Career," n.p., OHS.

27   "like a leashed animal": *Guthrie Leader*, Jan. 5, 1926.

27   "high-class gentleman": Pawnee Bill to James A. Finch, n.d., NARA-CP.

27   "Some did hate": C. K. Kothmann to James A. Finch, n.d., NARA-CP.

29   "I couldn't begin": M. B. Prentiss to James A. Finch, Sept. 3, 1935, NARA-CP.

29   "I never had better": Hale to Wilson Kirk, Nov. 27, 1931, ONM.

29   "We were mighty": *Tulsa Tribune*, June 7, 1926.

29   "willing to do": J. George Wright to Charles Burke, June 24, 1926, NARA-CP.

30   "How did she go": Testimony of Mollie Burkhart before tribal attorney and other officials, NARA-FW.

30   "When you brought": Coroner's inquest testimony of Bryan Burkhart, in bureau report, Aug. 15, 1923, FBI.

31   "You understand": Grand jury testimony of Ernest Burkhart, NARA-FW.

31   "the greatest criminal": Boorstin, *Americans*, 81.

32   "perhaps any": James G. Findlay to William J. Burns, April 23, 1923, FBI.

32   "the meanest man": McConal, *Over the Wall*, 19.

32   "diseased mind": *Arizona Republican*, Oct. 5, 1923.

33   "This may have": Private detective logs included in report, July 12, 1923, FBI.

33   "absolutely no": Ibid.

34   "Honorable Sir": *Pawhuska Daily Capital*, July 29, 1921.

34   "ANNA BROWN": *Pawhuska Daily Capital*, July 23, 1921.

34   "There's a lot": Quoted in Crockett, *Serial Murderers,* 352.

34   "If you want": Roff, *Boom Town Lawyer in the Osage,* 106.

35   "would not lie": Ibid., 107.

35   "sausage meat": Grand jury testimony of F. S. Turton, NARA-FW.

35   "the hands of parties": *Pawhuska Daily Capital,* May 30, 1921.

36   *"Have pity"*: Frank F. Finney, "At Home with the Osages," Finney Papers, UOWHC.

4: UNDERGROUND RESERVATION

37   The money had: In describing the history of the Osage, I benefited from several excellent accounts. See Louis F. Burns, *History of the Osage People;* Mathews, *Wah'kon-Tah;* Wilson, *Underground Reservation;* Tixier, *Tixier's Travels on the Osage Prairies;* and Bailey, *Changes in Osage Social Organization.* I also drew on field reports and Tribal Council documents held in the Records of the Osage Indian Agency, NARA-FW.

37   "we must stand": Louis F. Burns, *History of the Osage People,* 140.

37   "finest men": Ibid.

37   "It is so long": Quoted in Ambrose, *Undaunted Courage,* 343.

38   "to make the enemy": Mathews, *Osages,* 271.

38   Lizzie also grew up: Existing records do not indicate her Osage name.

39   "industrious": Probate records of Mollie's mother, Lizzie, "Application for Certificate of Competency," Feb. 1, 1911, NARA-FW.

39   "The race is": Tixier, *Tixier's Travels on the Osage Prairies,* 191.

39   "the beast vomits": Ibid., 192.

39   "I am perfectly": Quoted in Brown, *Frontiersman,* 245.

40   "Why don't you": Wilder, *Little House on the Prairie,* 46–47.

40   "The question will": Quoted in Wilson, *Underground Reservation,* 18.

40   "broken, rocky": Isaac T. Gibson to Enoch Hoag, in *Report of the Commissioner of Indian Affairs to the Secretary of the Interior for the Year 1871,* 906.

40   "My people": Mathews, *Wah'kon-Tah,* 33–34.

41   "The air was filled": Quoted in Louis F. Burns, *History of the Osage People,* 448.

41   the most significant: The Office of Indian Affairs was renamed the Bureau of Indian Affairs in 1947.

42   "This little remnant": Gibson to Hoag, in *Report of the Commissioner of Indian Affairs to the Secretary of the Interior for the Year 1871,* 487.

42   "It was like": Finney and Thoburn, "Reminiscences of a Trader in the Osage Country," 149.

42   "every buffalo dead": Quoted in Merchant, *American Environmental History,* 20.

42   "We are not dogs": Mathews, *Wah'kon-Tah,* 30.

43   "Tell these gentlemen": Information on the Osage delegation, including any quotations, comes from Mathews's account in ibid., 35–38.

44   "Likewise his daughters": Frank F. Finney, "At Home with the Osages."

46   "There lingers memories": Ibid.

46   "The Indian must conform": Louis F. Burns, *History of the Osage People*, 91.

47   "for ambush": Mathews, *Wah'kon-Tah*, 79.

47   "big, black mouth": Mathews, *Sundown*, 23.

48   "It is impossible": Quoted in McAuliffe, *Deaths of Sybil Bolton*, 215–16.

49   "His ears are closed": Mathews, *Wah'kon-Tah*, 311.

49   "A RACE FOR LAND": *Daily Oklahoma State Capital*, Sept. 18, 1893.

49   "Men knocked": *Daily Oklahoma State Capital*, Sept. 16, 1893.

51   "Let him, like these whites": Quoted in Trachtenberg, *Incorporation of America*, 34.

51   "great storm": *Wah-sha-she News*, June 23, 1894.

52   "to keep his finger": Russell, "Chief James Bigheart of the Osages," 892.

52   "the most eloquent": Thoburn, *Standard History of Oklahoma*, 2048.

52   "That the oil": Quoted in *Leases for Oil and Gas Purposes, Osage National Council*, 154.

53   "I wrote": *Indians of the United States: Investigation of the Field Service*, 398.

53   Like others on the Osage tribal roll: Many white settlers managed to finagle their way onto the roll and eventually reaped a fortune in oil proceeds that belonged to the Osage. The anthropologist Garrick Bailey estimated that the amount of money taken from the Osage was at least $100 million.

53   "Bounce, you cats": Quoted in Franks, *Osage Oil Boom*, 75.

53   "ack like tomorrow": Mathews, *Life and Death of an Oilman*, 116.

53   "It was pioneer days": Gregory, *Oil in Oklahoma*, 13–14.

54   "Are they dangerous": Quoted in Miller, *House of Getty*, 1881.

5: THE DEVIL'S DISCIPLES

56   "the foulness": Probate records of Anna Brown, "Application for Authority to Offer Cash Reward," NARA-FW.

56   "We've got to stop": H. L. Macon, "Mass Murder of the Osages," *West*, Dec. 1965.

56   "failing to enforce": *Ada Weekly News*, Feb. 23, 1922.

57   "turned brutal crimes": Summerscale, *Suspicions of Mr. Whicher*, xii.

57   "to detect": For more on the origin of the phrase "the devil's disciples," see Lukas, *Big Trouble*, 76.

57   "depart from": Pinkerton's National Detective Agency, *General Principles and Rules of Pinkerton's National Detective Agency*, LOC.

57   "miserable snake": McWatters, *Knots Untied*, 664–65.

58   "I fought in France": Shepherd, "Lo, the Rich Indian!"

58   "My name is": William J. Burns, *Masked War*, 10.

59   "perhaps the only": *New York Times*, Dec. 4, 1911.

60   "a thousand times": Quoted in Hunt, *Front-Page Detective*, 104.

60   That summer: Descriptions of the activities of the private eyes derive

from their daily logs, which were included in bureau reports by James Findlay, July 1923, FBI.

60   "Mathis and myself": Report by Findlay, July 10, 1923, FBI.

60   "Everything was": Grand jury testimony of Anna Sitterly, NARA-FW.

61   "This call seems": Report by Findlay, July 10, 1923, FBI.

61   "General suspicion": Ibid.

62   "Consequently I left": Ibid.

62   "The watchful Detective": Pinkerton's National Detective Agency, *General Principles and Rules of Pinkerton's National Detective Agency*, LOC.

62   "weakens the whole": Ibid.

62   "shot her": Report by Findlay, July 13, 1923, FBI.

63   "clue that seems": Ibid.

63   "We are going": Report by Findlay, July 10, 1923, FBI.

63   "she came out": *Mollie Burkhart et al. v. Ella Rogers*, Supreme Court of the State of Oklahoma, NARA-FW.

63   "a love that": Ibid.

64   "prostituting the sacred bond": Ibid.

65   "Burns was the first": "Scientific Eavesdropping," *Literary Digest*, June 15, 1912.

65   "a little baby": Grand jury testimony of Bob Carter, NARA-FW.

66   "The fact he": In proceedings of *Ware v. Beach*, Supreme Court of the State of Oklahoma, Comstock Family Papers.

66   "Operative shadowed": Report by Findlay, July 13, 1923, FBI.

67   "endowed with": Christison, *Treatise on Poisons in Relation to Medical Jurisprudence, Physiology, and the Practice of Physic*, 684.

67   "agitated and trembles": Ibid.

68   "untrained": Oscar T. Schultz and E. M. Morgan, "The Coroner and the Medical Examiner," *Bulletin of the National Research Council*, July 1928.

68   "kind-hearted": *Washington Post*, Nov. 17, 1935.

68   "Be careful": *Washington Post*, Sept. 6, 1922.

69   "the most brutal": *Washington Post*, July 14, 1923.

69   "CONSPIRACY BELIEVED": *Washington Post*, March 12, 1925.

6: MILLION DOLLAR ELM

70   "'MILLIONAIRES' SPECIAL'": *Pawhuska Daily Journal*, March 18, 1925.

70   "PAWHUSKA GIVES": *Pawhuska Daily Capital*, June 14, 1921.

70   "MEN OF MILLIONS": *Pawhuska Daily Capital*, April 5, 1923.

70   "Osage Monte Carlo": Rister, *Oil!*, 190.

70   "Brewster, the hero": *Daily Oklahoman*, Jan. 28, 1923.

71   "There is a touch": *Ada Evening News*, Dec. 24, 1924.

72   "Come on boys": *Daily Journal-Capital*, March 29, 1928.

72   "It was not unusual": Gunther, *The Very, Very Rich and How They Got That Way*, 124.

73   "the oil men": Quoted in Allen, *Only Yesterday*, 129.

73   "I understand": Quoted in McCartney, *The Teapot Dome Scandal*, 113.

73   "Veterans of": *Pawhuska Daily Capital*, April 6, 1923.

73   On January 18: My description of the auction is drawn from local newspaper articles, particularly a detailed account in the *Daily Oklahoman*, Jan. 28, 1923.

74   "the finest building": Thoburn, *Standard History of Oklahoma*, 1989.

74   "What am I": *Daily Oklahoman*, Jan. 28, 1923.

76   "Where will it": Shepherd, "Lo, the Rich Indian!"

76   "The Osage Indian": Brown, "Our Plutocratic Osage Indians."

76   "merely because": Quoted in Harmon, *Rich Indians*, 181.

77   "enjoying the bizarre": Ibid., 185.

77   some of the spending: For more on this subject, see ibid.

77   "the greatest, gaudiest": F. Scott Fitzgerald, *The Crack-Up* (1945; repr., New York: New Directions, 2009), 87.

78   "To me, the purpose": Gregory, *Oil in Oklahoma*, 40.

78   "The last time": Ibid., 43.

78   "like a child": *Modifying Osage Fund Restrictions*, 73.

78   "racial weakness": From the decision in the case of *Barnett v. Barnett*, Supreme Court of Oklahoma, July 13, 1926.

78   "Let not that": *Indians of the United States: Investigation of the Field Service*, 399.

79   "I have visited": H. S. Traylor to Cato Sells, in *Indians of the United States: Investigation of the Field Service*, 201.

79   "Every white man": Ibid., 204.

79   "There is a great": *Modifying Osage Fund Restrictions*, 60.

80   "We have many little": *Pawhuska Daily Capital*, Nov. 19, 1921.

80   "a flock of buzzards": Transcript of proceedings of the Osage Tribal Council, Nov. 1, 1926, ONM.

80   "Will you please": *Pawhuska Daily Capital*, Dec. 22, 1921.

80   "bunched us": *Indians of the United States: Investigation of the Field Service*, 281.

7: THIS THING OF DARKNESS

81   One day, two men: My description of the discovery of Roan's body and the autopsy comes from the testimony of the witnesses present, including the lawmen. For more information, see records at NARA-FW and NARA-CP.

81   "He must be drunk": Grand jury testimony of J. R. Rhodes, NARA-FW.

81   "I seen he": Ibid.

82   "Roan considered": Pitts Beatty to James A. Finch, Aug. 21, 1935, NARA-CP.

82   "We were good": Lamb, *Tragedies of the Osage Hills*, 178.

83   "Henry, you better": Testimony of William K. Hale, *U.S. v. John Ramsey and William K. Hale*, Oct. 1926, NARA-FW.

83   "truly a valley": *Tulsa Daily World,* Aug. 19, 1926.

83   "his hands folded": Grand jury testimony of J. R. Rhodes, NARA-FW.

83   "$20 in greenback": Ibid.

83   "HENRY ROAN SHOT": *Osage Chief,* Feb. 9, 1923.

84   *"Man's judgment errs"*: Charles W. Sanders, *The New School Reader, Fourth Book: Embracing a Comprehensive System of Instruction in the Principles of Elocution with a Choice Collection of Reading Lessons in Prose and Poetry, from the Most Approved Authors; for the Use of Academies and Higher Classes in Schools, Etc.* (New York: Vison & Phinney, 1855), 155.

84   And so she decided: Mollie's secrecy regarding her marriage to Roan was later revealed in *U.S. v. John Ramsey and William K. Hale,* Oct. 1926, NARA-FW.

85   "Travel in any direction": *Daily Oklahoman,* Jan. 6, 1929.

85   "do away with her": Report by Findlay, July 13, 1923, FBI.

85   "paralyzing fear": Unpublished nonfiction account by Grove with White, NMSUL.

85   "dark cloak": *Manitowoc Herald-Times,* Jan. 22, 1926.

85   Bill Smith confided: My description of Bill and Rita Smith during this period and of the explosion is drawn largely from witness statements made to investigators and during court proceedings; some details have also been gleaned from local newspaper accounts and the unpublished nonfiction account by Grove with White. For more information, see records at NARA-CP and NARA-FW.

85   "Rita's scared": Unpublished nonfiction account by Grove with White, NMSUL.

86   "Now that we've moved": Ibid.

86   "expect to live": Report by Wren, Oct. 6, 1925, FBI.

86   "county's most notorious": *Osage Chief,* June 22, 1923.

86   "I'm going to die": Shoemaker, *Road to Marble Hills,* 107.

88   "It seemed that the night": Unpublished nonfiction account by Grove with White, NMSUL.

88   "It shook everything": Statement by Ernest Burkhart, Jan. 6, 1926, FBI.

89   "It's Bill Smith's house": Quoted in Hogan, *Osage Murders,* 66.

89   "It just looked": Quoted in Gregory, *Oil in Oklahoma,* 56.

89   "Come on men": *Osage Chief,* March 16, 1923.

90   "He was halloing": Grand jury testimony of David Shoun, NARA-FW.

90   "Rita's gone": Unpublished nonfiction account by Grove with White, NMSUL.

90   "Some fire": Report by Wren, Dec. 29, 1925, FBI.

90   "blown to pieces": Grand jury testimony of Horace E. Wilson, NARA-FW.

90   "I figured": Grand jury testimony of F. S. Turton, NARA-FW.

90   "The time of the deed": Report by Burger and Weiss, Aug. 12, 1924, FBI.

92   "They got Rita": Report by Frank Smith, James Alexander Street, Burger, and J. V. Murphy, Sept. 1, 1925, FBI.

92   "He just kind": Grand jury testimony of Robert Colombe, NARA-FW.

92   "I tried to get": Grand jury testimony of David Shoun, NARA-FW.

92   "beyond our power": *Osage Chief,* March 16, 1923.

92   "should be thrown": Report by Wren, Dec. 29, 1925, FBI.

93   "loose upon": *Indiana Evening Gazette,* Sept. 20, 1923.

93   Amid this garish corruption: Details of Vaughan's investigation and murder were drawn from several sources, including FBI records, newspaper accounts, the Vaughan family's private papers, and interviews with descendants.

93   "parasite upon": Advertisement for Vaughan's candidacy for county attorney, Vaughan Family Papers.

93   "help the needy": Student file of George Bigheart, accessible on Dickinson College's Carlisle Indian School Digital Resource Center website and held in Record Group 75, Series 1327, at NARA-DC.

94   "OWNER VANISHES": *Tulsa Daily World,* July 1, 1923.

94   "Yes, sir, and had": Grand jury testimony of Horace E. Wilson, NARA-FW.

95   "shot in lonely": *Literary Digest,* April 3, 1926.

96   "dark and sordid": *Manitowoc Herald-Times,* Jan. 22, 1926.

96   "bloodiest chapter": John Baxter, "Billion Dollar Murders," Vaughan Family Papers.

96   "I didn't want": Grand jury testimony of C. A. Cook, NARA-FW.

96   "WHEREAS, in no": Report by Frank V. Wright, April 5, 1923, FBI.

96   part-Kaw, part-Osage: Charles Curtis would later serve as vice president of the United States during the administration of Herbert Hoover.

97   "Demons": Palmer to Curtis, Jan. 28, 1925, FBI.

97   "Lie still": Testimony of Frank Smith, included in Ernest Burkhart's clemency records, NARA-CP.

98   "a horrible monument": Bureau report titled "The Osage Murders," Feb. 3, 1926, FBI.

98   "in failing health": Mollie Burkhart's guardian records, Jan. 1925, NARA-CP.

8: DEPARTMENT OF EASY VIRTUE

103   "important message": White to Hoover, Nov. 10, 1955, FBI/FOIA.

104   "as God-fearing": Tracy, "Tom Tracy Tells About—Detroit and Oklahoma."

105   "bureaucratic bastard": Quoted in Gentry, *J. Edgar Hoover,* 112.

105   "In those days": Transcript of interview with Tom White, NMSUL.

105   "rough and ready": James M. White (Doc White's grandnephew), interview with author.

106   "bullet-spattered": Hastedt, "White Brothers of Texas Had Notable FBI Careers."

106   During the Harding: For more information on J. Edgar Hoover and the early history of the FBI, see Gentry's *J. Edgar Hoover;* Ungar's *FBI;* Powers's *Secrecy and Power;* and Burrough's *Public Enemies.* For more background on the Teapot Dome scandal, see McCartney's *Teapot Dome Scandal;* Dean's *Warren G. Harding;* and Stratton's *Tempest over Teapot Dome.*

106   "illegal plots": Quoted in Lowenthal, *Federal Bureau of Investigation,* 292.

107   "Every effort": Quoted in Gentry, *J. Edgar Hoover,* 129.

108   "gilded favoritism": *Cincinnati Enquirer,* March 14, 1924.

108   "I was very much": J. M. Towler to Hoover, Jan. 6, 1925, FBI/FOIA.

108   "You brought credit": Hoover to Verdon Adams, Oct. 19, 1970, FBI/FOIA.

109   "We were a bunch": Quoted in Burrough, *Public Enemies,* 51.

110   "any continued": C. S. Weakley to Findlay, Aug. 16, 1923, FBI.

110   "unfavorable comment": W. D. Bolling to Hoover, April 3, 1925, FBI.

110   "undercover man": Report by Weiss and Burger, May 24, 1924, FBI.

111   "We expect splendid": Ibid.

111   "a number of officers": Findlay to Eberstein, Feb. 5, 1925, FBI.

111   "responsible for failure": Hoover to Bolling, March 16, 1925, FBI.

111   "I join in": Palmer to Curtis, Jan. 28, 1925, FBI.

111   "acute and delicate": Hoover to White, Aug. 8, 1925, FBI/FOIA.

111   "This Bureau": Hoover to White, May 1, 1925, FBI/FOIA.

112   "I want you": Transcript of interview with White, NMSUL.

112   "office is probably": Hoover to White, Sept. 21, 1925, FBI/FOIA.

112   "I am human": White to Hoover, Aug. 5, 1925, FBI/FOIA.

112   "There can be no": Hoover to Bolling, Feb. 3, 1925, FBI.

9: THE UNDERCOVER COWBOYS

113   "The two women": Report by Weiss and Burger, April 29, 1924, FBI.

115   "unbroken chain": Transcript of interview with White, NMSUL.

115   "almost universal": Report by Weiss and Burger, Aug. 12, 1924, FBI.

115   "I'll assign as many": Transcript of interview with White, NMSUL.

115   These agents were still: Information on the members of Tom White's team comes largely from the agents' personnel files, which were obtained through the Freedom of Information Act; White's FBI reports, letters, and writings; newspaper accounts; and the author's interviews with descendants of the agents.

116   White first recruited: The former New Mexico sheriff was named James Alexander Street.

116   White then enlisted: Eugene Hall Parker was the former Texas Ranger who was part of White's undercover team.

116   "where there is": Personnel file of Parker, April 9, 1934, FBI/FOIA.

116   In addition, White: The deep undercover operative was an agent named Charles Davis.

116   "Pistol and rifle": Personnel file of Smith, Aug. 13, 1932, FBI/FOIA.

116   "the older type": Personnel file of Smith, Oct. 22, 1928, FBI/FOIA.

116   "He is exceedingly": Louis DeNette to Burns, June 2, 1920, FBI.

117   "Unless you measure": Hoover to Wren, March 28, 1925, FBI/FOIA.

117   "The Indians, in general": Report by Weiss and Burger, Dec. 31, 1923, FBI. Prior to Tom White's taking over the investigation, Burger had worked on the case with Agent Tom F. Weiss; all of Burger's reports were filed jointly with him.

117   "any of these dissolute": Report by Weiss, Nov. 19, 1923, FBI.

118   "PROCEED UNDER COVER": Harold Nathan to Gus T. Jones, Aug. 10, 1925, FBI.

10: ELIMINATING THE IMPOSSIBLE

119   One after the other: My descriptions of the bureau's investigations into the murders come from several sources, including FBI reports; agent's personnel files; grand jury testimony; court transcripts; and White's private correspondence and writings.

119   Finally, Agent Wren arrived: Wren also pretended at times to be representing certain cattle interests.

119   "Wren had lived": White to Hoover, Feb. 2, 1926, FBI/FOIA.

120   "My desk was": Grand jury testimony of Horace E. Wilson, NARA-FW.

120   "I don't know": Ibid.

120   "made a diligent": Grand jury testimony of David Shoun, NARA-FW.

121   "When you have eliminated": Arthur Conan Doyle, *The Sign of Four* (London: Spencer Blackett, 1890), 93.

121   "It is a matter": Report by Weiss, Sept. 1, 1923, FBI.

122   "I never had a quarrel": Report by Burger and Weiss, April 22, 1924, FBI.

122   "very self-contained": Ibid.

122   "Were you thick": Report by Weakley, Aug. 7, 1923, FBI.

122   "We interviewed": Report by Weiss and Burger, Feb. 2, 1924, FBI.

122   "unusually shrewd": Ibid.

123   "Talks and smokes": Ibid.

123   "This arrangement": Ibid.

123   "He may efface": Tarbell, "Identification of Criminals."

123   When Hoover became: The bureau's Identification Division initially collected fingerprints from files maintained by the U.S. Penitentiary in Leavenworth penitentiary and by the International Association for Chiefs of Police.

124   "the guardians of civilization": Quoted in Powers, *Secrecy and Power,* 150.

124   "We have his picture": Report by Weiss and Burger, Feb. 2, 1924, FBI.

124   He reported back: Morrison initially claimed, falsely, that Rose implicated her boyfriend.

124   "Why'd you do it": Report by Weiss and Burger, Feb. 2, 1924, FBI.

124   "If he is not": Report by Weiss and Burger, Aug. 16, 1924, FBI.

11: THE THIRD MAN

126   "I do not understand": Hoover to White, June 2, 1926, FBI.

126   "interesting observation": Hoover to Bolling, June 1925, FBI.

129   "paid by suspects": Weiss and Burger to William J. Burns, March 24, 1924, FBI.

130   "We old fellows": Grand jury testimony of Ed Hainey, NARA-FW.

130   "There was Indians": Trial testimony of Berry Hainey, *State of Oklahoma v. Kelsie Morrison*, OSARM.

130   "They went straight": Report by Weakley, Aug. 15, 1923, FBI.

130   "perjured himself": Report by Weiss and Burger, Jan. 8, 1924, FBI.

131   "Third man is": Report by Weiss and Burger, Jan. 10, 1924, FBI.

131   "Stop your foolishness": Ibid.

12: A WILDERNESS OF MIRRORS

133   "strangle": Report by Smith, Sept. 28, 1925, FBI.

133   "seen part": Ibid.

133   "information contained": Findlay to Burns, Dec. 19, 1923, FBI.

133   "handed to": Eustace Smith to Attorney General, March 15, 1925, FBI.

134   "reprehensible": Report by Weiss and Burger, July 2, 1924, FBI.

134   "sole object": Ibid.

134   "frightened out": Report by Weiss and Burger, July 12, 1924, FBI.

134   "son-of-bitches": Report by Weiss and Burger, July 2, 1924, FBI.

134   "Look out": Report by Weiss and Burger, Aug. 16, 1924, FBI.

134   "Keep your balance": Transcript of interview with White, NMSUL.

135   "has known": Report by Weiss and Burger, Feb. 11, 1924, FBI.

135   "It is quite": Report by Weiss and Burger, April 11, 1924, FBI.

135   "Pike will have": Report by Weiss and Burger, Aug. 14, 1924, FBI.

136   "shape an alibi": Grand jury testimony of Elbert M. Pike, NARA-FW.

136   "discuss this case": Report by Weiss, Nov. 19, 1923, FBI.

13: A HANGMAN'S SON

138   "Mr. White belongs": Daniell, *Personnel of the Texas State Government*, 389.

138   "I was raised": Adams, *Tom White*, 6.

139   "BLOOD, BLOOD": *Austin Weekly Statesman*, March 31, 1892.

139   "If a mob attempts": *Bastrop Advertiser*, Aug. 5, 1899.

141   "RAVISHED IN BROAD": *Austin Weekly Statesman*, Sept. 1, 1892.

141   "Truth to tell": *Austin Weekly Statesman*, Nov. 22, 1894.

142   "hung by the neck": *Austin Weekly Statesman*, Nov. 16, 1893.

142   "Let the law": *Austin Weekly Statesman,* Jan. 11, 1894.

142   "Sheriff White has been": *Dallas Morning News,* Jan. 13, 1894.

142   "Ed Nichols is": Ibid.

143   "He kicked": Adams, *Tom White,* 8.

143   "Every school boy": Quoted in Parsons, *Captain John R. Hughes,* 275.

144   "Get all the evidence": Leonard Mohrman, "A Ranger Reminisces," *Texas Parade,* Feb. 1951.

144   "the same as a cowpuncher": Transcript of interview with Tom White, NMSUL.

144   "Here was a scene": Quoted in Robinson, *Men Who Wear the Star,* 79.

144   Tom learned to be a lawman: Tom White practiced firing his six-shooter. It was the Rangers who had recognized the revolutionary power of these repeat revolvers, after long being overmatched by American Indian warriors who could unleash a barrage of arrows before the lawmen could reload their single-shot rifles. In 1844, while testing out a Colt five-shooter, a group of Rangers overran a larger number of Comanche. Afterward, one of the Rangers informed the gun maker Samuel Colt that with improvements the repeat revolver could be rendered "the most perfect weapon in the world." With this Ranger's input, Colt designed a lethal six-shooter—"a stepchild of the West," as one historian called it—that would help to irrevocably change the balance of power between the Plains tribes and the settlers. Along its cylinder was engraved a picture of the Rangers' victorious battle against the Comanche.

144   You picked up: To hone his aim, White practiced shooting on virtually any moving creature: rabbits, buzzards, even prairie dogs. He realized that being an accurate shot was more important than being the fastest draw. As his brother Doc put it, "What good is it to be quick on the draw if you're not a sure shot?" Doc said a lot of the legends about Western gunmen were "hooey": "All that business about Wyatt Earp being a quick draw artist is exaggerated. He was just a good shot."

146   "You don't never": Adams, *Tom White,* 19.

146   "the lawless element": Ben M. Edwards to Frank Johnson, Jan. 25, 1908, TSLAC.

146   "We had nothing": Hastedt, "White Brothers of Texas Had Notable FBI Careers."

146   "avoid killing": Adams, *Tom White,* 16.

147   "An officer who": Quoted in Parsons, *Captain John R. Hughes,* xvii.

147   "the Sheriff has": Thomas Murchinson to Adjutant General, March 2, 1907, TSLAC.

147   "I am shot all": Quoted in Alexander, *Bad Company and Burnt Powder,* 240.

148   "Tom's emotional struggle": Adams, *Tom White,* 24.

148   "proved an excellent": Adjutant General to Tom Ross, Feb. 10, 1909, TSLAC.

149   "fell, and did not get up": *Beaumont Enterprise,* July 15, 1918.

149   "One wagon sheet": Adjutant General to J. D. Fortenberry, Aug. 1, 1918,
       TSLAC.

14: DYING WORDS

152   "If Bill Smith": Grand jury testimony of David Shoun, NARA-FW.

152   "often leave": Ibid.

152   "If she says": Ibid.

152   "He never did say": Grand jury testimony of James Shoun, NARA-FW.

152   "Gentlemen, it is a mystery": Grand jury testimony of David E. Johnson,
       NARA-FW.

152   "You know, I only": Ibid.

152   "I would hate": Grand jury testimony of James Shoun, NARA-FW.

153   "If he did": Report of Smith, Street, Burger, and Murphy, Sept. 1, 1925,
       FBI.

153   "You understand in your study of": Grand jury testimony of David Shoun,
       NARA-FW.

153   "Did he know what": Ibid.

154   "The blackest chapter": *Survey of Conditions of Indians,* 23018.

155   "an orgy of graft": Gertrude Bonnin, "Oklahoma's Poor Rich Indians: An
       Orgy of Graft and Exploitation of the Five Civilized Tribes and Others,"
       1924, HSP.

155   "shamelessly and openly": Ibid.

155   "A group of traders": *St. Louis Post-Dispatch,* May 10, 1925.

156   "For her and her": Memorandum by Gertrude Bonnin, "Case of Martha
       Axe Roberts," Dec. 3, 1923, HSP.

156   "There is no hope": Ibid.

156   "Your money": Shepherd, "Lo, the Rich Indian!"

15: THE HIDDEN FACE

157   "controlled everything": Report by Wren, Davis, and Parker, Sept. 10,
       1925, FBI.

158   "Hells bells": Grand jury testimony of John McLean, NARA-FW.

158   "drunken Indian": Ibid.

158   "I don't think it": Grand jury testimony of Alfred T. Hall, NARA-FW.

159   "I knew the questions": *Tulsa Tribune,* Aug. 6, 1926.

159   "Photographs taken by means": Bert Farrar to Roy St. Lewis, Dec. 22,
       1928, NARA-FW.

160   "Absolutely": Grand jury testimony of John McLean, NARA-FW.

160   "Bill, what are you": Grand jury testimony of W. H. Aaron, NARA-FW.

160   "Hell, yes": *U.S. v. John Ramsey and William K. Hale,* Oct. 1926, NARA-FW.

160   "If I were you": Unpublished nonfiction account by Grove with White,
       NMSUL.

160   "notorious relations": Report by Burger and Weiss, Aug. 12, 1924, FBI.
161   "I, like many": Hale's application for clemency, Nov. 15, 1935, NARA-CP.
161   "is absolutely controlled": Report by Wright, April 5, 1923, FBI.
161   "capable of anything": Report by Weiss and Burger, Jan. 10, 1924, FBI.
162   "MOLLIE appears": Report titled "The Osage Murders," Feb. 3, 1926, FBI.

16: FOR THE BETTERMENT OF THE BUREAU

164   "many new angles": Edwin Brown to Hoover, March 22, 1926, FBI/FOIA.
164   "a crook and": Report by Wren, Oct. 6, 1925, FBI.
165   "dominated local": Report titled "Osage Indian Murder Cases," July 10, 1953, FBI.
165   "conditions have": Hoover to White, Nov. 25, 1925, FBI/FOIA.
165   "slender bundle": Quoted in Nash, Citizen Hoover, 23.
165   Hoover wanted the new: For more information regarding Hoover's transformation of the bureau, see Gentry, J. Edgar Hoover; Powers, Secrecy and Power; Burrough, Public Enemies; and Ungar, F.B.I. For more on the dark side of Progressivism, also see Thomas C. Leonard's journal articles "American Economic Reform in the Progressive Era" and "Retrospectives."
166   "days of 'old sleuth'": San Bernardino County Sun, Dec. 31, 1924.
166   "scrapped the old": Quoted in Powers, Secrecy and Power, 146.
166   "He plays golf": San Bernardino County Sun, Dec. 31, 1924.
166   "I regret that": Hoover to White, Sept. 21, 1925, FBI/FOIA.
166   "I have caused": Hoover to White, May 1, 1925, FBI/FOIA.
167   "You either improve": Quoted in Gentry, J. Edgar Hoover, 149.
167   "I believe that when": Hoover to White, April 15, 1925, FBI/FOIA.
167   "I'm sure he would": Quoted in Gentry, J. Edgar Hoover, 67.
169   "supposed to know": Tracy, "Tom Tracy Tells About—Detroit and Oklahoma."
169   "honest till": Adams, Tom White, 133.
169   "I feel that I": White to Hoover, Sept. 28, 1925, FBI/FOIA.
169   "with the betterment": White to Hoover, June 10, 1925, FBI/FOIA.
169   "I do not agree": Memorandum for Hoover, May 12, 1925, FBI/FOIA.
170   "The first thing": Quoted in Gentry, J. Edgar Hoover, 170.
170   "directed against": Quoted in Powers, Secrecy and Power, 154.

17: THE QUICK-DRAW ARTIST, THE YEGG, AND THE SOUP MAN

171   "diaspora": Mary Jo Webb, interview with author.
171   "I made peace": Osage Chief, July 28, 1922.
172   "Gregg is 100 percent": Report by Weiss and Burger, Aug. 12, 1924, FBI.
172   "A very small man": White to Grove, June 23, 1959, NMSUL.
172   "a cold cruel": Criminal record of Dick Gregg, Jan. 9, 1925, KHS.

172   "gone places": White to Grove, June 23, 1959, NMSUL.

173   "my life would": Report by Weiss and Burger, July 24, 1924, FBI.

173   "Bill Smith and": Statement by Dick Gregg, June 8, 1925, FBI.

173   "That's not my style": Quoted in article by Fred Grove in *The War Chief of the Indian Territory Posse of Oklahoma Westerners* 2, no. 1 (June 1968).

174   "on the level": White to Grove, June 23, 1959, NMSUL.

174   "an outlaw": Ibid.

174   "Johnson knows": Report by Weiss and Burger, Aug. 14, 1924, FBI.

174   "HENRY GRAMMER SHOOTS": Lamb, *Tragedies of the Osage Hills*, 119.

175   "CHEROKEES NO MATCH": *Muskogee Times-Democrat,* Aug. 5, 1909.

175   "that Indian deal": Report by Burger, Nov. 30, 1928, FBI.

176   The legendary quick-draw: There were also suspicions that Grammer had been shot as well and had a bullet wound near his left armpit.

176   "taking care": Grand jury testimony of John Mayo, NARA-FW.

176   "Hale knows": Report by Weiss and Burger, July 2, 1924, FBI.

178   "damned neck": Report by Weiss and Burger, Aug. 16, 1924, FBI.

178   "making all the propaganda": Report by Wren, Nov. 5, 1925, FBI.

178   "I'm too slick": Document titled "Osage Indian Murder Cases," July 10, 1953, FBI.

178   "like he owned": Transcript of interview with White, NMSUL.

18: THE STATE OF THE GAME

179   "We've been getting": Unpublished nonfiction account by Grove with White, NMSUL. In bureau records, Lawson's first name name is spelled Burt; in other records, it is sometimes spelled Bert. To avoid confusion, I have used Burt throughout the text.

180   "hot Feds": White to Grove, May 2, 1959, NMSUL.

180   "We understand from": Unpublished nonfiction account by Grove with White, NMSUL.

180   "Some time around": Report by Smith and Murphy, Oct. 27, 1925, FBI.

181   "Have confession": White to Hoover, Oct. 24, 1925, FBI.

181   "Congratulations": Hoover to White, Oct. 26, 1925, FBI.

182   "Once, when he": Homer Fincannon, interview with author.

182   "not to drink": Report by Wren, Oct. 6, 1925, FBI.

183   "illness is very suspicious": Edwin Brown to George Wright, July 18, 1925, NARA-CP.

183   "Understand I'm wanted": Unpublished nonfiction account by Grove with White, NMSUL.

184   "like a leashed": *Guthrie Leader,* Jan. 6, 1926.

185   "You could look": Transcript of interview with White, NMSUL.

185   "We all picked Ernest": Statement by Luhring in grand jury proceedings, NARA-FW.

185   "small-town dandy": Transcript of interview with White, NMSUL.

185   "We want to talk": Unpublished nonfiction account by Grove with White, NMSUL.
187   "If he didn't": Gentry, *J. Edgar Hoover,* 386.
187   "perfect": *Tulsa Tribune,* Jan. 5, 1926.
187   "too much Jew": Report by Weiss and Burger, April 30, 1924, FBI.
189   "Blackie, have": Grand jury testimony of Smith, Jan. 5, 1926, NARA-CP.
190   "After being so warned": Statement by Ernest Burkhart, Jan. 6, 1926, FBI.
190   "I relied on": Unpublished nonfiction account by Grove with White, NMSUL.
190   "Hale had told": Statement by Ernest Burkhart, Feb. 5, 1927, NARA-CP.
190   "Just a few days": Statement by Ernest Burkhart, Jan. 6, 1926, FBI.
190   "You have got": Grand jury testimony of Frank Smith, NARA-FW.
190   "All that story": Transcript of interview with White, NMSUL.
191   "When it happened": Statement by Ernest Burkhart, Jan. 6, 1926, FBI.
191   "I know who killed": Grand jury testimony of Frank Smith, NARA-FW.
191   "There's a suspect": Unpublished nonfiction account by Grove with White, NMSUL.
191   "like a nervy": *Tulsa Tribune,* March 13, 1926.
191   "I guess": Grand jury testimony of Smith, NARA-FW.
191   "a little job": Statement by John Ramsey, Jan. 6, 1926, FBI.
192   "white people": Unpublished nonfiction account by Grove with White, NMSUL.
192   "It is an established": Memorandum by M. A. Jones for Louis B. Nichols, Aug. 4, 1954, FBI.
193   "Weren't you giving": Grand jury testimony of James Shoun, NARA-FW.
193   "We are all your friends": Testimony of Mollie Burkhart before tribal attorney and other officials, NARA-FW.
194   "My husband": Macon, "Mass Murder of the Osages."
194   "ever saw until": Quoted in Gregory, *Oil in Oklahoma,* 57.
195   "We have unquestioned": Unpublished nonfiction account by Grove with White, NMSUL.
195   "money will buy": Report by Weiss and Burger, Feb. 2, 1924, FBI.
195   "We don't think": Unpublished nonfiction account by Grove with White, NMSUL.
195   "I'll fight it": Ibid.

19: A TRAITOR TO HIS BLOOD

196   "an evidently": *Literary Digest,* Jan. 23, 1926.
196   "more blood-curdling": *Evening Independent,* Jan. 5, 1926.
196   "King of the Killers": Holding, "King of the Killers."
197   "Hale kept my husband": Lizzie June Bates to George Wright, Nov. 21, 1922, NARA-FW.
197   "OSAGE INDIAN": *Reno Evening-Gazette,* Jan. 4, 1926.

197   "OLD WILD WEST": *Evening Independent,* March 5, 1926.

197   "The Tragedy": White to Hoover, Sept. 18, 1926, FBI.

197   "We Indians": Bates to Wright, Nov. 21, 1922, NARA-FW.

197   "Members of the Osage": Copy of resolution by the Society of Oklahoma Indians, NARA-FW.

198   "When you're up": Quoted in Irwin, *Deadly Times,* 331.

198   "Townspeople": *Lima News,* Jan. 29, 1926.

198   "not only useless": Edwin Brown to A. G. Ridgley, July 21, 1925, FBI.

199   "ablest legal talent": *Sequoyah County Democrat,* April 9, 1926.

200   "When a small-natured": Sargent Prentiss Freeling vertical file, OHS.

200   "I never killed": Lamb, *Tragedies of the Osage Hills,* 174.

200   "not to worry, that he": Statement by Burkhart in deposition, Feb. 5, 1927, NARA-CP.

200   The bureau put: One night in December 1926, Luther Bishop, a state lawman who had assisted on the Osage murder cases, was shot and killed in his house. His wife was charged with the murder but was later acquitted by a jury. Dee Cordry, a former police investigator and an author, examined the case in his 2005 book, *Alive If Possible—Dead If Necessary.* He suspected that Hale, in a final act of revenge, ordered the killing.

200   "Long face": Report by W. A. Kitchen, March 2, 1926, FBI.

200   "Kelsie said": Report by Smith, Feb. 8, 1926, FBI.

200   "get her out": Grand jury testimony of Dewey Selph, NARA-FW.

200   "We'd better": Unpublished nonfiction account by Grove with White, NMSUL.

201   "Before this man": White to Hoover, March 31, 1926, FBI.

201   "Whatever you do": Report by Burger, Nov. 2, 1928, FBI.

201   "bumped off": Grand jury testimony of Burkhart, NARA-FW.

201   "I'll give you": Transcript of interview with White, NMSUL.

201   "We think": White to Hoover, June 26, 1926, FBI.

201   "intentionally guilty": Wright to Charles Burke, June 24, 1926, NARA-CP.

201   "That is all": Testimony of Mollie Burkhart before tribal attorney and other officials, NARA-FW.

202   "Dear husband": Mollie to Ernest Burkhart, Jan. 21, 1926, NARA-FW.

202   "It appeared": Unpublished nonfiction account by Grove with White, NMSUL.

202   "Bill, I have": Ibid.

202   "Very few, if any": White to Hoover, July 3, 1926, FBI.

203   "Seldom if ever": *Tulsa Tribune,* March 13, 1926.

203   "new and exclusive": *Bismarck Tribune,* June 17, 1926.

203   "Hale is a man": *Tulsa Tribune,* March 13, 1926.

203   "*Judge Not*": Quoted in Hogan, *Osage Murders,* 195.

204   "Your honor, I demand": Unpublished nonfiction account by Grove with White, NMSUL.

204 "traitor to his": *Tulsa Daily World*, Aug. 20, 1926.

204 "This man is my client": *Tulsa Daily World*, March 13, 1926.

204 "He's not my attorney": Unpublished nonfiction account by Grove with White, NMSUL.

204 "high-handed and unusual": Leahy memorandum, clemency records, NARA-CP.

205 "nerve went": White to Hoover, June 5, 1926, FBI.

205 "I never did": Testimony from Ernest Burkhart's preliminary hearing, included in *U.S. v. John Ramsey and William K. Hale*, NARA-FW.

205 "Hale and Ramsey": Transcript of interview with White, NMSUL.

205 "I looked back": *Tulsa Tribune*, May 30, 1926.

206 "quite a tyrant": Quoted in Gentry, *J. Edgar Hoover*, 117.

206 "PRISONER CHARGES": *Washington Post*, June 8, 1926.

207 "ridiculous": White to Grove, Aug. 10, 1959, NMSUL.

207 "fabrication from": White to Hoover, June 8, 1926, FBI.

207 "I'll meet the man": Unpublished nonfiction account by Grove with White, NMSUL.

207 "the whole damn": Kelsie Morrison testimony, in *State of Oklahoma v. Morrison*, OSARM.

207 "bump that squaw": Morrison's testimony at Ernest Burkhart's trial, later included in ibid.

208 "He raised her": Ibid.

209 "I stayed in the car alone": Statement by Katherine Cole, Jan. 31, 1926, NARA-FW.

210 "Don't look": My description of Burkhart changing his plea derives from trial coverage in local papers, Grove's nonfiction manuscript, and a 1927 letter written by Leahy and held at the NARA-CP in Burkhart's clemency records.

210 "I'm through lying": *Tulsa Daily World*, June 10, 1926, and Grove's nonfiction manuscript.

210 "I wish to discharge": *Tulsa Daily World*, June 10, 1926.

211 "I'm sick and tired": Unpublished nonfiction account by Grove with White, NMSUL.

211 "I feel in my heart": *Daily Journal-Capital*, June 9, 1926.

211 "Then your plea": *Tulsa Daily World*, June 10, 1926.

211 "BURKHART ADMITS": *New York Times*, June 10, 1926.

211 "was very much": White to Hoover, June 15, 1926, FBI.

211 "Too much credit": Quoted in a 1926 missive from Short to Luhring, NARA-FW.

212 "That put us": Transcript of interview with White, NMSUL.

212 "whose mind": *Tulsa Daily World*, Aug. 19, 1926.

20: SO HELP YOU GOD!

213   "The stage is set": *Tulsa Tribune,* July 29, 1926.

213   "not testify against him": Report by Burger, Nov. 2, 1928, FBI.

215   "The attitude of": *Tulsa Tribune,* Aug. 21, 1926.

215   "It is a question": Ibid.

215   "Gentlemen of the jury": *Tulsa Daily World,* July 30, 1926.

215   "the veteran of legal battles": *Tulsa Tribune,* July 29, 1926.

216   "Hale said to me": *Tulsa Daily World,* July 31, 1926.

216   "I never devised": Lamb, *Tragedies of the Osage Hills,* 179.

216   "the ruthless freebooter": *Tulsa Daily World,* Aug. 19, 1926.

216   "The richest tribe": *Daily Journal-Capital,* Aug. 20, 1926.

216   "five to one": *Tulsa Tribune,* Aug. 21, 1926.

216   "Is there any": For this quotation and other details from the scene, see
       Oklahoma City Times, Aug. 25, 1926.

217   "I will kill": Report by H. E. James, May 11, 1928, FBI.

217   "Such practices": *Daily Oklahoman,* Oct. 8, 1926.

218   "this whole defense": Oscar R. Luhring to Roy St. Lewis, Sept. 23, 1926,
       NARA-FW.

218   "Will you state your name": *U.S. v. John Ramsey and William K. Hale,* Oct.
       1926, NARA-FW.

218   "Your wife is": Ibid.

218   "I don't work": Statement by Ernest Burkhart at his 1926 trial, NMSUL.

219   "The time now": Closing statement of Oscar R. Luhring, *U.S. v. John
       Ramsey and William K. Hale,* Oct. 1926, NARA-FW.

219   "There never has been": Ibid.

219   "Hale's face": *Daily Oklahoman,* Oct. 30, 1926.

219   "A jury has found": *Tulsa Daily World,* Oct. 30, 1926.

220   "'KING OF OSAGE'": *New York Times,* Oct. 30, 1926.

220   "one of the greatest": Leahy to U.S. Attorney General, Feb. 1, 1929, FBI/
       FOIA.

220   "if I ever get the Chance": Morrison to Hale, included in *State of Oklahoma
       v. Kelsie Morrison,* OSARM.

220   "watered": Testimony of Bryan Burkhart, *State of Oklahoma v. Kelsie Mor-
       rison,* OSARM.

220   "Did you go out": Ibid.

221   "Sheriffs investigated": *St. Louis Post-Dispatch,* Nov. 4, 1926.

221   "There is, of course": Hoover to White, Jan. 9, 1926, FBI.

222   "NEVER TOLD": Newspaper article, n.p., n.d., FBI.

222   "Look at her": Memorandum by Burger, Oct. 27, 1932, FBI.

222   "So another": *The Lucky Strike Hour,* Nov. 15, 1932, accessed from http://
       www.otrr.org/.

222   "a small way": Hoover to White, Feb. 6, 1926, FBI/FOIA.

223   "We express": Quoted in Adams, *Tom White,* 76.

223 "I hate to give up": Mabel Walker Willebrandt to Hoover, Feb. 15, 1927, FBI/FOIA.

223 "I feel that": Hoover to Willebrandt, Dec. 9, 1926, FBI/FOIA.

224 "giant mausoleum": Earley, *The Hot House*, 30.

224 "Why, hello": *Daily Oklahoman*, n.d., and transcript of interview with White, NMSUL.

21: THE HOT HOUSE

225 "How do you raise": Adams, *Tom White*, 84.

225 "ugly, dangerous": Rudensky, *Gonif*, 32.

226 "Warden White showed": Ibid., 33.

226 White tried to improve: Believing it was imperative for prisoners to keep busy, White allowed Robert Stroud, a convicted murderer, to maintain an aviary in his cell with some three hundred canaries, and he became known as the Birdman. In a letter, Stroud's mother told White how grateful she was that someone who understood "human nature and its many weaknesses" was in a position of authority over her son.

226 "The Warden was strict": Adams, *Tom White*, 133.

226 "I had a ray": Rudensky, *Gonif*, 27.

226 "I have no": Autobiography written by Carl Panzram, Nov. 3, 1928, Panzram Papers, SDSUL.

226 "I could hang a dozen": Nash, *Almanac of World Crime*, 102.

226 "He does high": Leavenworth report on Hale, Oct. 1945, NARA-CP.

227 "treated as": White to Morris F. Moore, Nov. 23, 1926, NARA-CP.

227 "Would I be imposing to ask your": Mrs. W. K. Hale to White, Sept. 29, 1927, NARA-CP.

227 "It was a business": Deposition of Hale, Jan. 31, 1927, NARA-CP.

227 "evidence of repression": Leavenworth report on Hale, Aug. 1, 1941, NARA-CP.

227 He allegedly arranged: Hale appealed his conviction, and in 1928 an appeals court shockingly overturned his verdict. A man who had assisted the defense team subsequently confessed that Hale had someone who had "done the fixing." But Hale was promptly tried again and convicted, as was Ramsey.

229 "IT IS FURTHER": Probate records of Mollie Burkhart, File No. 2173, NARA-FW.

229 On December: My descriptions of the escape attempt are drawn primarily from FBI records obtained through the Freedom of Information Act; a transcript of an interview with one of the convicts that was conducted by the author David A. Ward; Tom White's letters; newspaper accounts; and Adams, *Tom White*.

230 "I know you're going": *Dunkirk Evening Observer*, Dec. 12, 1931.

230 "Shoot him": Adams, *Tom White*, 114.

230   "White asked me": *Pittsburgh Press,* Dec. 14, 1939.

231   "I am sure": *Dunkirk Evening Observer,* Dec. 12, 1931.

231   "come back": Ward, *Alcatraz,* 6.

231   "The funny part": Ibid.

231   "He had begun": Adams, *Tom White,* 109–10.

231   "The experience affected": *Pittsburgh Press,* Dec. 14, 1939.

232   "The days of the small Bureau": Gentry, *J. Edgar Hoover,* 169.

232   "I looked up": Quoted in ibid., 58.

233   "We do not have to": White to Hoover, July 1, 1938, FBI/FOIA.

233   "appreciate a personal": Special Agent in Charge in El Paso to Hoover, Feb. 12, 1951, FBI/FOIA.

234   "I would be glad": White to Hoover, Sept. 3, 1954, FBI/FOIA.

234   "certainly bear": Hoover to White, Sept. 9, 1954, FBI/FOIA.

234   "confronted with": Gus T. Jones to Hoover, June 16, 1934, FBI/FOIA.

234   "unjust, unfair": Wren to Hoover, Aug. 2, 1932, FBI/FOIA.

234   "Often when I read of you": Wren to Hoover, Oct. 4, 1936, FBI/FOIA.

235   "After the Director": White to Hoover, Nov. 10, 1955, FBI/FOIA.

235   "I would like to keep": White to Grove, Aug. 10, 1959, NMSUL.

235   "I hope this": White to Hoover, March 20, 1958, FBI/FOIA.

237   "We should furnish": M. A. Jones to Gordon Nease, April 4, 1958, FBI/FOIA.

237   "Sickness of any kind": Bessie White to Grove, Sept. 21, 1959, NMSUL.

237   "I am hoping": Tom White to Grove, Jan. 4, 1960, FBI/FOIA.

237   "I am sincerely sorry": J. E. Weems to Grove, June 28, 1963, NMSUL.

237   "born on this land": White to Hoover, Feb. 15, 1969, FBI/FOIA.

237   "He died as he had lived": Adams, *Tom White,* in postscript.

237   "militate against": Special Agent in Charge in El Paso to Hoover, Dec. 21, 1971, FBI/FOIA.

22: GHOSTLANDS

241   "Stores gone": Morris, *Ghost Towns of Oklahoma,* 83.

242   "only shreds and tatters": Louis F. Burns, *History of the Osage People,* xiv.

244   Over several weekends: For more detailed information on Osage dances, see Callahan, *Osage Ceremonial Dance I'n-Lon-Schka.*

245   "To believe": Louis F. Burns, *History of the Osage People,* 496.

248   "Mrs. Mollie Cobb": *Fairfax Chief,* June 17, 1937.

248   "anyone convicted": Copy of Osage Tribal Council Resolution, No. 78, Nov. 15, 1937, NARA-FW.

248   "The parole of Ernest": *Kansas City Times,* Dec. 21, 1937.

248   "should have been hanged": *Daily Journal-Capital,* Aug. 3, 1947.

249   "It will be a far cry": *Oklahoma City Times,* Oct. 26, 1959.

249   "HEADRIGHTS KILLER": *Daily Oklahoman,* Feb. 14, 1966.

251 "OSAGE OIL WEALTH": *Literary Digest,* May 14, 1932.

251 "In five years": *Hamilton Evening Journal,* Sept. 28, 1929.

254 *"Because she died"*: Paschen's "Wi'-gi-e," in *Bestiary.*

254 "I think somewhere": Webb-Storey, "Culture Clash," 115.

23: A CASE NOT CLOSED

258 "PAWHUSKA MAN'S": *Daily Oklahoman,* July 2, 1923.

258 "sufficient evidence": Report by Smith, Sept. 28, 1925, FBI.

261 "Mr. Burt is one": *Hearings Before the Joint Commission of the Congress of the United States,* 1505.

262 "very intimate": Report by Weiss and Burger, April 11, 1924, FBI.

262 "split on the boodle": Ibid.

262 "murderer": Report by Wren, Nov. 5, 1925, FBI.

263 "I think Herb Burt": Report by Smith, April 3, 1926, FBI.

24: STANDING IN TWO WORLDS

265 "He had property": Tallchief, *Maria Tallchief,* 4.

265 "firebombed and everyone": Ibid., 9.

268 "I am in perfect health": Hale to Wilson Kirk, Nov. 27, 1931, ONM.

271 "This dope is": Report by Findlay, July 13, 1923, FBI.

271 "Vaughan who is": Ibid.

271 "Mr. Comstock had": Ibid.

272 "shrewd, immoral": Report by Burger, Aug. 12, 1924, FBI.

272 "prime mover": Report by Findlay, July 13, 1923, FBI.

272 "He could hear": Ibid.

272 "Minnie was making": Ibid.

273 "From the evidence": Report by Burger, Aug. 12, 1924, FBI.

273 "I am as smart": Report by Burger, Aug. 13, 1924, FBI.

273 "unprincipled, hypocritical": Report by Weiss and Burger, Jan. 10, 1924, FBI.

273 "We are strongly": Ibid.

273 "liable to die": Report by Weiss and Burger, Dec. 26, 1923, FBI.

273 "refusing to allow": Report by Weiss and Burger, Jan. 2, 1924, FBI.

273 "under his influence": Report by Weiss and Burger, Jan. 10, 1924, FBI.

274 "she does know": Report by Weiss and Burger, Dec. 26, 1923, FBI.

274 "isolated murder": Report by Burger, Aug. 13, 1924, FBI.

25: THE LOST MANUSCRIPT

276 "We don't disturb": U.S. District Court for the Northern District of Oklahoma, *U.S. v. Osage Wind, Enel Kansas, and Enel Green Power North America,* Sept. 30, 2015.

276 "defendants have not": Ibid.

277   "For the first time": *Tulsa World,* Feb. 25, 2015.
278   "scarcely stepped": *Pawhuska Daily Capital,* Jan. 30, 1919.
278   "GREWSOME FIND ENDS": Quoted in "The Murder of Mary Denoya-Bellieu-Lewis," PPL.

26: BLOOD CRIES OUT

281   "knew that was": E. E. Shepperd to U.S. Attorney's Office, Jan. 8, 1926, NARA-FW.
281   "Members of the family": *Daily Oklahoman,* Oct. 25, 1926.
282   "drugs, opiates": Quoted in Wilson, *Underground Reservation,* 144.
282   "one of the most beautiful": Quoted in McAuliffe, *Deaths of Sybil Bolton,* 109.
282   "In connection with": Bureau report titled "Murder on Indian Reservation," Nov. 6, 1932, FBI.
283   "Over the sixteen-year period": McAuliffe, *Deaths of Sybil Bolton,* 251.
283   "I don't know": Ball, *Osage Tribal Murders.*
283   "There are so many": Interview by F. G. Grimes Jr. and Edwin Brown, June 17, 1925, FBI.
285   "Bill, you know": Report by Smith, Oct. 30, 1926, FBI.
285   "Walking through": Robert Allen Warrior, "Review Essay: The Deaths of Sybil Bolton: An American History," *Wicazo Sa Review* 11 (1995): 52.
286   "You should be ashamed": McAuliffe, *Deaths of Sybil Bolton,* 137.
286   "Harry didn't do it": Ibid., 139.
286   "I did not prove": From McAuliffe's revised and updated edition of *The Deaths of Sybil Bolton,* which was renamed *Bloodland: A Family Story of Oil, Greed, and Murder on the Osage Reservation* (San Francisco: Council Oak Books, 1999), 287.
291   "There are men": Quoted in Wallis, *Oil Man,* 152.

SELECTED BIBLIOGRAPHY

Ackerman, Kenneth D. *Young J. Edgar: Hoover, the Red Scare, and the Assault on Civil Liberties*. New York: Carroll & Graf, 2007.

Adams, Verdon R. *Tom White: The Life of a Lawman*. El Paso: Texas Western Press, 1972.

Adcock, James M., and Arthur S. Chancellor. *Death Investigations*. Burlington, Mass.: Jones & Bartlett Learning, 2013.

Alexander, Bob. *Bad Company and Burnt Powder: Justice and Injustice in the Old Southwest*. Denton: University of North Texas Press, 2014.

Allen, Frederick Lewis. *Only Yesterday: An Informal History of the 1920s*. New York: John Wiley & Sons, 1997.

Ambrose, Stephen E. *Undaunted Courage: Meriwether Lewis, Thomas Jefferson, and the Opening of the American West*. New York: Simon & Schuster, 2002.

Anderson, Dan, Laurence J. Yadon, and Robert B. Smith. *100 Oklahoma Outlaws, Gangsters, and Lawmen, 1839–1939*. Gretna, La.: Pelican, 2007.

Babyak, Jolene. *Birdman: The Many Faces of Robert Stroud*. Berkeley, Calif.: Ariel Vamp Press, 1994.

Bailey, Garrick Alan. *Changes in Osage Social Organization, 1673–1906*. University of Oregon Anthropological Papers 5. Eugene: Department of Anthropology, University of Oregon, 1973.

———. "The Osage Roll: An Analysis." *Indian Historian* 5 (Spring 1972): 26–29.

Bailey, Garrick Alan, Daniel C. Swan, John W. Nunley, and E. Sean Standing Bear. *Art of the Osage*. Seattle: St. Louis Art Museum in association with University of Washington Press, 2004.

Bailey, Garrick Alan, and William C. Sturtevant, eds. *Indians in Contemporary*

Society. Vol. 2, *Handbook of North American Indians.* Washington, D.C.: Smith-
    sonian Institution, 2008.

Baird, W. David. *The Osage People.* Phoenix: Indian Tribal Series, 1972.

Ball, Larry D. *Desert Lawmen: The High Sheriffs of New Mexico and Arizona, 1846–
    1912.* Albuquerque: University of New Mexico Press, 1996.

Bates, James Leonard. *The Origins of Teapot Dome: Progressives, Parties, and Petro-
    leum, 1909–1921.* Urbana: University of Illinois Press, 1964.

Blum, Howard. *American Lightning: Terror, Mystery, the Birth of Hollywood, and the
    Crime of the Century.* New York: Three Rivers Press, 2008.

Boatright, Mody C., and William A. Owens. *Tales from the Derrick Floor: A People's
    History of the Oil Industry.* Garden City, N.Y.: Doubleday, 1970.

Boorstin, Daniel J. *The Americans: The Democratic Experience.* New York: Vintage,
    1974.

Breuer, William B. *J. Edgar Hoover and His G-Men.* Westport, Conn.: Praeger,
    1995.

Brown, Meredith Mason. *Frontiersman: Daniel Boone and the Making of America.*
    Baton Rouge: Louisiana State University Press, 2009.

Burchardt, Bill. "Osage Oil." *Chronicles of Oklahoma* 41 (Fall 1963): 253–69.

Burns, Louis F. *A History of the Osage People.* Tuscaloosa: University of Alabama
    Press, 2004.

————. *Osage Indian Customs and Myths.* Tuscaloosa: University of Alabama
    Press, 2005.

Burns, William J. *The Masked War: The Story of a Peril That Threatened the United
    States.* New York: George H. Doran, 1913.

Burrough, Bryan. *Public Enemies: America's Greatest Crime Wave and the Birth of the
    FBI, 1933–34.* New York: Penguin, 2009.

Caesar, Gene. *Incredible Detective: The Biography of William J. Burns.* New York:
    Prentice-Hall, 1989.

Callahan, Alice Anne. *The Osage Ceremonial Dance I'n-Lon-Schka.* Norman: Uni-
    versity of Oklahoma Press, 1993.

Cecil, Matthew. *Hoover's FBI and the Fourth Estate: The Campaign to Control the Press
    and the Bureau's Image.* Lawrence: University Press of Kansas, 2014.

Chapman, Berlin B. "Dissolution of the Osage Reservation, Part One." *Chronicles
    of Oklahoma* 20 (Sept.–Dec. 1942): 244–54.

————. "Dissolution of the Osage Reservation, Part Two." *Chronicles of Oklahoma*
    20 (Sept.–Dec. 1942): 375–87.

————. "Dissolution of the Osage Reservation, Part Three." *Chronicles of Okla-
    homa* 21 (March 1943): 78–88.

————. "Dissolution of the Osage Reservation, Part Four." *Chronicles of Oklahoma*
    21 (June 1943): 171–82.

Christison, Sir Robert. *A Treatise on Poisons in Relation to Medical Jurisprudence,
    Physiology, and the Practice of Physic.* Edinburgh: Adam Black, 1832.

Collins, Michael L. *Texas Devils: Rangers and Regulars on the Lower Rio Grande, 1846–1861.* Norman: University of Oklahoma Press, 2008.

Connelly, William L. *The Oil Business as I Saw It: Half a Century with Sinclair.* Norman: University of Oklahoma Press, 1954.

Cope, Jack. *1300 Metropolitan Avenue: A History of the United States Penitentiary at Leavenworth, Kansas.* Leavenworth, Kans.: Unicor Print Press, 1997.

Cordry, Dee. *Alive If Possible—Dead If Necessary.* Mustang, Okla.: Tate, 2005.

Cox, James. *Historical and Biographical Record of the Cattle Industry and the Cattlemen of Texas and Adjacent Territory.* St. Louis: Woodward & Tiernan, 1895.

Cox, Mike. *Time of the Rangers.* New York: Tom Doherty Associates, 2010.

Crockett, Art. *Serial Murderers.* New York: Pinnacle Books, 1993.

Daniell, L. E. *Personnel of the Texas State Government, with Sketches of Distinguished Texans, Embracing the Executive and Staff, Heads of the Departments, United States Senators and Representatives, Members of the Twenty-First Legislature.* Austin: Smith, Hicks & Jones, 1889.

Daugherty, H. M., and Thomas Dixon. *The Inside Story of the Harding Tragedy.* New York: Churchill, 1932.

Dean, John W. *Warren G. Harding.* New York: Times Books, 2004.

Debo, Angie. *And Still the Waters Run: The Betrayal of the Five Civilized Tribes.* Princeton, N.J.: Princeton University Press, 1991.

Demaris, Ovid. *The Director: An Oral Biography of J. Edgar Hoover.* New York: Harper's Magazine Press, 1975.

Dennison, Jean. *Colonial Entanglement: Constituting a Twenty-First-Century Osage Nation.* Chapel Hill: University of North Carolina Press, 2012.

Dickerson, Philip J. *History of the Osage Nation: Its People, Resources, and Prospects: The East Reservation to Open in the New State.* Pawhuska, Okla.: P. J. Dickerson, 1906.

Dickey, Michael. *The People of the River's Mouth: In Search of the Missouria Indians.* Columbia: University of Missouri Press, 2011.

Doherty, Jim. *Just the Facts: True Tales of Cops and Criminals.* Tucson: Deadly Serious Press, 2004.

Earley, Pete. *The Hot House: Life Inside Leavenworth Prison.* New York: Bantam Books, 1993.

Ellis, William Donohue. *Out of the Osage: The Foster Story.* Oklahoma City: Western Heritage Books, 1994.

Finney, Frank F. "John N. Florer." *Chronicles of Oklahoma* 33 (Summer 1955): 142–44.

———. "The Osages and Their Agency During the Term of Isaac T. Gibson Quaker Agent." *Chronicles of Oklahoma* 36 (Winter 1958–59): 416–28.

———. "Progress in the Civilization of the Osage." *Chronicles of Oklahoma* 40 (Spring 1962): 2–21.

Finney, James Edwin, and Joseph B. Thoburn. "Reminiscences of a Trader in the Osage Country." *Chronicles of Oklahoma* 33 (Summer 1955): 145–58.

Finney, Thomas McKean. *Pioneer Days with the Osage Indians: West of '96*. Pawhuska, Okla.: Osage County Historical Society, 1972.

Fixico, Donald Lee. *The Invasion of Indian Country in the Twentieth Century: American Capitalism and Tribal Natural Resources*. Niwot: University Press of Colorado, 1998.

Foley, William E., and C. David Rice. *The First Chouteaus: River Barons of Early St. Louis*. Urbana: University of Illinois Press, 2000.

Forbes, Gerald. "History of the Osage Blanket Lease." *Chronicles of Oklahoma* 19 (March 1941): 70–81.

Foreman, Grant. "J. George Wright." *Chronicles of Oklahoma* 20 (June 1942): 120–23.

Franks, Kenny Arthur. *The Osage Oil Boom*. Oklahoma City: Western Heritage Books, 1989.

Franks, Kenny Arthur, Paul F. Lambert, and Carl N. Tyson. *Early Oklahoma Oil: A Photographic History, 1859–1936*. College Station: Texas A&M University Press, 1981.

Friedman, Lawrence M. *Crime and Punishment in American History*. New York: Basic Books, 1993.

Gaddis, Thomas E., and James O. Long, eds. *Panzram: A Journal of Murder*. Los Angeles: Amok Books, 2002.

Gage, Beverly. *The Day Wall Street Exploded: A Story of America in Its First Age of Terror*. New York: Oxford University Press, 2009.

Gentry, Curt. *J. Edgar Hoover: The Man and the Secrets*. New York: W. W. Norton, 2001.

Getty, Jean Paul. *As I See It: The Autobiography of J. Paul Getty*. Los Angeles: J. Paul Getty Museum, 2003.

———. *How to Be Rich*. New York: Jove Books, 1983.

———. *My Life and Fortunes*. New York: Duell, Sloan & Pearce, 1963.

Gilbreath, West C. *Death on the Gallows: The Story of Legal Hangings in New Mexico, 1847–1923*. Silver City, N.M.: High-Lonesome Books, 2002.

Glasscock, Carl Burgess. *Then Came Oil: The Story of the Last Frontier*. Indianapolis: Bobbs-Merrill, 1938.

Graves, W. W. *Life and Letters of Fathers Ponziglione, Schoenmakers, and Other Early Jesuits at Osage Mission: Sketch of St. Francis' Church; Life of Mother Bridget*. St. Paul, Kans.: W. W. Graves, 1916.

———. *Life and Letters of Rev. Father John Schoenmakers, S.J., Apostle to the Osages*. Parsons, Kans.: Commercial, 1928.

Graybill, Andrew R. *Policing the Great Plains: Rangers, Mounties, and the North American Frontier, 1875–1910*. Lincoln: University of Nebraska Press, 2007.

Gregory, Robert. *Oil in Oklahoma*. Muskogee, Okla.: Leake Industries, 1976.

Gross, Hans. *Criminal Psychology: A Manual for Judges, Practitioners, and Students*. Montclair, N.J.: Patterson Smith, 1968.

Grove, Fred. *The Years of Fear: A Western Story*. Waterville, Maine: Five Star, 2002.

Gunther, Max. *The Very, Very Rich and How They Got That Way.* Hampshire, U.K.: Harriman House, 2010.

Hagan, William T. *Taking Indian Lands: The Cherokee (Jerome) Commission, 1889–1893.* Norman: University of Oklahoma Press, 2003.

Hammons, Terry. *Ranching from the Front Seat of a Buick: The Life of Oklahoma's A. A. "Jack" Drummond.* Oklahoma City: Oklahoma Historical Society, 1982.

Hanson, Maynard J. "Senator William B. Pine and His Times." Ph.D. diss., Oklahoma State University, 1983.

Harmon, Alexandra. *Rich Indians: Native People and the Problem of Wealth in American History.* Chapel Hill: University of North Carolina Press, 2010.

Harris, Charles H., and Louis R. Sadler. *The Texas Rangers and the Mexican Revolution: The Bloodiest Decade, 1910–1920.* Albuquerque: University of New Mexico Press, 2004.

Hastedt, Karl G. "White Brothers of Texas Had Notable FBI Careers." *Grapevine,* Feb. 1960.

Hess, Janet Berry. *Osage and Settler: Reconstructing Shared History Through an Oklahoma Family Archive.* Jefferson, N.C.: McFarland, 2015.

Hicks, J. C. "Auctions of Osage Oil and Gas Leases." M.A. thesis, University of Oklahoma, 1949.

Hofstadter, Richard. *The Age of Reform: From Bryan to F.D.R.* New York: Knopf, 1955.

Hogan, Lawrence J. *The Osage Indian Murders: The True Story of a Multiple Murder Plot to Acquire the Estates of Wealthy Osage Tribe Members.* Frederick, Md.: Amlex, 1998.

Horan, James D. *The Pinkertons: The Detective Dynasty That Made History.* New York: Crown, 1969.

Hoyt, Edwin. *Spectacular Rogue: Gaston B. Means.* Indianapolis: Bobbs-Merrill, 1963.

Hunt, William R. *Front-Page Detective: William J. Burns and the Detective Profession, 1880–1930.* Bowling Green, Ohio: Popular Press, 1990.

Hunter, J. Marvin, and B. Byron Price. *The Trail Drivers of Texas: Interesting Sketches of Early Cowboys and Their Experiences on the Range and on the Trail During the Days That Tried Men's Souls, True Narratives Related by Real Cowpunchers and Men Who Fathered the Cattle Industry in Texas.* Austin: University of Texas Press, 1985.

Hynd, Alan. *Great True Detective Mysteries.* New York: Grosset & Dunlap, 1969.

Indian Rights Association. *Forty-Fourth Annual Report of the Board of Directors of the Indian Rights Association (Incorporated) for the Year Ending December 15, 1926.* Philadelphia: Office of the Indian Rights Association, 1927.

Irwin, Lew. *Deadly Times: The 1910 Bombing of the "Los Angeles Times" and America's Forgotten Decade of Terror.* New York: Rowman & Littlefield, 2013.

Johnson, David R. *American Law Enforcement: A History.* Wheeling, Ill.: Forum Press, 1981.

————. *Policing the Urban Underworld: The Impact of Crime on the Development of the American Police, 1800–1887.* Philadelphia: Temple University Press, 1979.

Johnston, J. H. *Leavenworth Penitentiary: A History of America's Oldest Federal Prison.* Leavenworth, Kans.: J. H. Johnston, 2005.

Jones, Mark, and Peter Johnstone. *History of Criminal Justice.* New York: Elsevier, 2012.

Jones, Mary Ann. "The Leavenworth Prison Break." *Harper's Monthly,* July 1945.

Kessler, Ronald. *The Bureau: The Secret History of the FBI.* New York: St. Martin's Paperbacks, 2003.

Keve, Paul W. *Prisons and the American Conscience: A History of U.S. Federal Corrections.* Carbondale: Southern Illinois University Press, 1991.

Knowles, Ruth Sheldon. *The Greatest Gamblers: The Epic of American Oil Exploration.* Norman: University of Oklahoma Press, 1980.

Kraisinger, Gary, and Margaret Kraisinger. *The Western: The Greatest Texas Cattle Trail, 1874–1886.* Newton, Kans.: Mennonite Press, 2004.

Kurland, Michael. *Irrefutable Evidence: Adventures in the History of Forensic Science.* Chicago: Ivan R. Dee, 2009.

Kvasnicka, Robert M., and Herman J. Viola, eds. *The Commissioners of Indian Affairs, 1824–1977.* Lincoln: University of Nebraska Press, 1979.

La Flesche, Francis. *The Osage and the Invisible World: From the Works of Francis La Flesche.* Edited by Garrick Alan Bailey. Norman: University of Oklahoma Press, 1995.

————. *The Osage Tribe: Rite of the Chiefs; Sayings of the Ancient Men.* Washington, D.C.: Bureau of American Ethnology, 1921.

Lamb, Arthur H. *Tragedies of the Osage Hills.* Pawhuska, Okla.: Raymond Red Corn, 2001.

Lambert, Paul F., and Kenny Arthur Franks. *Voices from the Oil Fields.* Norman: University of Oklahoma Press, 1984.

Lenzner, Robert. *The Great Getty: The Life and Loves of J. Paul Getty, Richest Man in the World.* New York: New American Library, 1987.

Leonard, Thomas C. "American Economic Reform in the Progressive Era: Its Foundational Beliefs and Their Relationship to Eugenics." *History of Political Economy* 41 (2009): 109–41.

————. "Retrospectives: Eugenics and Economics in the Progressive Era." *Journal of Economic Perspectives* 19 (2005): 207–24.

Lloyd, Roger Hall. *Osage County: A Tribe and American Culture, 1600–1934.* New York: iUniverse, 2006.

Lombroso, Cesare. *Criminal Man.* Translated by Mary Gibson and Nicole Hahn Rafter. Durham, N.C.: Duke University Press, 2006.

Look Magazine, ed. *The Story of the FBI.* New York: E. Dutton, 1947.

Lowenthal, Max. *The Federal Bureau of Investigation.* Westport, Conn.: Greenwood Press, 1971.

Lukas, J. Anthony. *Big Trouble: A Murder in a Small Western Town Sets Off a Struggle for the Soul of America*. New York: Touchstone Books, 1998.

Lynch, Gerald. *Roughnecks, Drillers, and Tool Pushers: Thirty-Three Years in the Oil Fields*. Austin: University of Texas Press, 1991.

Mackay, James A. *Allan Pinkerton: The First Private Eye*. New York: J. Wiley & Sons, 1997.

Mathews, John Joseph. *Life and Death of an Oilman: The Career of E. W. Marland*. Norman: University of Oklahoma Press, 1989.

———. *The Osages: Children of the Middle Waters*. Norman: University of Oklahoma Press, 1973.

———. *Sundown*. Norman: University of Oklahoma Press, 1988.

———. *Talking to the Moon*. Norman: University of Oklahoma Press, 1981.

———. *Twenty Thousand Mornings: An Autobiography*. Norman: University of Oklahoma Press, 2012.

———. *Wah'kon-Tah: The Osage and the White Man's Road*. Norman: University of Oklahoma, 1981.

McAuliffe, Dennis. *The Deaths of Sybil Bolton: An American History*. New York: Times Books, 1994.

McCartney, Laton. *The Teapot Dome Scandal: How Big Oil Bought the Harding White House and Tried to Steal the Country*. New York: Random House Trade Paperbacks, 2009.

McConal, Patrick M. *Over the Wall: The Men Behind the 1934 Death House Escape*. Austin: Eakin Press, 2000.

Merchant, Carolyn. *American Environmental History: An Introduction*. New York: Columbia University Press, 2013.

Miller, Russell. *The House of Getty*. New York: Henry Holt, 1985.

Millspaugh, Arthur C. *Crime Control by the National Government*. Washington, D.C.: Brookings Institution, 1937.

Miner, H. Craig. *The Corporation and the Indian: Tribal Sovereignty and Industrial Civilization in Indian Territory, 1865–1907*. Norman: University of Oklahoma Press, 1989.

Miner, H. Craig, and William E. Unrau. *The End of Indian Kansas: A Study of Cultural Revolution, 1854–1871*. Lawrence: University Press of Kansas, 1990.

Morgan, R. D. *Taming the Sooner State: The War Between Lawmen and Outlaws in Oklahoma and Indian Territory, 1875–1941*. Stillwater, Okla.: New Forums Press, 2007.

Morn, Frank. *"The Eye That Never Sleeps": A History of the Pinkerton National Detective Agency*. Bloomington: Indiana University Press, 1982.

Morris, John W. *Ghost Towns of Oklahoma*. Norman: University of Oklahoma Press, 1978.

Nash, Jay Robert. *Almanac of World Crime*. Garden City, N.Y.: Anchor Press, 1981.

———. *Citizen Hoover: A Critical Study of the Life and Times of J. Edgar Hoover and His FBI*. Chicago: Nelson-Hall, 1972.

Nieberding, Velma. "Catholic Education Among the Osage." *Chronicles of Oklahoma* 32 (Autumn 1954): 290–307.

Noggle, Burl. *Teapot Dome: Oil and Politics in the 1920's.* New York: W. W. Norton, 1965.

Office of the Commissioner of Indian Affairs. *Report of the Commissioner of Indian Affairs to the Secretary of the Interior, for the Year 1871.* Washington, D.C.: Government Printing Office, 1872.

Ollestad, Norman. *Inside the FBI.* New York: Lyle Stuart, 1967.

Osage County Historical Society. *Osage County Profiles.* Pawhuska, Okla.: Osage County Historical Society, 1978.

Osage Tribal Council, United States, Bureau of Indian Affairs, and Osage Agency. *1907–1957, Osage Indians Semi-centennial Celebration: Commemorating the Closing of the Osage Indian Roll, the Allotment of the Lands of the Osage Reservation in Severalty and the Dedication of the Osage Tribal Chamber.* Pawhuska, Okla.: Osage Agency Campus, 1957.

Osage Tribal Murders. Directed by Sherwood Ball. Los Angeles: Ball Entertainment, 2010. DVD.

Parker, Doris Whitetail. *Footprints on the Osage Reservation.* Pawhuska, Okla.: the author, 1982.

Parsons, Chuck. *Captain John R. Hughes: Lone Star Ranger.* Denton: University of North Texas Press, 2011.

Paschen, Elise. *Bestiary.* Pasadena, Calif.: Red Hen Press, 2009.

Pawhuska Journal-Capital. *Cowboys, Outlaws, and Peace Officers.* Pawhuska, Okla.: Pawhuska Journal-Capital, 1996.

———. *Reflections of Pawhuska, Oklahoma.* Pawhuska, Okla.: Pawhuska Journal-Capital, 1995.

Pinkerton, Allan. *Criminal Reminiscences and Detective Sketches.* New York: Garrett Press, 1969.

———. *Thirty Years a Detective.* Warwick, N.Y.: 1500 Books, 2007.

Powers, Richard Gid. *G-Men: Hoover's FBI in American Popular Culture.* Carbondale: Southern Illinois University Press, 1983.

———. *Secrecy and Power: The Life of J. Edgar Hoover.* New York: Free Press, 1988.

Prettyman, William S., and Robert E. Cunningham. *Indian Territory: A Frontier Photographic Record by W. S. Prettyman.* Norman: University of Oklahoma Press, 1957.

Prucha, Francis Paul. *The Churches and the Indian Schools, 1888–1912.* Lincoln: University of Nebraska Press, 1979.

Ramsland, Katherine M. *Beating the Devil's Game: A History of Forensic Science and Criminal Investigation.* New York: Berkley Books, 2014.

———. *The Human Predator: A Historical Chronicle of Serial Murder and Forensic Investigation.* New York: Berkley Books, 2013.

Red Corn, Charles H. *A Pipe for February: A Novel.* Norman: University of Oklahoma Press, 2002.

Revard, Carter. *Family Matters, Tribal Affairs.* Tucson: University of Arizona Press, 1998.

Rister, Carl Coke. *Oil! Titan of the Southwest.* Norman: University of Oklahoma Press, 1957.

Roff, Charles L. *A Boom Town Lawyer in the Osage, 1919–1927.* Quanah, Tex.: Nortex Press, 1975.

Rollings, Willard H. *The Osage: An Ethnohistorical Study of Hegemony on the Prairie-Plains.* Columbia: University of Missouri Press, 1995.

— ——. *Unaffected by the Gospel: Osage Resistance to the Christian Invasion (1673–1906): A Cultural Victory.* Albuquerque: University of New Mexico Press, 2004.

Rudensky, Red. *The Gonif.* Blue Earth, Minn.: Piper, 1970.

Russell, Orpha B. "Chief James Bigheart of the Osages." *Chronicles of Oklahoma* 32 (Winter 1954–55): 884–94.

Sbardellati, John. *J. Edgar Hoover Goes to the Movies: The FBI and the Origins of Hollywood's Cold War.* Ithaca, N.Y.: Cornell University Press, 2012.

Shirley, Glenn. *West of Hell's Fringe: Crime, Criminals, and the Federal Peace Officer in Oklahoma Territory, 1889–1907.* Norman: University of Oklahoma Press, 1990.

Shoemaker, Arthur. *The Road to Marble Halls: The Henry Grammer Saga.* N p.: Basic Western Book Company, 2000.

Spellman, Paul N. *Captain J. A. Brooks, Texas Ranger.* Denton: University of North Texas Press, 2007.

Stansbery, Lon R. *The Passing of 3-D Ranch.* New York: Buffalo-Head Press, 1966.

Starr, Douglas. *The Killer of Little Shepherds: A True Crime Story and the Birth of Forensic Science.* New York: Alfred A. Knopf, 2010.

Sterling, William Warren. *Trails and Trials of a Texas Ranger.* Norman: University of Oklahoma Press, 1959.

Stratton, David H. *Tempest over Teapot Dome: The Story of Albert B. Fall.* Norman: University of Oklahoma Press, 1998.

Strickland, Rennard. *The Indians in Oklahoma.* Norman: University of Oklahoma Press, 1980.

Sullivan, William, and Bill Brown. *The Bureau: My Thirty Years in Hoover's FBI.* New York: Pinnacle Books, 1982.

Summerscale, Kate. *The Suspicions of Mr. Whicher: A Shocking Murder and the Undoing of a Great Victorian Detective.* New York: Bloomsbury, 2009.

Tait, Samuel W. *The Wildcatters: An Informal History of Oil-Hunting in America.* Princeton, N.J.: Princeton University Press, 1946.

Tallchief, Maria. *Maria Tallchief: America's Prima Ballerina.* With Larry Kaplan. New York: Henry Holt, 1997.

Tarbell, Ida M. *The History of the Standard Oil Company.* Edited by David Mark Chalmers. New York: Harper & Row, 1966.

———. "Identification of Criminals." *McClure's Magazine,* March 1894.

Thoburn, Joseph Bradfield. *A Standard History of Oklahoma: An Authentic Narrative of Its Development from the Date of the First European Exploration Down to the Present Time, Including Accounts of the Indian Tribes, Both Civilized and Wild, of the Cattle Range, of the Land Openings and the Achievements of the Most Recent Period.* Chicago: American Historical Society, 1916.

Thomas, James. "The Osage Removal to Oklahoma." *Chronicles of Oklahoma* 55 (Spring 1977): 46–55.

Thorne, Tanis C. *The World's Richest Indian: The Scandal over Jackson Barnett's Oil Fortune.* New York: Oxford University Press, 2003.

Tixier, Victor. *Tixier's Travels on the Osage Prairies.* Norman: University of Oklahoma Press, 1940.

Toledano, Ralph de. *J. Edgar Hoover: The Man in His Time.* New Rochelle, N.Y.: Arlington House, 1973.

Trachtenberg, Alan. *The Incorporation of America: Culture and Society in the Gilded Age.* New York: Hill and Wang, 2007.

Tracy, Tom H. "Tom Tracy Tells About—Detroit and Oklahoma: Ex Agent Recalls Exciting Times in Sooner State Where Indians, Oil Wells, and Bad Guys Kept Staff on the Go." *Grapevine,* Feb. 1960.

Turner, William W. *Hoover's FBI.* New York: Thunder's Mouth Press, 1993.

Ungar, Sanford J. *F.B.I.* Boston: Little, Brown, 1976.

Unger, Robert. *The Union Station Massacre: The Original Sin of J. Edgar Hoover's FBI.* Kansas City, Mo.: Kansas City Star Books, 2005.

U.S. Bureau of Indian Affairs and Osage Agency. *The Osage People and Their Trust Property, a Field Report.* Pawhuska, Okla.: Osage Agency, 1953.

U.S. Congress. House Committee on Indian Affairs. *Modifying Osage Fund Restrictions, Hearings Before the Committee on Indian Affairs on H.R. 10328.* 67th Cong., 2nd sess., March 27–29 and 31, 1922.

U.S. Congress. House Subcommittee of the Committee on Indian Affairs. *Indians of the United States: Investigation of the Field Service: Hearing by the Subcommittee on Indian Affairs.* 66th Cong., 2nd sess., 1920.

———. *Leases for Oil and Gas Purposes, Osage National Council, on H.R. 27726: Hearings Before a Subcommittee of the Committee on Indian Affairs.* 62nd Cong., 3rd sess., Jan. 18–21, 1913.

U.S. Congress. Joint Commission to Investigate Indian Affairs. *Hearings Before the Joint Commission of the Congress of the United States.* 63rd Cong., 3rd sess., Jan. 16 and 19 and Feb. 3 and 11, 1915.

U.S. Congress. Senate Committee on Indian Affairs. *Hearings Before the Senate Committee on Indian Affairs on Matters Relating to the Osage Tribe of Indians.* 60th Cong., 2nd sess., March 1, 1909.

———. *Survey of Conditions of the Indians in the U.S. Hearings Before the United States Senate Committee on Indian Affairs, Subcommittee on S. Res. 79.* 78th Cong., 1st sess., Aug. 2 and 3, 1943.

U.S. Dept. of Justice. Federal Bureau of Investigation. *The FBI: A Centennial His-*

tory, 1908–2008. Washington, D.C.: U.S. Government Printing Office, 2008.

Utley, Robert M. *Lone Star Justice: The First Century of the Texas Rangers*. New York: Berkley Books, 2003.

Wagner, E. J. *The Science of Sherlock Holmes: From Baskerville Hall to the Valley of Fear, the Real Forensics Behind the Great Detective's Greatest Cases*. Hoboken, N.J.: John Wiley & Sons, 2006.

Walker, Samuel. *Popular Justice: A History of American Criminal Justice*. New York: Oxford University Press, 1998.

Wallis, Michael. *Oil Man: The Story of Frank Phillips and the Birth of Phillips Petroleum*. New York: St. Martin's Griffin, 1995.

———. *The Real Wild West: The 101 Ranch and the Creation of the American West*. New York: St. Martin's Press, 1999.

Ward, David A. *Alcatraz: The Gangster Years*. Berkeley: University of California Press, 2009.

Warehime, Lester. *History of Ranching the Osage*. Tulsa: W. W. Publishers, 2001.

Webb, Walter Prescott. *The Texas Rangers: A Century of Frontier Defense*. Austin: University of Texas Press, 2014.

Webb-Storey, Anna. "Culture Clash: A Case Study of Three Osage Native American Families." Ed.D. thesis, Oklahoma State University, 1998.

Weiner, Tim. *Enemies: A History of the FBI*. New York: Random House, 2012.

Welch, Neil J., and David W. Marston. *Inside Hoover's FBI: The Top Field Chief Reports*. Garden City, N.Y.: Doubleday, 1984.

Welsh, Herbert. *The Action of the Interior Department in Forcing the Standing Rock Indians to Lease Their Lands to Cattle Syndicates*. Philadelphia: Indian Rights Association, 1902.

Wheeler, Burton K., and Paul F. Healy. *Yankee from the West: The Candid, Turbulent Life Story of the Yankee-Born U.S. Senator from Montana*. Garden City, N.Y.: Doubleday, 1962.

White, E. E. *Experiences of a Special Indian Agent*. Norman: University of Oklahoma Press, 1965.

White, James D. *Getting Sense: The Osages and Their Missionaries*. Tulsa: Sarto Press, 1997.

Whitehead, Don. *The FBI Story: A Report to the People*. New York: Random House, 1956.

Wiebe, Robert H. *The Search for Order, 1877–1920*. New York: Hill and Wang, 1967.

Wilder, Laura Ingalls. *Little House on the Prairie*. New York: Harper & Brothers, 1935. Reprinted, New York: HarperCollins, 2010.

Wilson, Terry P. "Osage Indian Women During a Century of Change, 1870–1980." *Prologue: Journal of the National Archives* 14 (Winter 1982): 185–201.

————."Osage Oxonian: The Heritage of John Joseph Mathews." *Chronicles of Oklahoma* 59 (Fall 1981): 264–93.

————. *The Underground Reservation: Osage Oil.* Lincoln: University of Nebraska Press, 1985.

Zugibe, Frederick T., and David Carroll. *Dissecting Death: Secrets of a Medical Examiner.* New York: Broadway Books, 2005.

ILLUSTRATION CREDITS

72   Courtesy of the Bartlesville Area History Museum
75   (top) Courtesy of Guy Nixon
75   (bottom) Courtesy of the Osage County Historical Society Museum
77   Courtesy of Raymond Red Corn
82   Credit: Corbis
87   Courtesy of the Montana Historical Society
88   Courtesy of the Federal Bureau of Investigation
91   (top) Credit: Corbis
91   (bottom) Credit: Corbis
95   Courtesy of Melville Vaughan
97   Courtesy of the Osage Nation Museum
104   Courtesy of the Western History Collections, University of Oklahoma
        Libraries, Rose No. 1525
109   Courtesy of the Library of Congress
117   Courtesy of Frank Parker Sr.
121   Courtesy of the Federal Bureau of Investigation
127   Courtesy of Homer Fincannon
131   Courtesy of the National Archives at Kansas City
134   Courtesy of Alexandra Sands
138   Courtesy of James M. White
140   Austin History Center, Austin Public Library
145   (top) Courtesy of James M. White
145   (bottom) Courtesy of the Western History Collections, University of
        Oklahoma Libraries, Rose No. 1525
149   Courtesy of the Western History Collections, University of Oklahoma
        Libraries, Rose No. 1806
155   Courtesy of Raymond Red Corn
163   Courtesy of the Oklahoma Historical Society, Oklahoman Collection
168   Unknown
173   Courtesy of the Kansas Historical Society
174   Courtesy of the Bartlesville Area History Museum
175   Courtesy of the National Cowboy and Western Heritage Museum
177   Courtesy of the Federal Bureau of Investigation
184   Courtesy of the Oklahoma Historical Society, Oklahoman Collection
188   Credit: Corbis
199   Courtesy of the Oklahoma Historical Society, Oklahoman Collection
208   Courtesy of the Osage Nation Museum
212   Courtesy of Raymond Red Corn
214   Courtesy of the Oklahoma Historical Society, Oklahoman Collection
217   Courtesy of the Oklahoma Historical Society, Oklahoman Collection
228   Courtesy of Margie Burkhart
233   Credit: Neal Boenzi/*The New York Times*
236   Courtesy of Tom White III
242   Aaron Tomlinson
244   Courtesy of Archie Mason

David Grann unravels one of the greatest mysteries of exploration in

THE
LOST CITY
OF
Z

A LEGENDARY BRITISH
EXPLORER'S DEADLY QUEST TO
UNCOVER THE SECRETS OF THE AMAZON

Colonel Percy Harrison Fawcett, the inspiration behind Conan Doyle's
novel *The Lost World*, was among the last of a legendary breed of British
explorers. For years he explored the Amazon and came to believe that its
jungle concealed a large, complex civilization, like El Dorado. Obsessed
with its discovery, he christened it the City of Z. In 1925, Fawcett headed
into the wilderness with his son Jack, vowing to make history.
They vanished without a trace.

For the next eighty years, hordes of explorers plunged into the jungle,
trying to find evidence of Fawcett's party or Z. Some died from disease
and starvation; others simply disappeared. In this spellbinding true tale of
lethal obsession, David Grann retraces the footsteps of Fawcett and his
followers as he unravels one of the greatest mysteries of exploration.

'*A riveting, exciting and thoroughly compelling tale of adventure*'
John Grisham

'*Marvellous ... This is an engrossing book whose
protagonist could out-think Indiana Jones*'
Daily Telegraph

'*The best story in the world, told perfectly*'
Evening Standard

Paperback ISBN: 978-1-84739-443-9
eBook ISBN: 978-1-84737-805-7